CRIMINAL ORGANIZATIONS

CRIMINAL ORGANIZATIONS

Vice, Racketeering, and Politics in an American City

GARY W. POTTER
Eastern Kentucky University

WAVELAND
PRESS, INC.
Prospect Heights, Illinois

For information about this book, write or call:

Waveland Press, Inc.
P.O. Box 400
Prospect Heights, Illinois 60070
(708) 634-0081

Acknowledgements

This book is a collaborative effort that has passed through many phases and incarnations before arriving at its present form. I am indebted to a great many people for their assistance. Philip Jenkins of the Pennsylvania State University was the driving force behind the original research which makes up the bulk of this effort. Professor Jenkins and I, on a research initiation grant from the Institute for Human Development, collaborated on the original field study. It was with Philip that I walked the streets of "Morrisburg" in the wee hours of the morning visiting the various dens of iniquity, and it was Philip who inspired much, if not all, of the historical and scholarly content of this work. His generosity, coherence, and attention to detail has made much of my work possible.

Bill Chambliss looked at an early draft of the research report and encouraged continued investigation and thought. Bill's *On The Take: From Petty Crooks to Presidents* was the inspiration for this research and for much of the other work I have done in organized crime. As most readers will readily recognize, I am also indebted to Bill for first articulating the framework presented here and for not objecting when his ideas were liberally borrowed by neophytes trying to follow in his footsteps.

Steve Mastrofski at Penn State helped me organize much of the material into a coherent argument in two journal articles we produced a few years back. Steve's care as a scholar has no doubt

v

saved me from egregious logical error more than once and has been invaluable in assembling bibliographies.

Mittie Southerland at Eastern Kentucky University co-authored chapter 8 and contributed a great deal of assistance in calling my attention to the relevant organizational literature and helping construct a framework to explain the organization of vice.

I also owe thanks to my mentor, Dr. Walter Freeman, professor emeritus at Penn State, for keeping me constantly focused on the importance of community as a level of analysis. My friend and officemate Vic Kappeler at EKU (who tries to make sure that I don't run out of coffee, ideas, or work to do) deserves much of the credit for the completion of this book. A substantial contribution was also made by Karen Miller who read the manuscript several times, pointing out confusing or incomplete explanations and correcting my grammar, spelling, phraseology and choice of words. She also labored on the proofs of the book, another task which is often beyond my ken.

Carol Rowe at Waveland is the best editor I have ever worked with, generously reworking large segments of text, pointing out contradictions, and helping to dump the scholarly jargon that renders much of the literature incomprehensible to everyone but an esoteric few. Waveland Press makes writing fun, provides a great deal of encouragement to their authors, and makes a substantial contribution to reducing an author's work load. Without their help this book would still be in file folders in my filing cabinet.

And finally, for both this work and much of the other research I have done on organized crime, I am heavily indebted to those people who took the time to shepherd me around, explain the ways of the underworld, get me into places and into contact with people whom I otherwise would never have been able to interview or observe, and were patient enough to overlook my naïveté and clumsiness—my informants. In addition to helping with my research, these denizens of the underworld also convinced me long ago of a basic criminological truth: there's really not much difference between people we label as criminal and the rest of us. While doing this research I often was reminded that if we judged folks in this society on their manifest honesty, their lack of hypocrisy, and their ability to adapt to pervasive inequality and stratification, we might find that these social outcasts do much better than many "respectable" people who rob us of our integrity, our hope, and our money.

Table of Contents

The Concept of Organized Crime

Organized crime is a topic of immense interest in American society. It is widely portrayed in the entertainment media, heavily covered by journalists, and the subject of continual criminal investigations and inquiries by official criminal justice agencies. Our fascination with the covert world of organized crime has created a popular view of this phenomenon that has elevated it to legend. Unfortunately, the glamour of organized crime—and the glamour of those who fight it—as portrayed in books, movies, and television, bears little resemblance to reality. Elliot Ness may have played a role in the conviction of Al Capone on tax evasion charges, but he did not destroy the syndicate that Capone built in Chicago. Tom Dewey may have launched a political career on the Lepke execution, but he failed to eradicate labor racketeering. Robert Kennedy may have imprisoned Jimmy Hoffa and inconvenienced Carlos Marcello, Sam Giancana, and Santo Trafficante, but he did little to interdict the flow of heroin or curtail the other money-making ventures of organized crime. Americans have watched the Kefauver Committee expose interstate gambling syndicates and watched Joe Valachi spin tales of Mafia power, but organized crime continues unabated.

For half a century, law enforcement agencies have pursued, prosecuted, imprisoned and even executed organized criminals. We have established professional, well-funded agencies to investigate organized crime and to expose the many intricate conspiracies involving organized criminals. We spend billions on "closing the borders" to the drug trade, on "stinging" labor racketeers, and on auditing tax returns of gamblers. Yet organized crime continues to conduct business-as-usual. With all of the time, effort, and money that has been expended in this area, we are still confronted with two basic questions: What can we do about organized crime? and How will we know if we have been successful?

Of course, the answers to these questions are contingent upon more basic questions: What is organized crime? What do we know about organized crime in America? How much empirically verified information do we have and how much data is simply based on background assumptions and fundamental tenets of belief? How dependent is criminal justice policy on a "set of disputable facts rearranged into a set of 'proofs' of a criminal conspiracy" (Smith, 1975: 77)? As McCaghy and Cernkovich comment:

> During the medieval ages Christian theologians pondered the question, How many angels can dance on the point of a needle without jostling one another? Although we might argue the subject's importance, we must at least marvel at any attempt to solve such a problem. After all, there is little evidence on angels' width and dancing abilities. The modern-day equivalent of angel counting is "syndicate structuring." Today's Mafia watchers have about as much data as the angel counters did as they debate the nature of organized crime's organization (1987: 265).

However, some law enforcement officials and some academics think they know how many angels are dancing on the point of organized crime's needle. Policy makers, law enforcement officials, and academics studying this phenomenon have primarily answered the question "What is organized crime?" by pointing to a fundamentally flawed model of organized crime in America: an "alien conspiracy theory." If the model used to define the characteristics and activities of organized crime is flawed, the policies derived from that model will be similarly flawed.

The Alien Conspiracy Theory

Dwight Smith, in his book *The Mafia Mystique*, critiqued the model of organized crime that has dominated the perspective of scholars and policy makers since the end of World War II (Smith, 1976; 1975). According to the model, the essence of organized crime in America is embodied in a conspiracy of outsiders.

Organized crime is characterized as: a group of men motivated by criminality and a sense of loyalty foreign to an open, democratic society, united by an organized design for crime that is based on violence and focuses on crime and corruption (Smith, 1978).

This model asserts that organized crime was imported to the United States in the wave of Italian immigration in the late nineteenth and early twentieth centuries. Some of these immigrants belonged to feudal, secret, outlaw societies (the Mafia and Camorra, for example); these criminal foreigners planted the seeds from which contemporary organized crime groups have sprouted. Beginning as several small, often feuding criminal gangs, these groups grew in size and power during Prohibition, when people like Johnny Torrio and his apprentice Al Capone began uniting various factions into a single criminal conspiracy (Bequai, 1979). The Castellemarese War, a 1931 conflagration resulting from a long-standing feud between two major factions of New York's Italian gangs, served to coalesce organized crime into modern corporate-like groups, bureaucratically structured and governed by a national commission. This group, also referred to as Cosa Nostra, is today believed to dominate vice as well as racketeering, fraud, and the corrupting of a host of legitimate enterprises—all producing enormous profits and exerting tremendous influence on both the under- and upperworlds.

Although there have been many contributors to this characterization of American organized crime, the law enforcement community has been its driving force, finding eager adherents among ambitious politicians, blue ribbon panels, journalists, academics, and purveyors of popular entertainment. The Federal Bureau of Narcotics was the first to project the national policy implications of this alien conspiracy in 1946 (Smith, 1976). Subsequently, the Kefauver Senate hearings looking into organized crime's role in interstate gambling in 1951, the McClellan Committee's hearings on labor racketeering in 1957, and the investigations of the Appalachian "conference" of Mafia leaders that same year generated public expositions of this alien conspiracy. The testimony of Joseph Valachi, a self-proclaimed gangster turned informer, in 1963 wedded the alien conspiracy model to the term organized crime for many academics and policy makers. Valachi, more than anyone else, created the popular images now associated with the alien conspiracy model. The President's Crime Commission (President's Task Force Report, 1967) and Donald Cressey's Theft of the Nation (1969) were the principal vehicles through which this information was disseminated to the public. These accounts were soon popularized in a variety of journalistic and fictional works, including Mario Puzo's *The Godfather*. Evidence of the widespread acceptance of the conspiracy theory can be found in almost any recent news account of organized crime as well as in a host of academic and journalistic treatises (see, for example, Bonnano, 1983; Demaris, 1981; Chandler, 1975; Hammer, 1975; Pace and Styles, 1975; Cook, 1973; Sondern, 1959).

Four basic assertions define the parameters of organized crime from the official alien conspiracy perspective. First, **organized crime groups exhibit many structural features of legitimate corporate sector enterprises**. They are—even if secret— distinctly defined groups that have clear membership requirements and rituals. Organized into "families," their membership is stable and enduring. They are rationally and bureaucratically structured to achieve their principal objective—the enlargement of illicit profits: "Family organization is rationally designed with an integrated set of positions geared to maximize profits" (Task Force of Organized Crime, 1967: 6).

> The major difference between the diagram of an organized crime family and the chart of a major corporation is that the head of the enterprise—the "boss"—does not have a box over him labeled "stockholder." Many of the other boxes are paralleled in the underworld. The underboss serves a function similar to that of executive vice-president. The counselor, off to one side, is much like a vice-chairman of the board or a special assistant. He is an adviser but has no command authority. He is available to everyone for advice—but in his advice he always reflects the Boss's wishes. He also serves as a confidant of the Boss and as an oral historian. Ostensibly, he is a referee; impartial he is not.
>
> The lieutenants or captains further below are the equivalent of divisional vice-presidents or general managers. There are different staff jobs corresponding to the personnel director, public relations manager, general counsel, security officer and the like . . . (Salerno and Tompkins, 1969:84–85).

Organizational control is accomplished through a potent system of rewards and punishments that employ violence and bribery. Discipline relies upon a strict, clan-based feudal hierarchy that demands intense loyalty to superiors in exchange for access to financial rewards and protection from competing criminal groups and law enforcement. The "wise guy" code is the core of an occupational culture that makes superiors strictly accountable for lapses in subordinates' loyalty to the "firm." Thus, the conspiracy model fuses the feudal culture of Mafia origins with the sleek

Figure 1.1 Organizational Structure of *Cosa Nostra* Families

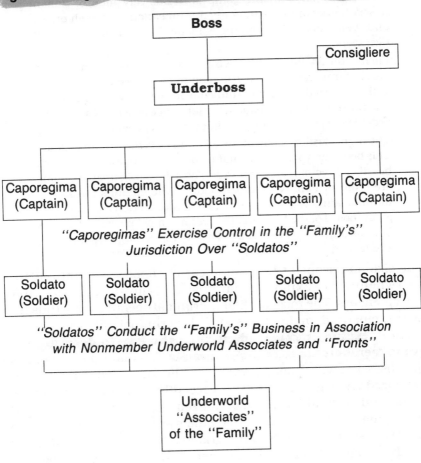

Adapted from U.S. Senate Permanent Subcommittee on Investigations, Committee on Governmental Affairs, *Hearings on Organized Crime and Use of Violence*, 96th Cong., 2d Sess., April, 1980, p. 117.

organizational forms that characterize the image of contemporary corporate enterprises of the upperworld.

A second feature of organized crime groups according to the official view is that, **like their upperworld counterparts, they seek to monopolize criminal enterprises by expanding in size and forming large cartels of national and international scope:**

Today the core of organized crime in the United States consists of 24 groups operating as criminal cartels in large cities across the nation. Their membership is exclusively men of Italian descent, they are in frequent communication with each other, and their smooth functioning is insured by a national body of overseers. . . .

Each of the 24 groups is known as a "family," with membership varying from as many as 700 men to as few as 20. Most cities with organized crime have only one family; New York has five. Each family can participate in the full range of activities in which organized crime generally is known to engage. . . .

The highest ruling body of the 24 families is the "commission." This body serves as a combination of legislature, supreme court, board of directors, and arbitration board; its principal functions are judicial. Family members look to the commission as the ultimate authority on organizational jurisdictional disputes. It is composed of the bosses of the nation's most powerful families but has authority over all 24 (Task Force on Organized Crime, 1967: 6–8).

The size and scope of this crime cartel enables it to intimidate, overwhelm, or exploit smaller-scale and would-be crime entrepreneurs. The most profitable criminal operations are thus the near-exclusive domain of this singular criminal alliance.

Third, **ethnic or racial identity is the key to determining group membership in organized crime**. This assertion illustrates the obsession with Italian heritage as the focal ethnic identity for organized crime groups. Until very recently the role of other ethnic, racial, and cultural groups in organized crime has been portrayed as insignificant. To the extent that others are involved, they are held to be very small operators or integrated into and subservient to the dominant families of the Italian cartel. Recent official revisions, discussed below, modify only the breadth of ethnic group participation, but retain the core assertion of ethnicity as the defining feature of group membership and operations.

Finally, the alien conspiracy model asserts that **organized crime groups undermine the very foundations of democracy by corrupting public officials and professionals to serve the criminal enterprise.** In the tradition of other alien conspiracy theories, this one portrays the organized criminal as a sinister foreign force that perverts essentially sound political and economic institutions, the functions of which are to ensure freedom and prosperity for the nation (Smith, 1976). Voicing this perspective, a journalist noted:

> Organized crime also has succeeded in corrupting legitimate businessmen who find that it is easier to do business with them than to try to buck them. Sometimes it simply involves selling their products to mob-controlled firms; other times it means paying bribes and kickbacks.
>
> Frank Perdue, the chicken magnate was unable to sell his birds to large New York grocery chains without doing business with distributor Dial Poultry, run in 1970 by the Mafia chieftain Paul Castellano, Jr. (Kahler, 1986).

According to this view, eliminating organized crime will largely eliminate corruption (Pace and Styles, 1975; Salerno and Tompkins, 1969).

The "Pluralist" Revision

In the last decade, the official depiction of organized crime in the United States has changed somewhat. Federal, state, and local law enforcement organizations have noted a growing pluralism in organized crime groups. In addition to "traditional" Mafia groups, they note the emergence of other groups that threaten the supremacy of the twenty-four families, especially in drug trafficking:

> The Mafia, the largest and best-established crime organization is up against forceful new competition from Asian and Latin American underworld groups that specialize in heroin, cocaine, and marijuana (Rowan, 1986: 26).

The California Attorney General's Annual Report to the Legislature for 1986 stated that "nontraditional" forms of organized crime (Colombians, Asian groups, motorcycle gangs, and the pornography syndicate) were becoming significant threats (*Organized Crime Digest*, 1986). Similarly, the Pennsylvania Crime Commission recently listed many of the same groups mentioned in the California report and added black groups operating in Pennsylvania (Pennsylvania Crime Commission, 1986). Perhaps the most comprehensive listing of "new" groups is found in the reports of the President's Commission on Organized Crime, which itemizes a variety of Cuban, Colombian, Japanese, Chinese, Vietnamese, Mexican, Russian, Canadian, Irish, black, and outlaw motorcycle gangs (1986).

What is most interesting about this recent shift in the official view of organized crime is not *how much* it has changed, but how steadfast it has been to the fundamental assertions of the alien conspiracy model in accounting for non-Italian groups. First, the new groups are defined as ethnically, racially, or culturally homogeneous. All have "alien" origins, are described in terms of some kind of culturally delineated "family" structure that resembles a rational corporate bureaucracy, and are rabidly expansionist in organization size and market share. Second, the recent acknowledgment that the Mafia does not have absolute hegemony in the illicit market for goods and services is based upon an underlying model of ethnic succession to other alien groups not yet as assimilated to mainstream American values. In fact, it is common for recent reports to tie the decline of Mafia power to the "Americanization" of the Italian community (Ianni, 1974; 1972b).

Why has this occurred? Enforcement officials offer several reasons. The Mafia has had difficulty generating dynamic replacements for the older leaders:

> The leadership is old, and the next generation of managers seems to lack spirit, dedication, and discipline. "Today you got guys in here who never broke an egg," a New Jersey Mafia leader complained in a conversation bugged by the FBI (Rowan, 1986: 24).

The new leadership is less interested in the high-risk aspects of the criminal enterprise and less inclined to resort to violence to maintain internal and external market control. They have an increasing interest in going the way of "sophisticated corporate America" according to an FBI spokesman (McFadden, 1987). Rather than intimidating and controlling competing groups, the new leadership makes deals with them, ceding certain markets or aspects of the production process in illicit goods and services. Also, federal officials point to recent enforcement efforts against the mob, such as surveillance of its leadership and prosecutions under the Federal Racketeer Influenced and Corrupt Organization (RICO) statute (Rowan, 1986). Finally, the new groups such as the Colombians, show the kind of criminal vitality and foreign connections that allegedly marked the Mafia in its earlier stages of development. The new groups are willing and eager to use violence where Mafiosi reputedly will not, and their foreign locations or connections outside the United States have made it easier to frustrate enforcement efforts and to operate with lower overhead costs.

The new crime groups are thus explained as part of a Darwinian struggle in which old groups give way to new and better adapted ones. As the new groups assume old Mafia functions, the Mafia leadership—to the extent that it can adapt—moves into new enterprises, such as the disposal of toxic wastes, securities and gem fencing, and fraud. Ultimately, we are left with a proliferation of distinct, ethnically defined criminal "corporations," some of which may die out or merge with other groups, or specialize in a specific sector of the illicit economy. The long-term fear is that a new, non-Italian ethnic hegemony may emerge.

It is interesting to note how federal law enforcement agencies scramble to account for new forces in illicit markets without seriously impairing their model of organized crime. There is a historical basis for their behavior. In the early twentieth century the same kind of alien conspiracy was touted as being responsible for America's drug problems. The temperance movement, for example, was a part of a nativist panic over the diminution of traditional, rural, middle-class, white, Protestant, native lifestyles in America. As Joseph Gusfield comments:

> The power of the Protestant, rural, native Americans was greater than that of the Eastern upper classes, the Catholic and Jewish immigrants, and the urbanized middle class. This was the lineup of the electoral struggle. In this struggle the champions of drinking represented cultural enemies and they had lost. . . .
>
> Increasingly the problem of liquor control became the central issue around which was posed the conflict between new and old cultural forces in American society. On the one side were the Wets—a union of cultural sophistication and secularism with Catholic lower-class traditionalism. These represented the new additions to the American population that made up the increasingly powerful political force of urban politics. On the other were the defenders of fundamental religion, or old moral values, of the ascetic, cautious, and sober middle class that had been the ideal of Americans in the nineteenth century (Gusfield, 1963: 122–23, 124).

So, like organized crime in the 1990s, liquor in the 1890s was a foreign, alien impingement on an otherwise righteous society.

The same fear of alien influence can be seen in discussions surrounding early narcotics legislation. Despite the fact that the 250,000 addicts in the United States at the turn of the century were predominantly middle-aged, middle-class, white women (Musto, 1973; Brecher, 1972), the problem of drugs was laid squarely at the feet of aliens:

> In the nineteenth century addicts were identified with foreign groups and internal minorities who were already actively feared and the objects of elaborate and massive social and legal restraints. Two repressed groups which were associated with the use of certain drugs were the Chinese and the Negroes. The Chinese and their custom of opium smoking were closely watched after their entry into the United States about 1870. At

first, the Chinese represented only one more group brought in
to help build the railroads, but, particularly after economic
depressions made them a labor surplus and a threat to American
citizens, many forms of antagonism arose to drive them out, or
at least to isolate them. Along with the prejudice came a fear
of opium smoking as one of the ways in which the Chinese were
supposed to undermine American society.

Cocaine was especially feared in the South by 1900 because of
its euphoric and stimulating properties. The South feared that
[African-American] cocaine users might become oblivious of
their prescribed bounds and attack white society . . .

Evidence does not suggest that cocaine caused a crime wave
but rather that anticipation of black rebellion inspired white
alarm. Anecdotes often told of superhuman strength, cunning,
and efficiency resulting from cocaine. One of the most terrifying
beliefs about cocaine was that it actually improved pistol
marksmanship. Another myth, that cocaine made blacks almost
unaffected by mere .32 caliber bullets, is said to have caused
Southern police departments to switch to .38 caliber revolvers.
These fantasies characterized white fear, not the reality of
cocaine's effects and gave one more reason for the repression
of blacks. (Musto, 1973: 5–7 and 65; cited in McCaghy and
Cernkovich, 1987).

Musto (1973) links similar fears toward Mexicans with the passage
of the Marijuana Tax Act of 1937.

The fear of immigrants and repressed racial and ethnic groups
in the United States was used to construct a conspiracy theory of
drug use, just as it was used to construct a conspiracy theory of
organized crime. The argument has always been the same: forces
outside of mainstream American culture are at work which seek
to pervert an otherwise morally sound, industrious, and democratic
people. It is a convenient and easily understood argument. It is, in
fact, the only depiction of organized crime that could gain
widespread popular appeal. To suggest that righteous citizens are
being perverted, intimidated, and forced into vice by alien forces
is far more palatable than suggesting that "native" demands for
illicit drugs, sex, and gambling invite the creation of organized
crime groups. Despite the minor alterations in the alien conspiracy
theory, we can clearly discern that its revisionist form is neither
new, clever, nor very different from the Mafia myth.

The Alien Conspiracy Discredited

The historical "proofs" of the alien conspiracy model range from the dubious to the preposterous. A detailed recounting of these proofs is not possible in this short discussion, but several of the most egregious errors will be highlighted.

Serious scholarship on the Sicilian Mafia has cast grave doubt on the claim that a highly structured and unified group of Sicilian gangsters was transplanted intact to the United States. First, none of the other nations which were the recipients of the waves of Sicilian immigration at the turn of the century (Australia and Britain, for example) developed organized crime groups anything like the Mafia. Second, organized crime already had a well-developed foothold in the major cities of the United States before the Sicilians arrived, indicating that it could not have been imported with the immigrants. Finally, the Sicilian Mafia appears to have been a far different group than the criminal conspiracy described by alien conspiracy theorists. A group rooted in the peasant traditions and feudal economy of Sicily would be virtually impossible to export to a democratic, industrial nation. It appears far more likely that the Sicilian Mafia were intermediaries between peasants and the aristocracy, usually serving the interests of the latter and consisting of many highly fragmented groups (Blok, 1974). Smith (1976; 1975) shows that the origins of the Mafia importation myth derive from strong nativist, anti-Italian sentiments, press sensationalism, and rampant rumor. The 1931 Castellemarese War, alleged to have restructured the old Mafia into its contemporary corporate form, has been discredited by thorough research that could find evidence of only three possibly related murders—not the forty which are alleged to have allowed the new breed of Americanized gangster to replace the "old Mustache Petes" (Block, 1978; Nelli, 1976). The Kefauver Committee hearings presented only law enforcement allegations—no evidence—to demonstrate the Mafia's existence, despite the fact that those hearings exposed non-Mafia organized crime syndicates in each and every city under investigation (Bell, 1964). Law enforcement testimony that the Appalachian conclave proved the existence of an overarching crime conspiracy has been shown to be based on very little reliable information easily amenable to other interpretations (Smith, 1975; Albini, 1971; Morris and Hawkins, 1970). Finally, the 1963 testimony of Joseph Valachi regarding the practices and structure of the Cosa Nostra has been shown to be riddled with contradictions, factual errors, and uncorroborated assertions (Albanese, 1985; Smith, 1975; Albini, 1971; Morris and Hawkins, 1970).

The official versions of organized crime share a heavy reliance on a few government-sponsored informants, selected police files, and surveillance transcripts—tied together with the tangled threads of law enforcement officials' speculations. Reuter (1986) points out the inherent biases in data collected by enforcement agencies that look only for the evidence that reinforces their basic assumptions about organized crime. Indeed, if law enforcement agencies had monitored a broader range of organized crime groups over the last forty years as assiduously as they did the Mafia families, they would know that a large number of these new groups are not new at all. Sometimes law enforcement agencies even *consciously* contribute to misinformation by falsifying files and reports through disinformation campaigns designed to create dissension in targeted groups or to present the agency in the best possible light (Villano, 1978; Capeci, 1976).

Aside from the flaws in the official version of organized crime's history, there is ample evidence that the structure and practices of crime groups bear little relationship to the tenets of the alien conspiracy theory. First, organized crime is **not** composed of clearly defined, tightly structured, stable families. Rather, **organized criminality occurs in an informal, loosely structured, open system**. It is highly reactive to fluctuations in its economic and political—as well as legal—environments. Although some individuals do show long-term patterns of collaboration in illicit activities, participation in any given operation is determined not so much by these collaborative patterns as by circumstances subject to frequent and rapid change: the growth or decline of a market for illicit goods and services, the availability of new manufacturers or distributors, opportunities arising from changes in the law and regulatory or enforcement practices, the need for special skills or contacts not readily available within the group, and, of course, the ambitions of potential participants. This leads, not to elaborate sub-rosa criminal empires, but to flexible, adaptive networks that readily expand and contract to deal with the uncertainties of the criminal enterprise. Rather than an immutable bureaucratic structure with a clearly defined hierarchy, the pattern of association more closely resembles what Albini (1971) has termed a "patron-client relationship." The patron exchanges information, connections (with government officials and legitimate business people), and access to a network of operatives (such as fences and enforcers) for the client's economic and political support. However, the client/criminal may cooperate with other, even competing, patrons, and may in turn be an independent patron in some other illicit enterprises. The wise-guy code of intense loyalty to the family is vastly overrated as a means of maintaining group cohesion. To be sure, such a code appears to exist, but not on a scale comparable to the sort of organizational loyalty thought to be promoted by major corporations like IBM or Hewlett-Packard (Peters and Wakeman, 1982). The scope of an organized criminal's enduring loyalty is usually limited to a few people. Membership rituals—to the extent that they occur at all—have little meaning in the context of a long-term socialization process (see, for example, Pileggi, 1985). Strict intergroup discipline is not the norm; competition, treachery, communication breakdowns, and other forms of "disorganization" are far more characteristic than the image of the sleek corporate machine (Reuter, 1983). The frequency of intragroup conflict, threats, violence, and fragmentation—documented even by proponents of the alien conspiracy model—are testimony to the contrary view.

A second major divergence from the conspiracy model is that **small, fragmented, and ephemeral enterprises tend to populate illegal markets—not large corporate syndicates** (Reuter, 1983; Block, 1979a). Small size minimizes exposure to the risk of getting caught and successfully prosecuted. Employees in illegal enterprises are the greatest threat to the operations. They make the best witnesses against others, so it is in the group's interest to limit the number of people who have knowledge about the group's operations and then to limit the amount of information available to them. By segmenting information so that most participants know only about their jobs, damage from a successful arrest or prosecution is controlled both vertically and horizontally in the operation. The best example is found in the heroin industry where production, importation, and distribution are discrete functions handled by completely different organized crime groups. Although this strategy is useful in thwarting law enforcement, it is not conducive to efficient corporate enterprise, which requires extensive information sharing.

In addition to limiting the number of employees and availability of information, organized crime groups tend to limit the geographic scope of their operations. The larger the geographic area, the more law enforcement and other public agencies take an interest in the operations, thus increasing the risks and costs (in terms of bribes) of doing business. Further, it is more costly to monitor employee loyalty and performance over large areas, given that the ways that legitimate organizations deal with these problems (telecommunications) are vulnerable to surveillance. Personal, undocumented communications are essential in organized crime, but traveling many hours to relay a message is simply not efficient. Thus, although illegality offers remarkable profit margins for risk takers, most organized crime groups are reluctant to expand geographically in rapidly rising markets, and it's often when such expansions are attempted that law enforcement achieves its greatest successes.

There are, of course, instances where the payoffs are sufficient to make the risks of apprehension attractive. For a period during Prohibition, an extensive cartel controlled the importation of Canadian whiskey to the United States, ranging from the northeast to the midwest (Abadinsky, 1985; Potter and Jenkins, 1985; Block and Chambliss, 1981). Some drug importers have distributed methamphetamines to much of the east coast. The Escobar and Ochoa cocaine cartel distributes its product across much of the western hemisphere and even has a substantial foothold in Europe. The so-called "Black Mafia" trafficks in heroin from Boston to Washington, D.C. Occasionally, bookmaking ventures involve several cities. Recently casino gambling (both legal and illegal) has been pursued on a multistate basis by several organized crime groups (Demaris, 1986; Pennsylvania Crime Commission, 1980). Probably the most dramatic and persistent example of monopolistic criminal enterprise was the Sturman pornography operations, which consisted of hundreds of corporate entities throughout the United States and as many as twenty thousand retail outlets (Potter, 1986). However, large geographic scope seems most feasible not in the operations end of illicit enterprise but in the financing. Meyer Lansky, through his financial wizardry, managed a low visibility collaboration with a small number of key figures in organized crime. Lansky, however, operated not as a "Don" or mob kingpin, but as an underworld investment banker whose principal influence was through selecting profitable enterprises which merited his support. Working through cooperative banks and investment institutions, which were overseen only by relatively underused or understaffed regulatory agencies, the financiers of criminal enterprise have long enjoyed a greater scope of freedom than their operational counterparts.

A third major problem with the alien conspiracy model is that it **overstates and misinterprets the role of ethnicity in determining the structure of organized crime**. As was noted earlier, even federal law enforcement agencies have come to acknowledge that the underworld is not dominated by a single ethnic group, the Mafia. However, even its recent adoption of ethnic pluralism retains the ethnic homogeneity of any group as the key defining feature. This claim ignores much of the evidence available on many crime groups comprised of or having substantial interactions with individuals of various ethnic backgrounds (Potter and Jenkins, 1984; Block, 1979b). Philadelphia's K and A Gang is a classic example of a multi-ethnic Irish-Jewish-Italian group. The Hampton crime group in Philadelphia, while primarily black and operating in an almost exclusively black area of the city, has James Creagh, an Irishman, as an active participant and major financier (Pennsylvania Crime Commission, 1986). One of the largest organized crime groups in the United States, Chicago's fabled "Outfit," has been composed of Italians, Irish, Jews, and Greeks (and at least one Welchman) since the days of Al Capone (Potter, 1986; Abadinsky, 1985). Meyer Lansky's long-term collaboration with Italian, Cuban, and Corsican gangsters also demonstrates the irrelevance of an ethnic component in a model of organized crime. Certainly the outlaw motorcycle gangs are also very mixed with regard to ethnicity and culture—some even wearing three-piece suits (Pennsylvania Crime Commission, 1986; 1983; 1980; Abadinsky, 1985)!

Finally, the alien conspiracy model **overplays the role of organized criminals as the corrupters of public officials and professionals**. Some studies show that positions of public trust are specifically sought for the opportunities that arise from collaboration with the underworld (Block and Scarpitti, 1985; Potter and Jenkins, 1985; Chambliss, 1978; Gardiner, 1970; Gardiner and Lyman, 1970). The Knapp Commission and recent exposes of Philadelphia Police Department corruption show how thoroughly institutionalized corruption can be among public officials. In the private sector, such institutions as Shearson/American Express, Merrill Lynch, the Miami National Bank, Citibank, and others have participated in illicit ventures (Moldea, 1986; *Organized Crime Digest*, 1986; Lernoux, 1984). Distinguishing the corrupter and the corruptee is even more problematic in the arena of state-organized crime, where those in public office seek the services of the underworld to perform the dirty work that they—for one reason or another—cannot do legitimately. State-organized crime has a long, if not honorable history (Chambliss, 1978). Revelations about the intelligence community's employment of organized criminals since World War II and its support for foreign narcotics exporters to the United States illustrate the point (Block, 1986; Lernoux, 1984; Kruger, 1980). The CIA's collaboration with Corsican organized crime figures in Marseilles, in order to break the power of left-wing trade unions, which resulted in the creation of the "French Connection" heroin network; its alliance with organized crime figures, including Lansky, in plots against Fidel Castro; its collaboration with Southeast Asian warlords and heroin producers during the Vietnam conflict; and, the Reagan administration's open collaboration with the Medellin Cocaine Cartel in support of the contra war in Nicaragua, are but a few of the best known examples. This is not to deny that members of the underworld initiate bribes and seek to control public figures, but it does suggest that the under- and upperworld criminals form a close, symbiotic bond that usually places the latter in the center, not the periphery, of the illicit enterprise. Society's legitimate and respected institutions are not just the pawns of organized crime; they are part of its fabric.

Of course, showing that many gangs have members from more than one ethnic group does not in and of itself disprove the claim that a single ethnic group dominates those gangs. This, however, misses the point that gang membership is often quite fluid and that groups dominated by different ethnic memberships work closely together in illegal enterprises. Several studies have shown how Italian groups work closely with Jewish, Irish, and black groups (Jenkins and Potter, 1987; Peterson, 1983; Block, 1979a).

To the extent that organized crime groups do show ethnic homogeneity, that fact does not logically lead to the conclusion that a secret brotherhood of ethnics consciously recruits only from its own group and excludes all others. Rather, ethnic homogeneity derives from the already demonstrated need of most illicit enterprises to remain geographically limited and from the demographics of urban areas where such enterprises are undertaken. Vice in a black neighborhood will be organized by blacks, by Italians in an Italian neighborhood, and so on. Although preference may be given to kinship in some crime organizations, recruitment of and interaction with "outgroup" criminals is based primarily on need, availability, and cost-effectiveness.

Perhaps the most important evidence against the relevance of ethnicity as an influential force in shaping organized crime is that the ethnicity of a group has no appreciable impact on the way it performs its illicit activities. This is due largely to the requirements for producing and distributing illegal goods and services which remain fairly constant across geographic areas. Black-run prostitution is very similar in structure to its Italian counterpart. Differences that do occur are based on differences in markets—not the producer's ethnicity (for example, in low income areas street walkers are prevalent while call girl services are most likely in high income areas; middle class neighborhoods are likely to be served by cocaine dealers, while inner city ghettos are likely to served by "crack" dealers). The same applies for drug trafficking, gambling,

Figure 1.2 Differing Propositions about Organized Crime Derived from the Alien Conspiracy Theory and Empirical Research on Organized Crime

Propositions from the Alien Conspiracy Theory	Propositions from Empirical Research on Organized Crime
Organized crime groups are similar in structure to large corporate bureaucracies in the legitimate economy.	Organized crime groups are loosely structured, informally organized, and open systems.
Organized crime groups try to secure a monopoly in the illicit market by constantly expanding in size and forming large criminal cartels.	Organized crime groups are small in terms of numbers of participants and geographical scope, and they tend to be highly fragmented.
Organized crime groups engage in a campaign of corruption aimed at public officials, police, professionals, and legitimate businessmen.	Corruption occurs in an open marketplace and is mutually agreed to and initiated.
Ethnicity and racial identity are key variables in selecting members for organized crime groups.	Ethnicity is not a determining factor in the composition of organized crime groups.

loansharking, fraud, racketeering, and a host of other criminal enterprises.

Reconceptualizing the Organized Crime Problem

To overcome many of the failings of present conceptions of organized crime, we must begin by viewing criminal organizations as participants in a variety of illicit industries. One must not assume, however, that identifying criminal organizations is tantamount to identifying the industry. The first step is to distinguish among the various "industries" with which organized crime is associated: various types of illicit drugs, gambling, racketeering, etc. The patterns and extent of organized crime involvement may be safely presumed to vary with the industry.

That is, at least, a safer working hypothesis.

The second step in reconceptualizing the organized crime problem is to break down each type of enterprise into its essential components. For example, the illicit drug industry may be divided into manufacturing, distribution, sales and marketing, finance, and product development. One may expect to see different levels of organized crime involvement in each of these areas and, indeed, different organized crime groups may be involved in each area. Further, these patterns vary from region to region and according to the particular drug. Under ideal circumstances, we would want to know the scope of the industry in each of its phases, the organization and individuals involved, the nature and extent of their activities, etc. It is difficult enough to obtain reliable data for legitimate and relatively open industries, such as petroleum; it is very difficult to go beyond surmise and speculation for illicit industries. If one is to understand the impact of policies directed at organized crime, one must know what is going on in the industry. The major problem in this attempt at understanding is that the entire enforcement mechanism for dealing with vice produces a very biased sample of information on participants and the scope of their activities. It is virtually impossible to make precise estimates of the level of activity. Estimating the street value of seized drugs or the proportion of illicit drugs removed from the market by enforcement efforts provides very little useful information. Instead, attention should be directed at the impact of various policies by searching for changes in patterns of operation or in the relationships among participants in the various phases of a particular activity. How do drug marketing practices change in the wake of a given enforcement policy or new market conditions? Does the assignment of tasks shift from one group to another? Was there an impact on the structure of the organized crime group? Were financial impacts noted?

It is clear that monitoring the various stages of a given illicit industry will produce markedly different types of information. One of the stages given insufficient attention in organized crime research and analysis is the "laundering" of funds. Today this is one of the most vulnerable aspects of illegitimate enterprises, such as gambling and drug dealing. These illicit activities generate enormous profits, which must be made to appear legitimate at some point if they are to be used in the legitimate economy (Lernoux, 1984).

Chambliss (1978), for example, reported that the distinction between organized crime, business, and government in Seattle was almost impossible to discern. The same patterns are evident elsewhere. Banks and other institutions of finance are the obvious and well-documented mechanism by which participants in illicit industries move between the under- and upperworlds (Block, 1979). As Dwight Smith, Jr. (1978: 164) concluded:

> [organized crime] represents in virtually every instance, an extension of a legitimate market spectrum into areas normally proscribed. Their separate strengths derive from the same fundamental considerations that govern entrepreneurship in the legitimate marketplace: a necessity to maintain and extend one's share of the market.

The implications of conceptualizing organized crime as a process and a business are clearly manifested in a number of ways. Rather than a macro search to prove that organized crime is a massive organization structured like a conglomerate and intent on swallowing all available markets while corrupting unsuspecting public servants, the emphasis should be on the micro element of truth in the assumption. This is an illicit "business" and all attendant features should be analyzed. The critical descriptive question changes from "who" to "how." How do organized crime networks successfully organize themselves to meet public demand? How do organized crime networks launder dirty money? Through what mechanism does reinvestment occur? What are the parameters of organized crime groups? What environmental contexts allow the processes of organized crime to operate with success? How do we evaluate and understand these environmental contexts, such as political and police corruption? How can we best conceptualize the symbiotic relationship between organized criminals and organized businessmen?

Organized Crime as a Social Subsystem

In view of the fact that it appears that the alien conspiracy theory is erroneous, inaccurate, and inappropriate to a description of organized crime, a more acceptable and satisfying mode of analysis must be developed. Within the context of the reconceptualization of the organized crime problem, it would be appropriate to suggest that organized crime, in contemporary American society, is a functional necessity. If this is the case, then organized crime should be studied within the context of the functions it performs in society and in the community.

Organized crime as a community subsystem is amenable to analysis in the same way we would analyze a United Fund drive or a local welfare system. In order to be regarded as a community subsystem, organized crime must meet certain functional requirements to continue in existence and, indeed, to prosper. The literature on community is quite specific in delineating these functional requirements. Warren (1973) delineates these functions as: 1) production-distribution-consumption; 2) socialization; 3) social control; 4) social participation; and 5) mutual support.

Production-distribution-consumption refers to the delivery of goods and services in the community. Organized crime plays a key role in this aspect of community life. In many respects, this function describes the reason for the existence of organized crime. The only difference between organized crime groups and other community groups is that the goods and services organized crime delivers are usually, and predominantly, illegal. Nonetheless, they are in great demand by the public, making the creation of organizations to meet that demand inevitable. In any study of organized crime, the production-distribution-consumption dimension of organized crime must be given considerable attention. Questions of how organizations are created, perform their logistical tasks, exact a profit, and meet consumer expectations must be looked at in detail. The role of the market in creating organized crime groups must be examined, and the importance of organized crime to other organizations and businesses performing this function must be addressed.

Socialization is the process by which values, acceptable patterns of behavior, and prevailing knowledge are transmitted in the community. We will see that organized crime plays an important role in this function. It socializes its own participants to life in an illegal economy and illicit environment, and it supports community socialization processes by reinforcing the definitions of acceptable behavior, within or outside of the law. In community studies, we often think of the local school system as the vital component of the socialization process. In terms of organized crime we can also examine an educational component, a component which teaches people how to make the fullest use of their talents in a specific social setting and economic market and a component which teaches people how to best adapt to the exigencies of social life.

Social control is the process by which the community influences its members toward conformance with established norms of behavior. It is important to remember that acceptable norms of behavior are not synonymous with legality. It is usually formal governmental agencies, such as the police, the courts, zoning boards and the like which perform this function. In reality, however, organized crime "picks up the slack" in many cases, providing protection against predatory crime when the police cannot, providing alternatives to predatory crime when the economy cannot, setting limits on illegal behavior and the amount of disruption present in the community when the law cannot. In many respects, organized crime operates as an ameliorative influence in the performance of this function where official agencies have failed.

Social participation is a function of providing access for community residents. Often we think of churches, voluntary civic organizations and the like as the primary modalities for social participation. In fact, organized crime also provides this function, often providing the most direct and socially acceptable means for granting social participation to groups that are otherwise excluded from community functions (minority and immigrant groups, for example). Organized crime, if conceived of as a massive social network running throughout the community, provides virtually unlimited opportunities for political, social, and economic participation in community life. It also plays a role, as we shall see, in facilitating the activities of other upperworld agencies in performing this function. Organized crime group members are often important actors and contributors to the activities of their churches, civic organizations, and local charities. Criminal organizations also cement patterns of social interaction arising from family, kinship, and other social groups in the community, adding business to the list of reasons for social solidarity.

Finally, organized crime plays a role in providing mutual support. Mutual support is the community function which provides for assistance in times of crises, aid for the infirm, assistance to the unemployed. Organized crime's role in providing this function may be more vital than any other community subsystem. Where the community has failed to provide adequate employment, sufficient retirement benefits, adequate information and assistance in finding housing and obtaining consumer goods, and adequate disposable income to prop up precarious small businesses, organized crime fills the void. As we shall see, organized crime may be one of the most effective social welfare agencies operating in the contemporary American community.

All of these factors come together to make organized crime a functional necessity in meeting the required functions at the community level. While this may be seen as a social pathology by some, it is quite simply a fundamental fact of community life. Organized crime is a functional necessity given the exigencies of contemporary social life in the United States.

Viewing organized crime as a functional necessity in the community also allows us to appreciate its role in other ways.

Figure 1.3 Organized Crime as a Community Subsystem

Community Function	Components of the Function	Type of Organized Crime Participation
Production-Distribution-Consumption	The delivery of goods and services in the community.	Delivery of strongly demanded but legally proscribed goods and services. Organized crime group interactions with legitimate businesses providing goods and services to the community.
Socialization	The process by which values, patterns of acceptable behavior, and prevailing knowledge are transmitted in the community.	Training people for "careers" in the illicit economy. Providing a means of adaptation for people in a stratified society. Passing on a sense of criminal "history" and illicit skills.
Social Control	The process by which the community promotes conformance with established norms of behavior.	Provides alternatives to predatory criminal careers. Provides protection from predatory crime. Provides controls on disruptive behaviors resulting from "vice" crimes.
Social Participation	The process by which community residents are granted access to community institutions.	Provides a means for upwards social mobility for those blocked from legitimate means of access. Provides wide-ranging social and business contacts. Participates in community charities.
Mutual Support	Provides for assistance in times of crises.	Provides information on available housing, consumer goods. Supplements incomes.

Warren (1973) argues that community subsystems are usually parts of the social system which extend far beyond the boundaries of the community. How they extend beyond the community is vitally important for understanding how both the subsystem itself and the community at large operate to meet their functional requirements. Warren isolates two types of patterns that integrate subsystems with social systems: a vertical pattern and a horizontal pattern.

Vertical patterns of integration refer to those connections that go beyond (and often above) the community. Organized crime plays an important role in fostering vertical integration. It connects that community to other organized crime groups operating in other communities and institutions at the state and national levels. It provides access to investment capital in major financial centers that otherwise would be denied to the local community. It ties the community to regional and even national industries, and it provides the community with a wide range of vertical political connections. As such, even though we may think of organized crime in negative and pejorative terms, it provides access for all kinds of community institutions to agencies and systems that might otherwise be closed to community actors.

In terms of horizontal integration (the pattern of structural and functional relationships between and among subsystems in the same community), organized crime is one of the few community subsystems that touches every other subsystem in one way or another. In providing vital functions at the community level, organized crime integrates other community institutions into the community social system.

Past studies of organized crime indicate the inadequacy of descriptions of organized crime that ignore its functional relationships with political, economic, and social systems and subsystems at the community level. In order to understand organized crime and to describe its operations and its persistence, it is necessary to understand its complex interrelationships and interactions with the rest of the community in a highly symbiotic relationship.

Chapter 2

What Do We Know about Organized Crime?

There are very few topics of interest in the area of crime and justice which have wider appeal and evoke more public fascination than organized crime. Organized crime is the basis for countless movies, television shows, books, newspapers and magazine articles and scholarly papers. The sheer volume of print and film products related to organized crime is staggering. Organized crime also has a lasting appeal and box office draw, as evidenced by recent releases of movies such as *Godfather III, Goodfellas, Prizzi's Honor, Billy Bathgate, The Untouchables, Miller's Crossing, Bugsy,* and *The Krays.*

Despite all the books that have been written, the articles that have been published, and the movies that have been made, we know very little about organized crime. Certainly we know the names of a few notorious crime figures such as Al Capone, Lucky Luciano, and Meyer Lansky. Many of us have become familiar with a few value-laden terms (although we may not know exactly what they mean), such as *Mafia, Cosa Nostra, omerta,* and *vendetta.* As discussed in chapter 1, we also have some vague idea about an international conspiracy of crime (structured much like a General Motors or Ma Bell), whose tentacles extend into even the most placid and bucolic

American communities, corrupting otherwise incorruptible citizens. The fact is, however, that very few of us—law enforcement officers, academics and the general public—know much about organized crime. For example, we can't really explain why we can't get rid of organized crime. After all, we seem to know who the bad guys are, and we put large numbers of them in jail, but when we turn around there's as much drug trafficking, illegal gambling, hijacking, and other types of organized crime as there was before. We seem to know a great deal about organized crime's role in illicit goods and services: pornography, prostitution, gambling, loansharking, fencing, organized theft, and drug dealing. What we can't explain, however, is why organized crime is so successful at delivering these goods and services to the general public and why the general public, which after all knows sin and evil when it sees them, continues to spend billions of dollars on vice despite our best law enforcement efforts to protect them from themselves. We seem to know that a business as big and as public as organized crime has to have some help from ostensibly legitimate business leaders, politicians, and law enforcement officers in order to survive. Nevertheless, we can't seem to understand how this happens, how these otherwise good and faithful servants of the public could be compromised by the mob.

As organized crime evolves to meet the demands of an ever-changing society, this lack of knowledge and understanding becomes even more pronounced. We used to take some comfort in the claim that organized crime was basically just the Mafia, but now we are told that we have to worry about myriad other groups: Cuban organized crime, Colombian cartels, Chinese "Mafias," black organized crime groups, prison gangs operating beyond the walls of the institution, outlaw motorcycle clubs, "Yuppie" cocaine rings, and the "Cornbread Mafia," among many, many others (President's Commission on Organized Crime, 1986).

Neither academics trying to provide scholarly answers nor law enforcement personnel trying to develop useful intelligence have been very successful in analyzing organized crime. The bottom line is that we do not understand its appeal or its persistence. It is obvious that organized crime is not an easy topic to research, but the problems inherent in the research topic have been compounded by two simple and systematic research errors: 1) we are using the wrong data; and 2) we are asking the wrong questions.

Research Problems and Dilemmas

Traditional research methods, which have proven to be valid and reliable in dealing with other topics in criminology, have limited utility in studying organized crime. How does one conduct survey research on the mob? Do we send questionnaires to a representative sample of drug traffickers? Do we ask for the cooperation of our local Mafia chapter or motorcycle gang in setting up structured interviews? What about the experimental method? Do we set up a community of rats and try to determine how they might organize to collect sports bets or distribute cocaine? Do we immerse ourselves in crunching numbers from data we know are not only suspect and incomplete, but in many cases simply wrong, in hopes of a little mathematical alchemy?

There are few sources of funding for research on organized crime. The National Institute of Justice provides some level of support for a couple of proposals each year. Occasionally, private foundations have funded research efforts, but there is no sense of urgency in establishing a research agenda on organized crime. The process of proposal writing and funding has compromised what research there is even further. The peer review process has stifled methodological innovation and risk taking. As a result, the limited research on organized crime has often been limited to the mundane and often irrelevant kinds of inquiries that can be conducted within the parameters of traditional "science."

Finally, the environment within which organized crime research takes place has been debilitating to quality work. Law enforcement intelligence analysts are under constant pressure to provide useful, tangible, tactical intelligence that will lead to arrests and convictions, not to an understanding of the dynamics of organized crime. Academics, operating under considerable pressure to publish in a timely fashion and in quantity, have shied away from research on organized crime which is usually very time consuming and uncertain as to the likelihood that it will produce useful data for publication.

Bad Data

Shackled by the research conditions described above, researchers initiating a project soon find that they are immersed in tainted data of questionable validity and almost no reliability. Most of the literature, both popular and scholarly, on organized crime draws its information from three basic sources: government reports, government-sponsored informants, and journalistic accounts. Each of these data sources is contaminated from the start. If relied upon as the exclusive sources of data, the research process is infected with validity and reliability problems that cannot be overcome.

Government Documents

Documents and reports from government agencies are suspect for a number of reasons (Albanese, 1985; Block, 1978; Rubinstein and Reuter, 1978a; Smith, 1975; Albini, 1971). First, these agencies are limited by secrecy. Because their information comes from ongoing investigations or criminal prosecutions, much information is withheld.

Second, law enforcement agencies are unlikely to include information in their public documents which contradicts the position that they are taking. These reports are edited and carefully refined; all data that might lead to alternative interpretations is expunged. It is in the interest of the agency in question to present its strongest possible case. This is fine for public relations purposes; however, it is not acceptable for scientific inquiry. These reports and documents are not subject to an external validation process which might raise questions of validity and reliability, which would insist upon rigorous checks of data quality, and which should suggest alternate interpretations of the data.

Third, official law enforcement agencies, particularly at the federal level have shown an inexorable tendency to engage in the construction of elaborate conspiracy theories which pander to popular fascination and fear. Dwight Smith has argued that there is a peculiar preoccupation among these agencies and the American public in general with the idea of conspiracies. As we learned in chapter 1, Smith applies the "alien conspiracy" mentality to organized crime. All that is needed for the construction of a conspiracy framework is a set of assumptions that can be rearranged into a set of "proofs" supporting a conspiratorial explanation (Smith, 1975). These "facts" make for interesting reading and are quickly picked up by newspapers, magazines, books, movies, and television. They thereby earn credence by the frequency of their repetition, even if there is little empirical justification for the assumptions supporting the conspiracy. In particular, Smith points to the case of the Federal Bureau of Narcotics as a premier constructor of conspiracies:

The notion of total suppression of illegal narcotics use through importation control was a self-proclaimed mission, and it had not been attained. How better to explain failure (and incidentally, to prepare the ground for increased future budgets) than to argue that, dedicated though it may be, the bureau was hard pressed to overcome an alien, organized, conspiratorial force which, with evil intent and conspiratorial methods had forced its way on an innocent public? (1975: 85).

Smith, of course, is arguing that a set of disputable facts were constructed in such a way as to "prove" the existence of a sinister, alien conspiracy called the Mafia. According to Smith, the initial problem which must be confronted in using government documents is this bureaucratic tendency to explain failure through conspiracy.

Fourth, the government has been known to present incorrect information from time to time for deliberate purposes. Anthony Villano (1978), in his fascinating book *Brick Agent*, talks about the use of disinformation by law enforcement agencies. The use of this strategy is more common than we might imagine. Villano, an FBI agent for over twenty years specializing in organized crime, states that the FBI regularly supplied false reports to the press and others in an attempt to create dissension and confusion among organized crime networks. In a similar incident, the *New York Times* revealed that in 1977 the Drug Enforcement Agency "leaked" information that organized crime figure Carmine Galante was making a move to take over the rackets in New York City. The report was false and the agency knew it was false. Nonetheless, they went ahead and disseminated the story in the hope that dissension and confusion would plague New York's organized crime groups. Apparently someone believed them; on July 12, 1979, Mr. Galante was assassinated. Disinformation readily finds its way into official reports and documents and into the press. While there may be good tactical reasons for the use of disinformation, lies are very bad data.

Fifth, there is always the suspicion of corruption and questionable police tactics which underlie official reports. Obviously, an agency compromised by the mob cannot be expected to report accurately on organized crime. Similarly, an agency protecting its informants and keeping its word in deals made with active criminals cannot be expected to present a very accurate portrait of organized crime.

Finally, far more important than bureaucratic tendencies toward conspiratorial theories and the use of disinformation campaigns is the fundamental question of what the government actually knows. There is a very real question of how much accurate information government sources have at their command, even when they are trying to tell the unvarnished truth. This point was vividly demonstrated by Rubinstein and Reuter:

> The difficulty the government had in obtaining accurate information on the reserve of the energy-producing companies in the wake of the 1973 oil boycott should serve as a sober reminder of how difficult it is to collect accurate information even from legitimate organizations operating in a highly regulated environment. The challenges are immeasurably greater in collecting information about people who are consciously involved in illegal activities (1978b: 57).

They go on to comment on a United States Department of Justice effort to determine the amount of illegal gambling revenues in the United States. After noting the totally unscientific basis for the final estimate, Rubinstein and Reuter conclude:

> In truth, we suspect that the real failing of the estimate was that no one really cared how it was developed, but only that it produce a large number. The assumption that the details of the calculation would not be subjected to any scrutiny led to a cavalier use of the available data. Also, the estimate had no possible consequences; it was produced for rhetorical purposes and has served these purposes very well (1978b: 62).

Nonetheless, in spite of these problems, the primary source for most of the scholarly writings on organized crime, at least the best known scholarly writings, is official government documents. The most important work derived from the use of this data is Cressey's (1969) *Theft of the Nation*. Cressey compiled his data while serving as a member of the Federal Task Force on Organized Crime. In addition to the problems inherent in using officially produced data (in this case data supporting the very controversial testimony of Joe Valachi), Cressey had an additional problem in that he was a government employee who was given access to data that no other scholar had or could review. The combination of these two factors have made his work suspect to a number of critics of the official version of organized crime. Cressey, to his credit, acknowledged the problem, admitting that he had shifted his role from that of a social scientist to that of a "propagandist" in the course of his work. In fact, it was Cressey himself who argued that a social scientist "who is given access to information ordinarily inaccessible must be prepared to shift his role" (1967b: 106). Cressey's work creates an ongoing problem in organized crime research in that it is the basis for much for the scholarly writing which followed his book's publication.

Government-Sponsored Informants

Government-sponsored informants present many of the same problems (Albanese, 1985; Block, 1978; Smith, 1975; Albini, 1971). While a Joe Valachi, or a Jimmy "the Weasel" Fratianno, or a Vinnie Teresa make good copy for the press and good subjects for best sellers, they make lousy data sources. Consider the many invalidating factors surrounding these individuals. First, they are cooperative witnesses because of compelling circumstances. They either plea bargain their way into informant status to escape imprisonment, or they seek government protection because they fear for their lives as a result of intra-mob transgressions. In either case, they are dependent on the government's good will for their survival. As a result, they are most cooperative witnesses. They are willing to participate in endless prodding for information, coaching on how best to present that information, refinement of the data they possess, and polishing of their public persona. In the end, the information they present is often less their own version of the truth and more of a scriptwriters' and directors' enhancement of the "important" truth they may possess. Even after this coaching and refinement, these stories are often shaky. A virtual cottage industry in criminology was created by the Valachi testimony as scholars tore it apart line by line and pointed out both factual errors and copious contradictions in his story.

Even a cursory examination of Valachi's actual testimony before the McClellan Committee, which was investigating the role of organized crime in drug trafficking, raises serious questions about his veracity. He contradicted himself over and over again; he was inconsistent on every key point which his testimony supposedly resolved. In some cases he was out-and-out wrong; in other cases it is highly doubtful that he could have been in a position to know much of the information about which he testified (Smith, 1979; Albini, 1971). Because of the extensive and detailed literature attacking the specifics of his story, a few examples should suffice to illustrate the depth of the difficulties (Smith, 1978; Albini, 1971):

1) Valachi claimed that the most important event in the life of an organized criminal was his initiation into Cosa Nostra. He described an elaborate ceremony at which all members were present so that they could recognize and welcome the initiate. However, later in his testimony Valachi was unable to recall being present at any such ceremonies, except his own initiation. This contradiction leaves few possible explanations to reconcile the conflict. Either such events were extremely rare, happening only

once every half century or so (to meet the facts of the Valachi story) or these initiations were really unimportant and ignored by most mob members destroying much of the Mafia mystique.

2) Valachi testified that the major service provided by Cosa Nostra was support for members who had been arrested or imprisoned, including bail money, legal fees, and financial support for families. Later in his testimony, despite the fact that Joe Valachi had been arrested numerous times, he testified that he had never received such support from the organization. Once again, the contradiction can only be resolved by suggesting that such services don't really exist or that Joe Valachi was singled out for very bad treatment by his colleagues.

3) Valachi testified that among the major rules governing Cosa Nostra families was a strict prohibition, punishable by death, against dealing in drugs. Later he gave extensive testimony about the drug trafficking activities of Vito Genovese and other Cosa Nostra leaders. Either the rule did not exist, or the organization was so weak it couldn't enforce it.

4) While much has been made of Valachi's testimony that the criminal organization he belonged to was called Cosa Nostra, it remains to this day unclear whether Cosa Nostra (roughly translated as "Our Thing") was the phrase Valachi used. Transcriptions of his testimony also refer to "Cases Nostra" ("Our House"), "Causa Nostra" ("Our Cause"), and several other versions. Other contradictions and improbabilities abound in the transcript. Even more vital than these inconsistencies are two other questions: Could Valachi have known these details of this elaborate conspiracy? and Why would Valachi have turned against his fellow Cosa Nostra members?

Joe Valachi had a conspicuously troubled and undistinguished criminal career. He had a long record of arrests, mostly on minor charges such as burglary and breaking and entering. He had spent much of his criminal career in prison. It is singularly unlikely that Joe Valachi would have been privy to the innermost secrets of any organization, let alone a hierarchically arranged, tightly organized, secret criminal conspiracy. Gordon Hawkins in his critique of the Mafia myth suggests that Valachi's level of knowledge and understanding of Cosa Nostra inner-workings would be about the same as the knowledge and understanding that a gas station attendant would have about top-level corporate decisions made by a major oil corporation.

Why Valachi chose to testify, however, is more useful in placing his revelations into context. While in the federal penitentiary in Atlanta, Valachi murdered a fellow inmate. Not only was he facing an additional homicide charge, but the rationale for the murder posed even greater dangers. Valachi had become convinced that Vito Genovese, also an inmate in the Atlanta penitentiary, had ordered his death. The man Valachi murdered had not been sent by Genovese. Now Valachi had reason to fear Genovese and had reason to fear a trial for murder. These circumstances compelled him to be a very compliant and useful government witness. In the years that followed, Valachi would go to great lengths to demonstrate to the government that he was a willing and useful ward of the Justice Department.

The net impact of Valachi's testimony on organized crime was modest at best. Valachi provided very little useful information, he provided almost no new information, in fact he only "confirmed and added depth and dimension to the knowledge or fragments of information the police already had" (Salerno and Tompkins, 1969: 310–311). Valachi, while in some instances telling investigators more than he really knew, in other instances "protected a few friends and acquaintances from the past by refusing to identify them or implicate them in specific crime" (Salerno and Tompkins, 1969). The bottom line is that not one organized crime figure was ever sent to jail as a result of the Valachi testimony.

While Valachi's information resulted in no convictions and did not appreciably advance knowledge of organized crime, it did serve some very important purposes for federal law enforcement agencies. Prior to Valachi's testimony, the Federal Bureau of Narcotics had only 225 special agents assigned to its operations. The Bureau's successor agency, the Drug Enforcement Administration, has 2,000 agents. The FBI also benefitted from the impression created by Valachi's testimony. They were able to justify a massive campaign against organized crime, including the use of illegal wiretaps and other abuses of power under the pretext of a campaign against this massive alien conspiracy, now called Cosa Nostra (Skolnick, 1978). This was a complete about face. Prior to Valachi's appearance, the FBI was denying that organized crime even existed and had made no effort to investigate it whatsoever:

> La Cosa Nostra was created as a public image. This simple device of giving the Mafia a new name worked wonders. Hoover was taken off the limb where he had perched so long, and citizens had a new menace to talk about with tales of blood oaths, contracts for murder, secret societies . . . (Messick, 1973: 8).

Hank Messick, veteran organized crime reporter and chronicler of Meyer Lansky, goes so far as to allege that the entire Valachi presentation was orchestrated by the Justice Department. Messick claims that Valachi was given a previously unpublished manuscript written by Nicola Gentile who had been a major Italian-American organized crime figure in the early twentieth century. Gentile returned to Sicily in 1936 after jumping bail in the United States: "This manuscript was given to Valachi to study, and he became an instant expert" (1979: 15).

Another celebrated case of an organized crime insider turning informant is that of Jimmy "the Weasel" Fratianno. Fratianno, allegedly the boss of the San Francisco Cosa Nostra family, turned state's evidence in the 1970s and collaborated with Ovid Demaris on a best selling biography which "told all," called *The Last Mafioso* (1980). Once again there are serious problems with the Fratianno story or stories. If one compares the text of his biography with testimony in numerous trials, such as the Funzi Tieri trial in New York, serious contradictions are easily discernible. Entire parts of his story are impossible, involving meetings with people and events that could not have taken place in the places or at the times specified (Albanese, 1985; Potter and Jenkins, 1985). Fratianno's knowledgeability has been called into question, most prominently by his own words. When testifying before the Kaufman Commission (President Reagan's commission investigating organized crime), he revealed that he knew little of money laundering and said "my friends usually kept their money in shoe boxes or buried it in the back yard." If this is the case, then Mr. Fratianno knows very little about organized crime. His story is filled with improbabilities. Are we really to believe that the "Weasel" intimidated Meyer Lansky—whose criminal worth approached $500 million and whose empire was worldwide—or "Doc" Stacher—a criminal with a violent past and a personal fortune of about $100 million? Fratianno's accounts are merely self-glorifying fantasies (Potter and Jenkins, 1985).

Journalistic Sources

Reliance on journalistic accounts of organized crime often compound the errors cited above (Galliher and Cain, 1974). Like government officials, journalists are not subject to the controls of the scientific method. They are primarily interested in selling newspapers and magazines and in prominently displayed by-lines. This means that they emphasize both the familiar and the sensational. The day-to-day mundane activity (which is, after all, the keystone of any business) of organized crime is ignored in their presentations. Most of these accounts tend to be snapshots of particular sensational incidents or notorious criminals. Organized crime, however, is a social process—constantly changing and adapting. A snapshot is of extremely limited explanatory value. Finally, journalists often repeat other people's errors. They print press releases from prosecutors, they interview government supplied informants and they recount the information in government reports, thereby compounding the errors in the original sources.

There are many examples of the press reproducing or inventing serious errors of fact. The gullible acceptance of the FBI's disinformation campaign against Carmine Galante is one example. The use of informants by journalists and the manipulations of those informants by the government agencies which supply them have been soundly criticized.

Controversy abounds over the information presented in a variety of popular sources about organized crime. Self-serving, salacious, and usually overstated biographies of mob figures are common. Some of these are outright fabrications, some are heavily embellished, and some are simply impossible to confirm or deny. For example, in 1974, Martin Gosch and Richard Hammer, two well-respected journalists with established credentials in covering organized crime, produced a book entitled *The Last Testament of Lucky Luciano*, supposedly "dictated by Charles 'Lucky' Luciano himself during the final months of his life." Gosch, a reporter for the *New York Times*, had contacted Luciano about a possible movie project. During those contacts Gosch said he conducted a series of interviews which culminated in the Luciano biography. Nicholas Gage, another reporter with impeccable credentials in the area of organized crime, challenged both the accuracy and authenticity of this work in a front page story in the *New York Times*:

> It is widely known that Mr. Gosch met on a number of occasions with Mr. Luciano on the aborted film project, and presumably the gangster recounted some of his experiences during these meetings. But contradictions and inaccuracies in the book raise question to the claim that Mr. Luciano told his whole life story to Mr. Gosch and that everything in the book attributed to Mr. Luciano actually came from him (Gage, 1974: 28).

While the authenticity and accuracy of the Gosch and Hammer book is important (particularly because it was a best-selling work), it pales in comparison with an even more disturbing inaccuracy that has been accepted as fact by both popular and scholarly writers.

This story (mentioned in chapter 1) has been repeated in virtually every comprehensive account of organized crime.

On September 10, 1931, Salvatore Maranzano, the self-proclaimed "boss of bosses" of the American Mafia, was murdered. According to the Castellemarese War story, Meyer Lansky and Bugsy Siegel, recruited assassins for the "hit" at the behest of Lucky Luciano. Cressey (1969: 44) reported: "On that day and the two days immediately following, some forty Italian-Sicilian gang leaders across the country lost their lives in battle." Fred Cook (1973: 107–108) labeled this event as the "Purge of the Greasers":

> Within a few short hours, the old-time crime bosses who had been born and reared in Sicily and were mostly illiterate—the "mustache Petes" or "the Greasers," as they were sometimes called—were liquidated by the new breed of Americanized, business-oriented gangsters of the Luciano-Costello-Adonis school.

Cook adds that, "beginning on September 11 and lasting through the next day, some thirty or forty executions were performed across the nation." A story in *New York Magazine* (Plate, 1972: 45) adds to the story: "During the bloodbath nearly 40 of the Old Guard were executed in various ingenious ways." This story, forms the linchpin of the Mafia conspiracy argument—and is treated in the popular literature as accepted fact. Unfortunately, it is entirely false.

Alan Block surveyed newspapers in eight major cities beginning two weeks prior to the Maranzano assassination and extending to two weeks after the murder. Block was trying to find stories relating to gangland murders that could be connected even remotely to the Maranzano assassination. He concluded: "While I found various accounts of the Maranzano murder, I could locate only three other murders that might have been connected" (1978: 460). As Block notes, three murders do not make a "purge." Humbert Nelli has (1976) also attacked the veracity of the alleged gang war story. He argues that the murders of some thirty to forty veteran Sicilian gangsters within a forty-eight-hour period is preposterous. It took at least four gunmen to kill Maranzano (who was unarmed), and many others had to know of the plot. To kill forty tough Sicilian gangsters who were often armed, always cautious and accompanied by bodyguards, would have required a conspiracy involving hundreds of people. If only one person let the information leak out, the entire purge would have been aborted. The proposed victims would have gone into hiding, barricaded themselves against attack, or struck preemptively at the assassins. The problem is succinctly summarized by Block who notes that "it is by no means clear why

Figure 2.1 Organized Crime Data Sources: Problems of Reliability

Data Source	Reliability Problems
Documents from Law Enforcement Agencies	• Some information is withheld because of ongoing investigations and prosecutions. • Information provided is edited and refined to make the agency look good and to remove any contradictory data. The data is not subjected to the rigor of scientific examination. • Law enforcement agencies play to the public's fascination with elaborate conspiracies. • Law enforcement agencies occasionally present "disinformation" as fact. • The acknowledged presence of corrupt relationships with organized crime groups and the use of questionable police tactics taints the data. • There is a basic question of government knowledgeability. How much do these agencies really know?
Government-Sponsored Informants	• These informants are providing information under duress. They are either involved in plea bargaining arrangements or are seeking the protection of the government from their mob associates. In either case they are very accommodating and pliable witnesses. • These informants are usually low-level organized crime operatives whose actual first-hand knowledge is in question.
Journalistic Sources	• Journalists tend to emphasize stories that are familiar to readers or sensational in their content. • Journalists do not subject their data to the rigor of the scientific method. • Journalists often uncritically repeat information from government agencies.

so many scholars have bought a story which so grossly violates historical respectability" (Inciardi, Block, and Hallowell, 1977: 100).

There is no other incident which more clearly represents the poverty of available data on organized crime. This "purge of the greasers" has been cited over and over as the cornerstone of the official construction of organized crime. If it is wrong—and it is— then the entire theoretical construct is also wrong.

Bad Questions

As if bad data were not enough, we frequently ask the wrong questions in organized crime research. This is a malady that infects intelligence analysts, academics, and journalists alike. A quick review of the holdings of any library on organized crime reveals two debilitating fascinations in the organized crime literature: the fascination with the notorious and the fascination with the hierarchy of the organization.

The vast preponderance of the organized crime literature, particularly that emanating from non-academic sources, deals with notorious characters and their atrocities, both real and imagined. Many of these works deal with organized criminals of some importance: Al Capone, Frank Costello, Mickey Cohen, Dutch Schultz, Bugsy Siegel, Meyer Lansky, and the like. Some of this literature deals with obscure individuals, whom the author(s) are trying to make into notorious figures, often with claims that stretch credulity. In either case, this fascination with villains grossly overemphasizes the role of individual actors in organized crime. The very term organized crime implies collaboration and coordination with others. The concept of criminal masterminds obfuscates the simple fact that it is networks of criminals who make up organized crime, not modern day versions of Sherlock Holmes' arch-rival, Professor Moriarty. Such a view also fails to understand the process of organizing crime and the complex series of interactions involving many individuals, both criminal and noncriminal, that goes into criminal organizations.

Even more debilitating than the fascination with the notorious is the fascination with hierarchy, a malady found equally distributed among journalists, academic criminologists, and intelligence analysts. The seemingly irresistible desire to force descriptions of organized crime into corporate hierarchies, neatly depicted in elegant flow charts, seriously overstates the tendency toward bureaucratization in organized crime. Most empirical research from primary sources, such as Albini's (1971) description of organized crime as a patron-client relationship, and Haller's (1987) depiction of organized crime as a series of overlapping partnerships, refutes this bureaucratic concept. This is not simply a matter of misinterpretation. Depicting organized crime as a corporate hierarchy leads to a fundamental and basic misunderstanding of organized crime itself. One of the great strengths of organized crime is its fluidity and responsiveness to social, political, and economic changes in its environment. The bureaucratic model insists on a chain-of-command and a decision-making hierarchy which makes this all but impossible.

Better Data, Better Methods, Better Questions

So, is it all hopeless? Are there no means of gathering valid and reliable data? Is there no way to provide accurate research findings on organized crime? Of course there is. The necessary ingredient is often overlooked—imagination. We have to pursue more daring and imaginative research designs and methods. We have to be willing to ask difficult and unpopular research questions.

Methodological Departures

As with all research problems, the place to start in addressing the deficiencies in organized crime research is with the methods. Despite all of the problems discussed above, organized crime continues as a topic of scholarly fascination in criminology, with important implications for criminal justice policy. The problems in using state-of-the-art research methods to describe organized crime should be taken as a challenge by social scientists. Organized crime as a research topic offers a rare opportunity to construct and utilize a truly interdisciplinary research methodology. Research on organized crime, if it is to be valid and reliable, must involve methods drawn from sociology, political science, history, and the community-based methodologies revived in the early 1960s. The opportunity to work on the development of such a methodology should make organized crime an even more compelling topic for research.

In the last twenty years there have been some interesting and provocative methodological departures in the study of organized crime. Some of the most promising empirical studies have made use of field research and participant observation methodologies.

Francis A. J. Ianni used basic participant observation methods and his Italian heritage in studying the "Lupollo Family" in New York City (Ianni, 1972a). Later, in his pioneering work on organized crime among blacks and Hispanics, Ianni made use of native informants (numbers runners, pimps, etc.) to collect information on crime networks (Ianni, 1974). The earlier study was based on three years of participant observation in an Italian organized crime group in New York City and provides the kind of insider's perspective not commonly found in the scholarly literature. Ianni set out to test some of Cressey's claims about the structure of organized crime and to test some of the other commonly held misconceptions emanating from works based on official sources. Not surprisingly, his work challenged many of the previously accepted truths about the structure of organized crime. In his second research effort, Ianni utilized a team of native informants as field researchers. He chose eight black and Puerto Rican ex-convicts "who had been involved in organized crime activities—running numbers, pushing dope, or hijacking goods—prior to their imprisonment" (1974: 17). Once again, he developed a strikingly different picture of organized crime than that presented in the official version.

William Chambliss (1978), in writing one of the best descriptions of an organized crime network ever produced, used the entire gamut of participant observation techniques in studying organized crime in Seattle. Chambliss immersed himself in that city's underworld and emerged with data that vividly described an organized crime network that reached into the upper echelons of Seattle's political and business communities. Chambliss provided a detailed account of the symbiotic relationship between organized criminals, the police, politicians, and business leaders.

Drug trafficking networks have also been subjected to analysis through the use of participant observation methodologies. Mieczkowski's (1986) description of heroin distribution in Detroit provides previously unfathomed insights into the means of coordination, the levels of organization, the socialization process in organized crime and the remarkable agility of organized crime in dealing with market fluctuations and law enforcement pressures. In a similar vein, Patricia Adler's (1985) compelling study of upper-level drug trafficking, derived from a field research methodology, provides a depth of understanding that other drug trafficking studies fail to achieve.

There have been other studies using field research techniques for data generation. Field research has been used in a study of organized crime and corruption in Reading, Pennsylvania (Gardiner, 1970) and Philadelphia (Potter and Jenkins, 1985). In addition, field research methods have been employed to study the gambling and loansharking industries (Reuter, 1983) and the pornography industry (Potter, 1986).

This does not mean that field research is free of pitfalls; it often fails. The time and effort spent gathering data and working the field can result in nothing usable. This method cannot be used successfully by everyone. Clearly some people are more at home and better able to adapt to deviant contexts than others. Finally, all research methods have problems of internal and external validity, and field research is particularly open to attack on its lack of generalizeability. However, as an initial step in research, particularly research on social processes occurring over time and space, field research remains an unparalleled method.

These field research studies, while very different from each other, offer a theme around which a new and perhaps more satisfying methodology for the study of organized crime can be developed. While field research has obvious limitations, its use as a descriptive tool is unparalleled. It is particularly appropriate in two kinds of studies: 1) research directed at a particular good or service (i.e., gambling, drug trafficking, prostitution), and 2) research directed at a specific locality (i.e., a specific city, county, or in some cases state). In addition, field research is appropriate for describing the criminal networks engaged in the delivery of illicit goods and services and for understanding the relationships between those networks on horizontal (between organized crime groups) and vertical (between crime groups and the business and political communities) axes. The objective is to design a methodology that allows the exposition of data which can be easily observed and the understanding of subtle nuances which can help to place that data in context.

Realizing the limits of field research, some scholars have looked to the use of multiple methods in describing organized crime. Albini (1971), for example, in his study of Detroit spoke with police officials, racketeers and others, while at the same time making careful use of official documents, journalistic accounts, and historical sources. Peter Reuter (1983), in his classic study of the gambling and loansharking markets in New York City, made extensive use of police records and case files, as well as cultivating informants.

Still others have turned to historical sources, either on their own or in concert with field research designs. Good history is vital to research on organized crime. Because organized crime is an ongoing and continually developing social process, histories can have great explanatory power in tracing that process and demonstrating the means of adaptation and change used by the mob. Haller's (1987) study of the Capone mob and Meyer Lansky's Broward County operations provides compelling insights into the nature of criminal organization, which he describes as an overlapping and pervasive series of partnerships, rather than as a massive, hierarchically arranged organization. Histories by Humbert Nelli (1976) and Virgil Peterson (1983) have also played a key role in emphasizing the changing nature of organized crime.

The limits of organized crime research are defined only by the limits of the researcher's imagination. Combining methodologies and pursuing interdisciplinary research designs provides the best hope for coming up with workable and useful information.

The Right Questions

It is important that we recognize the need for actual empirical investigation of organized crime. Almost every scholar who has tackled organized crime has recognized that "there is a pressing need for accumulation of case studies for hypothesis development and testing, and for the kind of research that moves forward by careful, additive processes" (Geis and Meier, 1977). It is of overriding importance for both policy formulation and continued research that a foundation of factual, empirically derived information be developed to describe both the extent and the nature of organized crime in the United States. Organized crime does not readily lend itself to survey research or experimental designs. Of the remaining alternatives it seems intuitively obvious that observational strategies, if carefully constructed to assure a high degree of reliability and validity, offer the best hope for creating a data base related to organized crime. The accumulation of specific case studies, either in terms of locality or by type of market activity, is the best available means to accumulate the knowledge necessary to understand organized crime in its social context.

Organized crime is a highly integrated institution in American society. Therefore research efforts should be directed by methodologies capable of assessing relationships in a temporal continuum, capable of understanding and making note of subtle nuances in behavior and attitude, and capable of studying organized crime as a social process. The use of field research and observational strategies does not require that we ignore all official pronouncements on organized crime. It merely requires that we relegate them to an appropriate place in the creation of a data base. No field researcher would take the unconfirmed, unverified word of an informant to build his or her case. Similarly, it can be argued that no researcher should use information contained in official sources without confirmation and verification, and without verifying the implications of that information by testing it in the real world. Organized crime must be conceptualized as what it really is, a social process occurring over time interlaced with social relations that must be appreciated and understood in order to comprehend organized crime as a social phenomenon.

Just as important as adopting useful methodologies capable of understanding subtle social nuances and interpreting social processes is asking the right questions about organized crime. We cannot enumerate all the right questions, but a few examples should serve as guides.

First, it seems imperative that we start asking the question, what's really happening out there? This means describing organized crime as it actually is, not reaching for an elaborate and convoluted argument. Empirical research on organized crime almost universally stresses the localized nature of the enterprise. Therefore, an accumulation of local case studies is an excellent contribution to the study of organized crime. There has already been a good start made on this process. John Gardiner's (1970) study of corruption in "Wincanton" not only describes the operation of local organized crime groups in detail but also explores the community's attitudes toward organized crime and the process of political corruption vital to the continuation of organized crime. Gardiner's work provides insights into corruption as a process that is not found elsewhere in the organized crime literature. Chambliss' work in Seattle and Albini's in Detroit have already been mentioned. They also contribute to the accumulation of documented case studies of organized crime as it actually works in American communities. Alan Block's (1979a) historical case study of the development of organized crime on the Lower East Side of New York provides important information on the localized nature of organized crime and its ephemeral nature. Other case studies of organized crime in Philadelphia and Chicago help to create a seminal database for future theory construction (Potter and Jenkins, 1985; Abadinsky, 1981).

Second, the pedestrian rather than the sensational aspects of organized crime must be researched. Organized crime is a constant in American society. We are long overdue in asking why this is. In the language of the sociologist, we must ask, is organized crime functional? Does it perform certain functions which are valued in the communities in which it operates? Such a consideration extends to questions of jobs, disposable income, meeting market demands for goods and services and investment capital. In addition, it is time to address the issue of power and organized crime. As Chambliss has suggested, organized crime's continuation provides a means for resolving certain social contradictions—contradictions emanating from moral entrepreneurs, the community power elite, and the law enforcement bureaucracy. We should not avoid the question, is organized crime functional for those with political and economic power and for the social control bureaucracy?

Third, research attention must be turned toward the economics of organized crime. Peter Reuter (1983), in his study of gambling in New York, concluded that the basic controls on that business were simple economic influences that impacted on all service industries. Other studies of organized crime's role in the garbage business, toxic waste disposal business, and the pornography industry provide similar seminal market case studies (Potter, 1986; Block and Scarpitti, 1985; Reuter, Rubinstein and Wynn, 1983). We need to understand these economic controls. We need to begin asking questions about illicit markets and industries. How do these markets work? How does organized crime respond so readily to changes in the market? How is it that organized crime is usually ready to exploit new markets as they open up? The increased profits realized by cocaine traffickers as a result of the introduction of crack should provide compelling evidence of the need for this type of approach.

Finally, we need to raise the issue of corruption in a comprehensive manner. It has become virtually axiomatic in the organized crime literature to state that organized crime could not exist without corruption. Corruption, just like economic markets, involves a complex series of interactions and processes, not a simple bribe handed over in a dark alley. We need to turn our attention away from the bad actors of the mob and look to the gatekeepers for the mob in the political system, in law enforcement, and in business. Writing books about the venality and crudeness of Little Nicky Scarfo (Philadelphia's alleged Cosa Nostra boss) may make for interesting reading, but writing books about money laundering, the subtle influences of organized crime on political leaders, and the accommodations between organized crime and law enforcement will make for important breakthroughs in our understanding of this phenomenon. Research efforts paralleling Penny Lernoux's (1984) important book, *In Banks We Trust*, and James Moldea's (1986) *Dark Victory: Ronald Reagan, MCA, and the Mob*, provide data which lend a greater understanding of the subtle market system in which favors are traded—another name for corruption.

The "Morrisburg" Study

The study which is presented in the following chapters attempts to elucidate the nature and structure of organized crime by means of a local case-study in "Morrisburg" (a pseudonym). The research presented here bears many similarities to the efforts described previously and also exhibits some important differences. Rather than directing the research at a specific group (as Ianni did in both of his works, or at a specific activity, as Rubinstein and Reuter have done), this study is a detailed investigation of the organization and delivery of a wide spectrum of illegal goods and services in the "Morrisburg" area. The data collected in "Morrisburg" point to several important conclusions about organized crime and the process of organizing crime:

1) Vice and organized crime activities are extremely prevalent, overt, and profitable. They are not controlled by any one clique but by a number of independent groups and entrepreneurs. While the leaders of the groups are easily identified by ethnicity, and while some of the groups show a preponderance of ethnic members, no one ethnic group holds hegemony.

2) Crime is syndicated within the city and region by means of a common access to finance and capital—to provide investment and money laundering facilities. The police and city bureaucracy also provide a centralizing and organizing role in coordinating bribes and payoffs.

3) Historically, "ethnic succession" seems a dubious concept. New groups do join the crime syndicate, but older networks do not withdraw. The blacks do not *replace* Italians, who in turn replaced the Jews. Instead, blacks *join* Italians, Jews, and others.

4) There are regional and natural ties within organized crime, although they do not result from the imperial ambitions of any Mafia commission or board of directors of a national crime syndicate. They arise for the convenience of local syndicates who need sources of capital further afield from their base of operation.

Chapter 3

"Morrisburg" and Organized Crime

"Morrisburg"[1] is a classic example of a declining industrial city in the rust-belt of the United States. In the nineteenth century, "Morrisburg" was celebrated as a boom town with flourishing coal, steel, and railroad industries. Throughout the nineteenth century and early twentieth century, "Morrisburg" exhibited a turbulent political life, both in terms of party politics and labor activity. The town was centrally located for railroad communications. After the demise of the railroads it became a central hub for the new system of interstates. Like so many other cities in the region, it began a rapid decline after World War II. Today it is a depressed city with high unemployment, an undereducated work force, and visible poverty.

[1]In field research, confidentiality is the greatest concern. In this case, it was maintained by using pseudonyms for the city involved, persons interviewed, living persons mentioned in the narrative, and business establishments. Pseudonyms are identified throughout the text with quotation (" ") marks. Names not in quotation marks are real names of people, places, or businesses.

The issue of confidentiality created some difficulty, however, in writing up the findings. In many cases, it was possible to verify the accuracy of information supplied by informants through published materials (i.e., books, investigative hearings, newspapers). To cite that information and those sources in the body of the text would surely give away the identity of the city and usually the identity of the informant or his or her associates. Therefore, a decision was made to list these sources in the bibliography, but not to cite specific references in the text. While this is an inconvenient practice, it is necessary to this type of research. The researcher's pledge of confidentiality must be all inclusive, superseding the requirements of scholarly prose.

"Morrisburg" is a city of about 95,000 people; its population has been on a continual downward spiral since 1950, with population declines averaging 7 percent between census reports. The per capita income in "Morrisburg" is about $4,500. "Morrisburg" has a mayor-council form of government which administers a budget of about $22 million a year. Expenditures on the police department are slightly over $3 million a year, and the "Morrisburg" police department employs about 135 uniformed officers and 20 additional police department personnel. Police officers work 40 hours a week and new officers start at a salary of about $13,500. Fully 96 percent of the police budget is spent on salaries and benefits.

"Morrisburg" has a rich tradition of organized vice and extortion. The mining villages clustered around "Morrisburg" had "black hand" extortion rings in the late nineteenth century and developed traditional organized crime groups active in gambling, loansharking, and extortion early in the twentieth century. Since the 1950s, local organized crime has attracted considerable national attention, first centering on the activities of a major gambling syndicate based in "Morrisburg," and later on the activities of "Joseph Marcantonio," a venerable gangster with national political connections who allegedly serves as the Godfather of a major Cosa Nostra family. "Marcantonio's" associates have very strong political ties—within "Morrisburg" itself, in neighboring "Birchwood," and in the state government. Members of the state legislature are often seen dining in "Marcantonio"-connected restaurants, and political scandals have been common, especially in "Birchwood."

At the time of the Kefauver hearings on interstate gambling (1951), crime in "Morrisburg" was a multi-ethnic affair, dominated by a gambling syndicate led by "Jacob Schiff" and his brothers. "Schiff" worked in close collaboration with a series of Irish, Slavic, and Italian partners, but then—as later—the syndicate held its power chiefly in alliance with city government and the police. The modern structure of organized crime in "Morrisburg" dates from the withdrawal of "Schiff" from local activities in the late 1950s. In the 1970s and 1980s, three main organized crime groups could be clearly discerned in "Morrisburg":

1) *The "Gianellis"*: The patriarch of the "Gianelli" clan was a close ally of the "Schiff" machine. His four sons kept up the gambling tradition, which today has been inherited by the third generation. The "gambling Gianellis" are today one of the area's most successful and prolific business clans. Although the "Gianellis" are an extended family of Italian descent, no Mafia theorists in law enforcement have ever connected them to any Cosa

Nostra or Mafia organization.

The "Gianelli" network is made up of the six surviving "Gianelli" family members and five other individuals who have key roles in bookmaking and numbers gambling. The group is ethnically mixed: the "Gianellis" and one other member are of Italian descent; one member has WASP lineage; two are Jewish; and one member has an Eastern European background. These eleven core members form the "Gianelli" gambling organization.

The "Gianelli" organization has direct links to other organized crime groups through a variety of mechanisms. "Dave Perlman" handles both bookmaking and numbers action as part of the "Gianelli" operation, plus heads his own hijacking gang. The link to the "Akbars" is less direct. The "Gianellis" are the landlord for an "Akbar"-run nightclub, and one of the younger "Gianellis" is friends with "Joe Akbar." Finally, they are linked to an organized crime group in Pittsburgh through joint participation in a Las Vegas junket operation.

2) *The "Akbars"*: The "Akbars" are two brothers, long active in vice, prostitution, and drug trafficking, who head another organized crime group. They have excellent criminal connections across the state, which have apparently been useful in money laundering. They also have well-established and long-standing friendships in the "Morrisburg" police department.

The "Akbars" have very limited participation at the top of their organization although they have many employees in prostitution and drug dealing. The two brothers have only one other major accomplice, a local woman who oversees their prostitution operations and often serves as a hostess in their nightclub.

The "Akbars" are closely linked to the "James Gang" by a mutual system of protection from police harassment through a "Morrisburg" police officer. They are linked to the "Gianellis" both as tenants and as business operators in close proximity to one another. They are tied to a major Philadelphia-area bookmaker by finances, very probably money-laundering activities.

3) *The "James Gang"*: "Michael James" is one of several individuals from "Morrisburg's" small black community (about 3 percent of the total population) who established a criminal foothold in the city, particularly as local drug distributors. The "James Ring" is also active in prostitution and counterfeiting and has a reputation for violence.

The "James Ring" has three components to their operations: prostitution, drug trafficking, and counterfeiting. All three involve "Michael James," but always in concert with different associates.

For example, his counterfeiting operations have been carried on in association with a local man of Greek descent. His prostitution activities are managed by two local women, both white and both veterans of the prostitution trade. His drug trafficking activities bring in three more associates, two black males and one Hispanic male. The organization is very mixed ethnically and has several individuals in its leadership positions. It is also interesting to note that at the lower echelons of the "James Ring," eighteen members of their drug trafficking operation were identified. Of those eighteen drug dealers, four were black, three were Italian, three were East European, five were Anglo-Saxon, and three were Irish—a very ecumenical mix of criminals. As mentioned above, the "James Ring" is linked to the "Akbars" through the police department. There are no other "Morrisburg"-area associations.

The blatant nature of vice and illegality in contemporary "Morrisburg" indicates great indifference on the part of local authorities. The conventional forms of vice, such as gambling, loansharking, and fencing, are widely available. In addition, the town is a center for the manufacture of illegal pornographic films (involving rape, extreme violence, and under-age subjects); it has a flourishing boy prostitution operation; and it is a key entrepot for the importation of heroin from Canada and its subsequent distribution throughout the northeastern United States.

In the discussion that follows, we will see how these three organized crime groups are closely connected through business relations, personal connections, and common links to the machinery of government and law enforcement.

The "Schiff" Era

The Kefauver Committee examined "Morrisburg" and held hearings there. In its report, the committee gave a thorough description of "Morrisburg's" organized crime operations. "Jacob Schiff" was the key figure, running a specialized lottery operation which covered several states. "Schiff" was based both in Florida and locally at his fortress-like estate in nearby "Morris Hills." Printing and selling "Schiff's" illegal lottery tickets was a huge local industry, employing hundreds of people and providing ancillary income for many small business owners and employees. The trade in the "Schiff" lottery ran to about $30 million a year, with over half of the proceeds going to "Schiff's" business associates. The members of the "Schiff" organization represented a wide range of

ethnic heritages. His local assistants were Irish; other key members
were Slavic and Italian. A major associate of "Schiff" was "Achielle
Gianelli."

The "Schiff" lottery operation, according to the Kefauver
Committee, served cities across the country including Chicago;
Alliance, Barnesville, Berea, Canton, Cleveland, Toledo, and
Youngstown (Ohio); Indianapolis; Rochester, Plattsburgh, Syracuse,
Niagara Falls, Oleon, Rome, Utica, Salamanca, Buffalo, Concern,
Geneva, Elmira, Johnson City, Beacon, Endicott, Ilion, and
Newburgh (New York); Boston, Worcester, and Falls River
(Massachusetts); Manchester and Concord (New Hampshire);
Elizabeth (New Jersey); Baltimore; Burlington (Vermont); Edgewood
(Rhode Island); and Allentown, Pittsburgh, Johnstown,
Williamsport, Jeanette, Lewistown, Monessen, Altoona, and Easton
(Pennsylvania).

At the time of the Kefauver Committee hearings, "Morrisburg"
vice was prominently featured because of major gambling raids
conducted by the state police—a law enforcement agency distinct
and alien from the local political organization. The raids did not
seriously impede "Schiff's" business. His runners were quickly
bailed out by "Achielle Gianelli," and business was soon back to
normal. The raids did, however, produce some interesting
observations, not the least of which identified some very compliant
police officers (several of whom have sons and nephews in the
"Morrisburg" criminal justice bureaucracy today). One Kefauver
witness was "Tommy Quinto" who had lived in "Morrisburg" since
1917 and had been a numbers banker since 1930. When he died
in 1983, his gambling business was still operating—an impressive
lifetime of illegality. (It is interesting to note that when summoned
to the Kefauver investigation, "Mr. Quinto" was surprised and
shocked to learn that his gambling business, which he freely
admitted to running, was illegal. He pointed out that no one had
ever brought it up in "Morrisburg," and he simply assumed that
the numbers game was a legal enterprise).

The "Schiff" organization provided the context within which
"Morrisburg's" present gambling syndicate run by the "Gianellis"
took root. "Jacob Schiff" had connections with some of the leading
crime syndicates of the time, in particular the Cleveland Four, Nig
Rosen's Philadelphia mob, and Meyer Lansky. It was "Schiff" who
gave "Morrisburg's" organized crime any national dimension it
possessed. As noted above, the patriarch of the "Gianelli" clan,
"Achielle Gianelli," at times worked for "Schiff." "Steve Gianelli,"
one of "Achielle's" sons, got his start in bootlegging in alliance with
"Schiff" and several Philadelphians, most importantly the fight

promoter and King of the Bootleggers, Max (Boo Boo) Hoff. Through their business relationships with the "Schiff" organization, the "Gianellis" developed close relations with other Philadelphia mobsters who later invested in "Morrisburg"-area businesses, such as Louis Stromberg (brother of Philadelphia syndicate chief Nig Rosen). In addition, the "Gianellis" often bankrolled fights in "Morrisburg" in association with Philadelphia-based fight promoter and Rosen mob veteran (Blinky) Palermo. In the late 1940s and early 1950s the "Gianellis" had become close to several New York organized crime figures, in particular Jack Parisi and Albert Anastasia, the reputed head of Murder, Inc. At least by the early 1940s, "Steve Gianelli, Sr." was a prominent layoff banker for local bookmakers and numbers operators, suggesting that he must already have had a good financial network. One source—"Harry Weinstein"—indicated that the "Gianellis" made up one part of a wider gambling syndicate which included the legendary Frank Erikson of New York, one of the largest bookmakers in the country who carried the appellation, "the bookmakers' bookmaker." According to the elder "Gianellis," organized crime in "Morrisburg" through the end of the 1950s was dominated by three key actors: "Jacob Schiff," "Achielle Gianelli," and "Mo Green" whose younger brother "Izzy" continues in business today.

New York, Money, and the Organizing of Crime

The question of how "Morrisburg" is linked to other organized crime groups is vitally important to understanding the later development of organized crime in "Morrisburg." In order to trace these links, it is important to look at the ties formed between "Schiff" and the "Gianellis" as far back as the 1930s. These outside connections are chiefly financial and involved significant links with organized crime operations directed by Meyer Lansky.

Beginning with "Jacob Schiff" himself, it is easy to discern close relationships with the New York gangs, particularly those clustered around Meyer Lansky, Bugsy Siegel, and Lepke Buchalter. "Schiff" was the target of a murder investigation in Cleveland in the 1930s, where it was alleged that he had carried out a contract at the behest of the Lansky group. When "Schiff" began to consolidate his power in "Morrisburg," the favor was apparently returned when three rivals were murdered by New York gunmen in "Morrisburg" in the mid-1930s. "Schiff" was also prominently featured in 1950s investigations of the heroin trade. Specifically, it was alleged that he had been a partner of Nig Rosen and other alumni of New York's

Lower East Side bootlegging gangs in a massive heroin importing network.

In fact, organized crime in "Morrisburg" has strong historical links with New York gangsters. Refugees from the New York area had a major role in creating an organized crime presence in the "Morrisburg"-area garment trade. By the early 1950s, New York gangsters like Harry Strauss, Lefty Strasser, and alleged New York Cosa Nostra bosses, Carlo Gambino and Thomas Lucchese had entered into garment industry partnerships with local activists such as "Schiff" and "Mo Green." Philadelphia was represented in the garment trade by Louis Stromberg. "Joseph Marcantonio" himself owned at least six local dress companies. By the 1950s, four organized crime figures dominated the "Morrisburg" garment trade: "Joseph Marcantonio," Albert Anastasia, Louis Stromberg, and "Morris Green."

There is every reason to believe that these four leaders collaborated very closely and had cordial and productive relations (at least as cordial as anyone could be with Anastasia). "Marcantonio," in partnership with Anastasia, used this garment industry concentration to create a particularly valuable trucking business that had exclusive contracts with "Morrisburg"-area garment manufacturers. Transportation was particularly important to the "Morrisburg" industry in that local plants were primarily used to cut patterns from fabric trucked in from New York. The patterns were then returned to New York for finishing and sewing. This company, "National Garment Carriers," still operates as a major trucking concern. Most of the garment factories that were owned by this cartel have passed to other contemporary organized crime figures in the 1970s and 1980s.

The importance of the men like "Jacob Schiff," the elder "Gianellis," and "Morris Green" to the organizing of local crime cannot be underestimated. One individual who puts their role in perspective is organized crime veteran "Gaspar Capparelli." "Capparelli" is a seventy-four-year-old man who has lived in the "Morrisburg" area for his entire life. In his criminal career, he was involved with bootlegging, gambling, and fencing operations. He was a partner of "Morris Green" in a local garment factory and knew all of the major actors in "Morrisburg's" developing organized crime groups. His comments on "Morris Green" and his associates are particularly revealing:

> "Morrisburg" was their city. If you took "Morris [Green]" and "Jacob Schiff" and the old "Gianellis" you had the most important people in the city. They were the kings. For them

anything was possible. They kept the place alive. You know they also helped with outside people. When things was falling apart they brought in the money to keep people in jobs, no bullshit, they didn't just talk, they did it. People depended on them. If you was an immigrant and didn't speak English, where was you going to work? Without the garment jobs these people, especially the women, would have starved. Also, you know these guys bailed people out. When a store or something came up short, there was money, lotsa times without any interest. I bet some was never paid back. These politicians, they said all these guys was criminals. Shit. What did they ever do for anybody? What do any of them do? The politicians and the unions are all bloodsuckers. The guys who do something, who help people, they call criminals. Maybe they should work for a living then they'd understand what's going on. That Bobby Kennedy, too. Now, I loved the Kennedy's. I give them money. But they didn't work none. Then they get all high and mighty about Hoffa and the other guys. Shit, they got their money from the same place. It stinks.

"Capparelli" also has vivid recollections of the role played by outside organized crime figures in the economic life of "Morrisburg" and of the connections between and among "Morris Green," Phil Strauss, Harry Strasser, Blinky Palermo, Albert Anastasia, the Strombergs and others:

[Harry Strasser was] the union guy, you know he had the garment contracts here, he made sure everybody had stuff worked out, that we didn't have to deal with the Commies. Sometimes, maybe it was in the forties, "Morris [Green]" said that people was coming to help out with the business. He said we had to do something to help out because the coal was in trouble and we needed jobs. So a whole bunch of people came in with "Morris." There was Lefty and Pittsburgh Phil, and there was Louis Stromberg and his brothers, and some others. They come in and they opened up some garment places, and they helped with the money for the coal. I think they give the money to the old men for the mines. They helped out with the unions.

These outside contacts gave dimension and form to the organizing of crime in "Morrisburg." They have important implications for contemporary crime operations as we shall see when we discuss their role in the coal industry (which was alluded to by "Capparelli"). Because of these connections, "Morrisburg" was a far more important center for organized crime activities than if it had depended only on the productivity of local vice networks. There has been a straight and thorough continuity in "Morrisburg" crime since the 1930s, when its local underworld merged into a loose syndicate of interests with the criminal machines of New York and Philadelphia. These links still survive with the heirs of early organized crime figures.

Organized Crime After "Schiff"

After "Schiff's" death in 1962, some of his local interests were consolidated in the "Campbell Corporation," an organization whose ostensible purpose is to manage the affairs of "Schiff's" "Morris Hills" estate. Several relatives of "Achielle Gianelli" have played important roles in the management of this corporation since "Schiff's" death. In fact, in the 1980s, the "Gianellis" made a mysterious $16,500 interest-free loan to this corporation.

Did "Schiff's" death mark the point of transition from the multi-ethnic gambling syndicate to another syndicate, perhaps one akin to the fabled Cosa Nostra? The answer is clearly no. Several "Schiff" associates continue to be active in organized crime in "Morrisburg," although the passage of time has brought with it an increase in discretion. The old syndicate activists have retained roles as financiers and fences; they continue to own a great deal of real estate, particularly real estate which houses contemporary vice operations. A number of other "Schiff" associates have been mentioned as heirs of some of the "Schiff" interests (see below). The most significant survivors are the "Gianellis."

The "Gianellis"

The "Gianellis" represent a complex, although localized, crime network. The family's genealogy is represented in Figure 3.2.

The "Gianellis' " illegitimate business activities are widespread. These illegitimate holdings are closely integrated with their legitimate business activities. The extent of "Gianelli" business holdings is described in Table 3.1. Seven business partners (separate from the core group of the organization discussed earlier, one Slavic, one Irish, one Wasp and four Italians) participate in business ventures with them (see Table 3.2).

The "Gianellis" run an impressive business network providing logistical support for gambling operations and money-laundering services, particularly through real estate and vending companies. Even the most casual glance at a "Gianelli"-run business confirms this impression. For example, the back room of the "Pine Record Store" contains sixteen telephones, ideal for a bookmaking

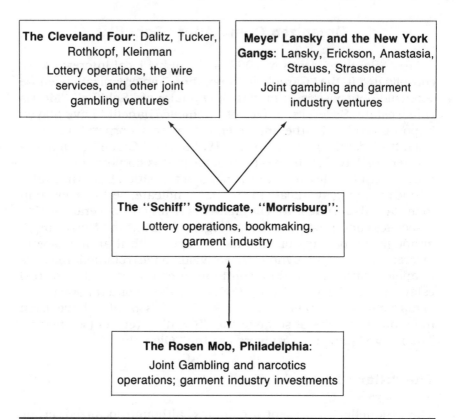

Figure 3.1 Connections between the "Schiff" Syndicate and Other Organized Crime Groups (circa 1950)

operation. When "Michael's Fashions" was raided, a thriving gambling business was uncovered. Moreover, all these activities make up only a small portion of "Gianelli" enterprises. Other licit and illicit operations in "Morrisburg" have the "Gianellis" as secret partners. Bars and pornography stores regularly obtain vending and video machines from "Gianelli" companies—or from firms like "Northern Vending," a front operating from "Agosto Gianelli's" home address (the partners in this corporation are the "Orlandos," another bookmaking organization).

What of the "Gianellis" themselves? "Michael Gianelli" agreed to an interview in which he provided a detailed account of his family's operations plus their outlooks and attitudes as well.

Table 3.1 "Gianelli"-Related Businesses and Ownership (1970s and 1980s)

	Tommy Gianelli	Agosto Gianelli	Steve Gianelli, Sr.	Harry Gianelli	Michael Gianelli	Steve Gianelli, Jr.
Vending Companies						
Gianelli Amusements						X
Al-Bro Vending		X				
Star Amusements	X					
University Billiards	X					
XYZ Vending						X
Gianelli Cigarettes				X		
Northern Vending	X					
Retail Outlets						
Pine Records			X	X		
Michael's Fashions					X	
Robot Car Wash		X				
Real Estate						
Borgia Apartments		X				
Tallyrand Apartments	X					
Bellevue Apartments		X				
Valley Apartments		X				

Figure 3.2 The "Gianellis": The Extended Family through Successive Generations

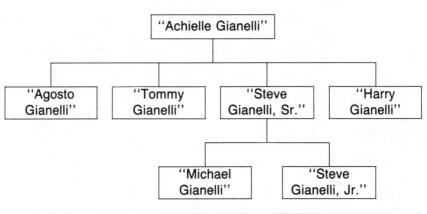

"Michael" is one of the younger members of the group. Although he has never been in prison, he has been arrested five times for gambling violations, including a major arrest in 1976. He is still an active bookmaker with a weekly volume which he estimates to be about $200,000. As do others in similar positions, the "Gianellis" consider themselves to be businessmen rather than criminals; they make little attempt to conceal their role in gambling. They argue that they provide a service which has been in heavy demand in "Morrisburg" for at least a century. They are respected members of the community, active in business, civic affairs, and politics.

What about the other products and services of organized crime? Individuals associated with the "Gianellis" have been implicated in loansharking, drugs, truck hijacking, and even prostitution. "Michael" maintains that these activities are outside of his family's business. He and his relatives are gamblers—to engage in other forms of vice would be asking for trouble. Why bring scrutiny on themselves, why encourage investigations, why create trouble for the police and the district attorney, he asks. To do so would only be bad for business. "Michael" steadfastly maintains that no "Gianelli" money goes to other forms of vice. He admits, however, that gambling associates who utilize "Gianelli" layoff services do sometimes finance other goods and services. For example, he points to "Harry Weinstein," who engages in loansharking and provides financing for the local drug network, in addition to gambling. "Michael's" feeling is that these other activities are "Weinstein's"

Table 3.2 "Gianelli" Business Partners

	Partner A	Partner B	Partner C	Partner D	Partner E	Partner F	Partner G
Vending Companies							
Gianelli Amusements	X	X					
Al-Bro Vending			X				
Star Amusements				X			
University Billiards				X			
XYZ Vending	X						
Retail Outlets							
Michael's Fashions					X	X	
Robot Car Wash					X		
Real Estate							
Borgia Apartments							X
Bellevue Apartments			X				
Valley Apartments			X				

business and no concern of his as long as they don't taint "Gianelli" enterprises. The same is true of "Dave Perlman," who is associated with "Gianelli" layoff banks, but is not one of their partners. "Perlman," as mentioned earlier, heads up a major hijacking ring in the "Morrisburg" area. "Michael" argues that "Morrisburg" is a relatively small city, and as such it would be impossible to avoid contacts with other criminal actors like the "Akbars," or even business dealings with "Perlman" and "Weinstein." Vice can be demarcated by the goods and services provided. For example, the

"Gianellis" do not loan money to gamblers, but they refer needy clients to a variety of other enterprises dealing in fencing and loansharking. In return, they expect gambling business to be steered their way.

The "Gianellis" strongly disapprove of the traffic in drugs from both a moral and business standpoint. "Michael" argues that a 10 percent return on safe investments in gambling is, overall, more profitable than 100 percent returns on drug purchases, which are simply too risky and unsure. Besides, the drug business, because of its very nature, brings in undesirable characters, such as "Michael James" and "Dave Earle." It also brings in the "Akbar" brothers, with whom the "Gianellis" have had dealings. They explain their relationship with the "Akbars" by saying that it would be improper and unwise to refuse favors to the "Akbars" in a limited political environment, as long as the favors do not jeopardize "Gianelli" enterprises. However, if the going gets too treacherous, the "Akbars" will be left to fend for themselves.

Occasionally, the crime networks overlap geographically, "Michael" points out that a bar may take bets for the "Gianellis" but may also be running prostitutes and drugs for the "Akbars." This is a situation the "Gianellis" regard as unfortunate. They have attempted to separate their writing establishments (places where bets are taken) from the rest of their organization. Writers are treated as independent entrepreneurs who work on a commission basis, not as direct employees of the "Gianellis." If they are arrested, the "Gianelli" crime organization will provide them with limited assistance relating to their gambling problems, but will not go beyond that.

"Michael" was pressed on the subject of prostitution because of the historical links between prostitution and gambling in "Morrisburg." He states that in the past the two were linked. This was when prostitution was respectable, meaning that it was run from well-organized brothels in red-light districts. In contemporary "Morrisburg," the organization in prostitution has broken down. Many prostitutes are independent, some work for the "James Gang," and some work as bar girls for the "Akbars." The "Gianellis" provide no protection or political muscle to the prostitutes and have no business interests in the enterprise. Additionally, "Michael" points out that the profits in prostitution are low and the risk is high because it is such a highly visible activity, unsanctioned by the community.

"Michael" was also asked about connections between "Morrisburg" organized crime groups and organized crime groups in other cities. He claims that both "Dave Messer," a suburban

Philadelphia bookmaker, and another major bookmaker in the eastern part of the state have occasionally made use of "Gianelli" layoff services, but for the most part there is little connection to outside gamblers. When asked about people associated with "Joseph Marcantonio" and his alleged Cosa Nostra family, "Michael" asserted that there were no "Marcantonio"-related gambling operations in the city. He said that there were social connections with the "DeSotos," close "Marcantonio" associates from neighboring "Birchwood." The only business connection he could think of involved occasional dealings related to the disposal of assets. For example, if a gambler paid his debt to the "Gianellis" in the form of property or securities, these assets are converted to cash by someone else. The "Gianellis" usually use local entrepreneurs for this service, men such as "Harry Weinstein" or "Izzy Green." Occasionally, especially in the case of precious metals or gems, "Marcantonio" was called in because of his special knowledge in this area. However, "Marcantonio" has been too conspicuous in recent years, and the "Gianellis" have stopped sending him any business.

When asked specifically about securities dealers and fences, "Michael" said that there were several in operation. At least three local jewelers handled small amounts of gems, and "Harry Weinstein" handled small property or securities transactions. Most major transactions were carried on through "Izzy Green," the brother of the late "Morris Green." The "Gianellis" regard the conversion business as too dangerous for direct involvement. In fact, "Michael" marveled at the fact that an "old operator" like "Green" was now employing members of a motorcycle gang as bodyguards, people that wouldn't even be allowed inside a "Gianelli"-owned establishment.

The "Akbars"

The "Akbars" first came to public attention in 1971 when "Tom Akbar" was working as a bartender at a "Morrisburg" club where the liquor license was owned by his brother "Joey." The club was fined several times for permitting lewd and lascivious entertainment, and "Tom" was arrested for pandering. "Tom" continued to run into trouble through the next decade for barroom violence and for pimping operations based in bars. His connections were revealed by a 1977–78 investigation in which he was charged with bribing a "Morrisburg" police captain named "Clements." "Tom Akbar" had approached "Clements" to try to arrange for the

dismissal of charges against several drug dealers. His relationship
with "Clements" was long-standing; "Clements" was his contact
in the police department. (It is interesting to note that one of the
drug traffickers whose release was sought in this transaction was
"Dave Earle," a prominent member of the "James Gang" and a
black drug dealer.) "Tom" was convicted of perjury in 1978 for lying
to a grand jury investigating corruption, while "Captain Clements"
was given a mild departmental reprimand.

By the end of the decade, the "Akbars" had established
interesting contacts in crime, particularly in the suburbs of
Philadelphia. "Tom" and "Joey" engaged the services of "Dave
Messer" (a major money mover and drug financier in addition to
the bookmaking mentioned by "Michael") to attempt to obtain a
legitimate bank loan to finance some of their illicit activities. On
their behalf, "Messer" approached a bank manager with whom he
had considerable dealings in an attempt to secure the loan. In the
early 1980s this relationship was apparently cemented in the
creation of a new drug network involving the "Akbars," "Messer,"
and black gamblers in a suburban Philadelphia city. It is instructive
to note that when this drug network was the target of raids, "Tom
Akbar" escaped detection as a result of being tipped off by friends
within the "Morrisburg" police department.

The "Akbars" have a long record of trouble with law enforcement
agencies. The "Akbars" have for nearly twenty years been
prominent figures in drugs and prostitution, with close connections
to the police, to the black crime network in "Morrisburg," and to
Philadelphia-based financing sources. They are not conspicuously
wealthy, but they are linked to much of the criminal activity in
"Morrisburg."

The "James Gang"

In 1974, a major heroin organization was broken up by state police.
The network was headed by one "Jim Robson." At his trial, a major
issue was the coercion of a government witness (a prostitute) by
"Michael James" and several colleagues. They allegedly forced her
to modify her testimony. One of these colleagues was "Dave Earle."

"Michael James" has a lengthy record which includes: running
a counterfeiting ring, running a prostitution ring, and being what
law enforcement officers say is the kingpin of drugs in
"Morrisburg." He was active in heroin and cocaine distribution, and
his prostitutes are often underage. Current opinion in "Morrisburg"
suggests that his convictions have done great damage to efforts to

consolidate a black-dominated crime network in the area.

Specific highlights of "Michael James" criminal history include: an indictment on counterfeiting charges; a fifty-three-count federal indictment for fraudulently collecting social security payments; an arrest for trafficking in cocaine; and an arrest for prostitution when a fifteen-year-old "Morrisburg" girl testified that she had turned over nine thousand dollars in prostitution income to "James."

Other members of the "James Gang" have also had considerable difficulty with the law as well. One of the leaders of the ring, "Dave Earle" was arrested for heroin distribution. In addition, twenty-one dealers associated with the group were arrested in "Morrisburg" and several million dollars worth of methamphetamines were confiscated.

Other Organized Crime Groups

There are, of course, other organized crime operations in "Morrisburg" not included in the three groups cited above. For the most part, these groups tend to be smaller, more specialized, less successful, and without the political and community ties necessary to attain prominence. Take, for example, the case of "Dave Perlman." "Dave Perlman" was indicted for participating in a gambling conspiracy in 1970 in association with the "Gianellis." Later, he was arrested (in 1975 and 1984) for activities associated with his hijacking ring. The "Perlman" hijacking gang includes seven other men—five Italians and two WASPs. These men are primarily professional thieves and have negligible roles in other organized crime activities in "Morrisburg." In 1983, "Perlman's" sons were actively engaged in a gang war with another small organized crime clique.

Another local organized crime group is headed by "Joe Orlando." "Joe Orlando" has been convicted for running a gambling operation estimated to be worth about $50,000 a day, which represents the totality of the "Orlando" group's activity. Two other "Orlandos" formed the vending machine company mentioned earlier based at the home address of "Agosto Gianelli." In 1971, control of "Morrisburg" racketeering was credited, by law enforcement sources, to "Steve Gianelli," "Tommy Quinto," and yet another "Orlando" brother. In the 1980s, "Joe Orlando" was in trouble again for his concealed ownership of a restaurant at 414 "Pine Street" that was being used as a money-laundering operation.

Other organized crime operations, such as those headed up by "Izzy Green" and "Harry Weinstein" also play a key role in the criminal life of "Morrisburg." All of these groups in one way or another are interrelated and have mutual dependencies. The "Gianellis," as the most powerful and most successful of the organized crime groups, occupy a position at the core of this web of illicit activity (see Figure 3.3), but this does not suggest that the "Gianellis" are dominant or exercise hegemony over organized crime, only that they do their business more efficiently and effectively than the other groups.

The Criminal Topography of "Morrisburg"

The streets of central city "Morrisburg" are arranged in a grid pattern. Major north-south streets include:

"Abundance Avenue"

"Center Street"

"Pine Street"

"Baum Street"

"Bush Street"

"Grape Street"

East-west avenues which cross these streets are:

"Benjamin Avenue"

"Colonial Avenue"

"Idaho Avenue"

"Vernon Avenue"

"Munster Avenue"

"Hamilton Avenue"

"Abundance Avenue" is the town's traditional strip or tenderloin. As so often is the case, close property relationships exist between and among vice establishments. Sometimes these relationships are overt and sometimes very discreet. The whole 500 block of "Abundance Avenue" is a vice complex in itself, providing drugs, gambling, and prostitution (see Figure 3.4). On the opposite side of the street is a celebrated local restaurant, "Benguerra's," long described by state law enforcement agencies as an organized crime hangout and believed to be owned by "Joseph Marcantonio." "Benguerra's" is indicative of the old tradition of maintaining vice operations in historic locales. Its side entrance stands at 108 "Munster Avenue," which was listed in the Kefauver hearings as the major horse-betting parlor of the "Gianellis." The whole area

Figure 3.3 Interrelationships among "Morrisburg's" Organized Crime Groups

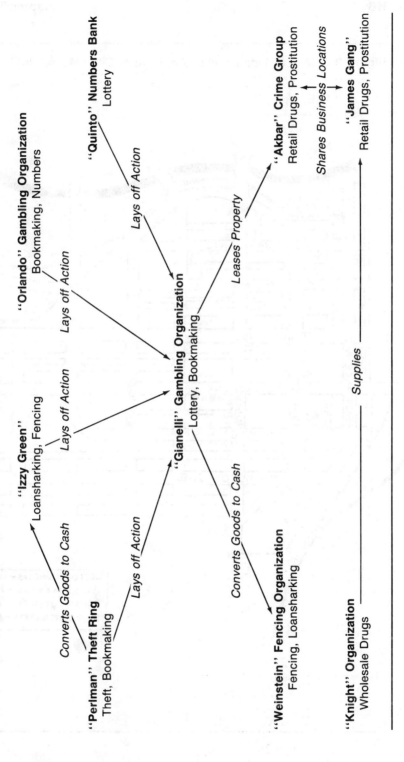

Figure 3.4 Map of Vice Locations in Central City "Morrisburg"

Table 3.3 Vice Locations in Center City "Morrisburg"

Address	Gambling	Prostitution	Drug Distribution
124 "Benjamin Avenue"	X		
117 "Colonial Avenue"	X		
238 "Colonial Avenue"	X		
246 "Colonial Avenue"		X	X
250 "Idaho Avenue"	X		
254 "Idaho Avenue"	X		
256 "Idaho Avenue"	X		
302 "Vernon Avenue"	X		
304 "Vernon Avenue"	X		
306 "Vernon Avenue"	X		
139 "Munster Avenue"	X		
141 "Munster Avenue"	X		
200 "Munster Avenue"	X		
306 "Munster Avenue"	X		
309 "Munster Avenue"	X		
509 "Baum Street	X		
511 "Baum Street"	X		
515 "Baum Street"		X	X
410 "Pine Street"	X		
546 "Pine Street"	X		
224 "Abundance Avenue"	X		
226 "Abundance Avenue"		X	
330 "Abundance Avenue"		X	X
512 "Abundance Avenue"	X		
524 "Abundance Avenue"	X	X	X
526 "Abundance Avenue"	X	X	X
528 "Abundance Avenue"	X	X	X
530 "Abundance Avenue"	X	X	X
532 "Abundance Avenue"	X	X	X
601 "Abundance Avenue"	X		
608 "Abundance Avenue"	X		
610 "Abundance Avenue"	X		

Table 3.4 Gambling Operations in Center City "Morrisburg"

Address	Lottery/ Numbers	Bookmaking	Illegal Machines
124 "Benjamin Avenue"	X		
117 "Colonial Avenue"	X		
238 "Colonial Avenue"		X	X
246 "Colonial Avenue"			X
250 "Idaho Avenue"	X		
254 "Idaho Avenue"	X		X
256 "Idaho Avenue"	X	X	
302 "Vernon Avenue"	X	X	
304 "Vernon Avenue"	X		
306 "Vernon Avenue"	X		
139 "Munster Avenue"	X		X
141 "Munster Avenue"		X	
200 "Munster Avenue"	X		X
306 "Munster Avenue"	X		
309 "Munster Avenue"	X		
509 "Baum Street"	X		
511 "Baum Street"	X		
515 "Baum Street"			X
410 "Pine Street"		X	
546 "Pine Street"	X	X	
224 "Abundance Avenue"	X		X
330 "Abundance Avenue"	X	X	
512 "Abundance Avenue"	X		X
524 "Abundance Avenue"	X	X	
526 "Abundance Avenue"	X	X	
528 "Abundance Avenue"	X	X	
530 "Abundance Avenue"	X	X	X
532 "Abundance Avenue"	X	X	
601 "Abundance Avenue"	X	X	
608 "Abundance Avenue"	X	X	
610 "Abundance Avenue"	X	X	

between "Abundance," "Munster," and "Hamilton" seems mob-connected; while just north stands a decrepit hotel that was once a favorite venue for organized crime conclaves and even housed a pre-Appalachian meeting get-together.

A quick summary of vice locations in "Morrisburg's" downtown is depicted in Tables 3.3 and 3.4. It is interesting to note that many of the bars and gambling establishments indicated in Table 3.3 are connected to, or share structural space with, garment manufacturing concerns. Such proximate locations may well indicate a financial or money-moving relationship between the "heirs" of "Jacob Schiff" and "Morris Green."

It should be clear that illicit entrepreneurial activity in "Morrisburg" is widespread and involves several major and many minor organized crime groups. Having described the general situation with regard to "Morrisburg's" organized crime community, let us now turn to the structure and functions of the various illicit enterprises as they can be observed on the streets.

Chapter 4

The Crimes of Organized Crime

While there is a great deal of debate in the scholarly literature about the actual structure of organized crime and the best components of a definition of organized crime, there is substantially more agreement on those activities that organized crime engages in on a regular basis. The business of organized crime involves primarily, although not exclusively, those goods and services that are in public demand but are also illegal (Reuter, 1983; Schur and Bedau, 1974; Geis, 1972). The fact that acts, such as gambling, prostitution, pornography, loansharking, fencing, and drug trafficking, are illegal creates a number of opportunities for organized crime groups to realize significant economic gain and also creates a set of social circumstances which allow criminal organizations to flourish.

In most cases, organized crime groups have as their primary activity, and almost certainly as their greatest sources of income, the provision of legally proscribed but strongly demanded goods and services. In fact, in a great many cases, organized crime groups are careful to avoid illicit activities where there is not a consensual relationship with the customer, such as extortion and robbery (Abadinsky, 1985; Ianni, 1974; Salerno and Tompkins, 1969). The main activities of traditional organized crime groups are gambling, loansharking, fencing, drug trafficking and illicit sexual services.

71

Gambling

For the last century and a half, gambling has been the cornerstone of organized crime, providing both power and capital for organized crime groups (McCaghy and Cernkovich, 1987; Ianni, 1974; Cressey, 1969; Salerno and Tompkins, 1969). In the 1930s and 1940s, many of the old bootleggers turned to gambling. They created gambling syndicates that virtually ran many American cities and owned both public officials and the police departments in those cities (Potter and Jenkins, 1985; Haller, 1979).

Gambling is a very big business which takes many forms—numbers betting, horse and sports betting, dice games, illegal machines, and casino operations. Unlike many other illicit services, gambling requires a clearly delineated organizational structure. In the numbers racket, for example, a typical "bank" requires the existence of a banker, his lieutenants, office men, pickup men and writers. A numbers syndicate operates in a fairly straightforward manner (Simon and Witte, 1982). The bets are placed with runners by customers. There are mobile runners who move around neighborhoods and collect daily action from steady customers and stationary runners who take bets at a place of business, such as a bar, diner, or newsstand. Runners work on a commission basis, most are paid about 25 percent of their receipts. In addition, most runners expect and receive "tips" from winners who are their regular customers. Pickups travel a larger area, much like a regional sales manager, and collect the action from the runners. They maintain records for each runner and return with the payoffs from the central numbers bank. Pickups also are paid on a commission basis, receiving between 5 and 10 percent of the action they collect. The pickup takes the day's receipts for his or her area to the numbers bank where officemen keep track of the bets and authorize the payoffs. At the top of this structure is the banker who arranges protection from the police and usually retains the services of both bail bondsmen and lawyers in addition to taking care of financial responsibilities. The average numbers bank requires forty to fifty employees. An elaborate financial network is also required (Abadinsky, 1985). Very often that financial network is separate from the numbers bank itself and provides a kind of insurance against a disastrously large win by buying up the betting action of individual numbers banks.

Bookmaking also requires a defined organization (Simon and Witte, 1982). Bets are often taken in otherwise legitimate businesses such as candy stores or dry cleaners by runners. The runners turn in their daily action to clerks who record the bets and keep track of the transactions. The bookmaker is the banker in this type of syndicate. It is the bookmakers who set the odds and place limits on the size of bets. They also must supply the working capital necessary for the bookmaking syndicate. Some very large bookmakers employ tabbers who keep their eye on the bets and change the odds or the point spreads on games to protect the bookmaker's profit margin. In fact, it has been suggested that this ancillary gambling activity provides the measure of survival for many marginal small businesses (Laswell and McKenna, 1971). Bets are collected frequently, often by individuals who come to the store for an otherwise legitimate purpose, such as servicing the vending machines. It is not uncommon for gambling organizations to own vending machine companies. Bookmaking syndicates on the east coast often have turnovers of several hundred million dollars a year, while large numbers banks often take in as much as $30 or $40 million. It is important to remember that all of this activity is based on the active support and consent of the public. If no one wished to gamble, there would be no gambling syndicates.

Gambling activity is very obvious throughout "Morrisburg." Betting activity is open and quite apparent in small bars, lunch counters, and newsstands, where the preponderance of numbers bets are placed. Bets are also placed in tobacco shops or other retail establishments doubling as bookmaking parlors. In "Morrisburg" the gambling network is a "Gianelli"-run machine. It should be clear from Figure 4.1 that "Gianelli" gambling operations are dependent upon their legitimate business holdings. The integration of these two components allows the "Gianellis" to carry out their illicit activities with maximum efficiency and also provides a built-in money-laundering service to legitimize profits from gambling.

Gambling in "Morrisburg" can be viewed in two segments. First, there is the organization of both bookmaking and the numbers racket through the "Gianelli" organization, as well as through some of their associates, such as the "Orlandos." Through their vending companies, the "Gianellis" dominate the video poker market. The video poker machines, in and of themselves, are quite legal and are ubiquitous devices in downtown bars. The practice of paying cash rewards to winners on these machines is, however, quite illegal— yet this system of payoffs is universal in "Morrisburg." The "Gianelli" operation certainly dominates gambling as an illicit enterprise both in terms of actual volume of business and in terms of organizational sophistication. The "Gianellis" are able to provide their associates with a full range of banking and money-laundering services plus political protection through a highly structured payoff

Figure 4.1 "Gianelli" Gambling Operations

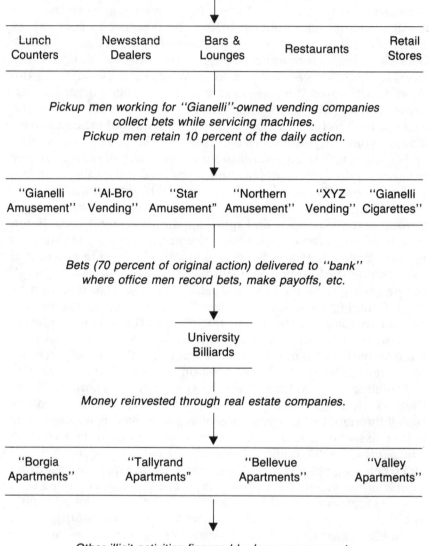

system that, over the years, has simply become part of the normal way of doing business in "Morrisburg."

However, the "Gianellis" are not the only gambling operators at work in "Morrisburg." Rubinstein and Reuter (1978a; 1978b) have pointed out that the need for elaborate organization in bookmaking has declined over the years, and there are far more independent bookmakers today than in the 1930s and 1940s. Gambling operators were more closely allied with one another during the days of the wire services. The pertinent issue in contemporary gambling is not whether any group has created a monopoly. Rather, it is an issue of longevity. The rate of bankruptcy among small, independent bookmakers is quite high, and their profit margin is only between 4.5 and 5 percent. Belonging to an organization such as the "Gianelli" group offers increased efficiency, greater centralization of services, and increased financial security. As Reuter and Rubinstein (1977) found there is no clear territoriality in the gambling business. The gambling business in "Morrisburg" is not a corporate structure dominated or controlled by one group. Rather, it is based on a network of associations and relationships. Those who are the best organized and have the strongest associations are also the most successful.

Gambling networks play a vital role in the economic and social life of "Morrisburg." Many of the small luncheonettes, bars, and newsstands could not survive if they did not handle gambling action in addition to their primary business. As Whyte (1961) pointed out, gambling performs many services for local businesses:

1) Local members of the business community very often are dependent on the money they receive from handling betting action. Silberman (1978) adds that gambling allows local merchants to compete with larger chain stores and supermarkets.

2) Customers are attracted to business establishments by the availability of numbers and other forms of gambling.

3) Gambling also provides employment for local men and women who are unable to secure other jobs. In fact, Laswell and McKenna (1971) found in their study of Bedford-Stuyvesant that the numbers racket was the largest single private employer in that community.

Gambling activities are clearly a big business in "Morrisburg." The gambling networks share common space, personnel, and organization with a large number of legitimate businesses. The gambling networks thus represent illicit activities that have become almost institutionalized in "Morrisburg's" political and social life.

Fencing and Loansharking

There are many who would argue that loansharking is a criminal activity entirely devoid of consent. Despite its bad reputation, loansharking is a business in which individuals agree, and in many cases beg, to become victims (McCaghy, 1987; Conklin, 1973). People seek out loansharks for a variety of reasons. Some entrepreneurs are seeking capital investment in ventures that are regarded as too risky for legitimate lending institutions. Other people have a history of bad credit, which precludes them getting a loan from a bank. Still others go to loansharks for a quick and temporary bailout to cover unexpected business reversals. What all of these clients have in common is insufficient collateral or liquidity. Larger loansharking operations employ runners on the streets to let the loans, plus accountants, attorneys, and a number of loansharks who bankroll the operations and provide for the payoffs necessary to maintain official protection (Simon and Witte, 1982).

In "Morrisburg," fencing, loansharking, and money moving are closely related. At the lowest level, fences are in rather traditional roles as jewelers, pawn brokers, and discount retail store operators. At the other end of the spectrum are individuals engaged in larger enterprises whose money often finances large criminal enterprises.

Three central city jewelers handle unregistered gems of doubtful ownership. They are willing to buy stones without seeing prior sales receipts, gem registration papers, or insurance registrations. Such stones are purchased for twenty-five cents on the dollar in appraised value. Some form of registration or receipt is then manufactured, and the stones are mounted and sold through normal retailing operations. The jewelers in question are located in the 200 block of "Bush Street," the 200 block of "Pine Street," and the 300 block of "Colonial Avenue." While it was difficult to ascertain the actual volume of such transactions, it can be inferred that it is relatively low.

Two discount clothing stores in the downtown area (army-navy stores) also handle small quantities of stolen articles such as watches, radios, televisions and the like. Once again, the level of activity is minimal.

The largest fences are individuals who deal in stolen securities and bonds, among other items. They also provide loansharking services and often manage investment opportunities in legitimate enterprises. One of these individuals is "Izzy Green," who operates several businesses. The major public front for this operation is a gold and silver purchasing company located in the 500 block of

"Hamilton Avenue." It has been suggested that he supplies some money to other criminal network participants to facilitate their entry into legitimate business, for illicit purchases, and for the conversion of assets to legitimate income. It is also rumored, although unconfirmed, that he maintains a significant interest in the local garment industry.

The other major figure is "Harry Weinstein," a long-standing fence and loanshark, who had also been a gambling associate of the "Gianellis." He provided a wide-ranging picture of "Morrisburg" organized crime.

As a gambler, "Harry" had used "Gianelli" layoff services, and from time to time even served as an active partner in some of their gambling enterprises. Over the thirty-five years in which he has been active in organized crime, he has used a variety of business fronts, including a clothing store, a bar, a smoke shop, and now a lunch counter.

"Harry" says that he is no longer active as a gambler because the profit margin for small operators is so small. Between buying protection and paying employees, he would be lucky to realize 3 percent in profits. He claims that in the last twenty years, a great many bookmakers and numbers bankers have gone out of business as the profitability of the enterprise shrinks. Loansharking and fencing are more profitable according to "Harry" because there is greater control over who is serviced and over the financial spread (profit margin) on each transaction.

He ceased his involvement in gambling in about 1970. However, prior to that time he had a series of interesting relationships with gamblers. When he came out of the army after World War II, he worked for "Jacob Schiff," who supplied him with a "stake" to open his own business in about 1949. He started selling "Schiff's" lottery tickets and augmented his income with bookmaking. He said "Schiff" did not handle his layoff business in bookmaking. Rather, he laid off to "Steve Gianelli," who "Harry" claims was part of a gambling syndicate including Abe Minker of Reading, Pennsylvania, and others, backed by New York's premier bookmaker, Frank Erikson. In the mid-1950s, he expanded his gambling operation, converting to more traditional numbers betting (rather than the treasury balance lottery) and operating a bookmaking business jointly with the "Gianellis." He claims that at that time, layoff action was handled by a group of eastern Pennsylvania gamblers, which included the older "Gianellis" and people from the Philadelphia area. This arrangement apparently continued with some minor variations until his retirement from gambling.

"Harry" claims that loansharking offers a comfortable money flow. He loans to two kinds of customers: (1) small businessmen who are overextended with the banks or their suppliers, and (2) gamblers with large debts, usually to the "Gianellis." He disputes the notion that loansharking involves the use of enforcers. He says that he has no such system and will simply not loan money without proper collateral, which could include interest in a business, an automobile title, a mortgage, etc. He also asserts that he very rarely has trouble collecting. According to "Harry," his customers are quite careful with him because he is their last course of liquid capital. So, while they may be able to "stiff" a bank, they always want to stay on good terms with him in case they need another bailout. He says his interest rate is more moderate than loansharks in big cities. He usually loans money for a month, three months at the most, and expects a return of 15–20 percent depending upon the risk involved.

"Harry" says that fencing is an even more dependable business. He deals only with professional thieves and not with amateurs. He pays for goods on a sliding scale related to the resaleability of the items involved. For example, he pays 40 percent of value on TVs, personal computers, etc., but only 25 percent on precious gems which are harder to unload. He keeps a modest stock of items in the back room of his luncheonette but insists that the vast majority of the goods are sold to respectable business people, who simply add them to their inventories. He claims to have a group of seventeen local businessmen who take anything he has that fits their inventory.

"Harry" says there are four or five large fences operating in "Morrisburg" and many merchants who fence on a small scale. Fencing and loansharking are often interrelated. While he is tied in with the "Gianelli" gambling network, he thinks that most fences and loansharks are independent operators, not part of any larger organization.

Loansharking in "Morrisburg" is clearly tied to the gambling network in many respects. Many of the loansharks work on a referral basis from the "Gianellis" and their associates. In many ways, the organization of loansharking in "Morrisburg" is similar to descriptions provided by other researchers. For example, in "Morrisburg" loansharks tend to specialize in their clientele, a result also reported by Rubinstein and Reuter:

> There is strong evidence for specialization by loansharks. Some deal with illegal entrepreneurs. One medium-level loanshark specialized in fur dealers, though he might make loans to other

small businessmen. Some specialize in lending money to gambling operators (1978b: Appendix, 3–5).

In "Morrisburg," most loansharks are independent entrepreneurs. Some had connections to larger crime organizations. As was the case with gambling, those with connections tended to be the most successful. Others were clearly independent with only tenuous relationships with other crime operators. It can be said with confidence that in "Morrisburg" loansharking is not controlled or dominated by any single organized crime group or syndicate.

Fencing has similar organizational characteristics. As Marilyn Walsh found in her study (1977) of fences, almost all fences were clearly independent entrepreneurs. In addition, the "Morrisburg" data also confirmed Walsh's findings that most fences have other illegitimate businesses, such as gambling or loansharking.

Fencing also provides one of the clearest connections between organized crime and upperworld businesses. Legitimate business people knowingly sell stolen property in a variety of settings (including retail stores, poolrooms, bars, etc.). This involvement by local merchants parallels the study done by Cartey (1970: 30–31) of fences in Brooklyn.

Another interesting finding is that many of the fences take the role of what Walsh (1977: 110) termed the "hood." A hood is a person with "a floating illegitimate status." Hoods are usually older and their active participation in other kinds of vice has either ended or is significantly reduced. Walsh argues that the hood is "analogous to the pensioner in the legitimate employment world."

In "Morrisburg," organized crime is quite traditional, with the most successful organized criminals and groups engaged in gambling, loansharking, and fencing. However, somewhat surprisingly, "Morrisburg" also has major organized crime interests in the high-risk enterprise of drug trafficking and in illegal sexual services.

Drug Trafficking

In looking at the drug trade in "Morrisburg," a few central questions about drug trafficking and its relationship to organized crime can be posed. For instance: Is there an organized crime role in drug distribution? What is that role? What precisely do organized criminals do in relationship to the distribution of drugs? Do organized criminals exercise territorial control in relation to drug trafficking? Are organized crime groups in competition with one another or is there a clear dominance of one group?

In "Morrisburg," it was possible to examine drug delivery organizations in some detail. Drug distribution organizations could be observed and the nature of trafficking could be discussed with key informants active in the drug trade. Questions that could be addressed because of the limited size of the drug trade in "Morrisburg" are: Who controls the drug flow? Who reaps the profits? How do the drugs get to the street? Once they are on the street, how are they distributed? Pursuing the answers to these questions is vital if we are to understand the relationship between drug trafficking and structural arrangements inherent in the organization of crime.

Drug Trafficking at the Source

Most illicit drugs are freely available in "Morrisburg" especially through the "Akbar" Organization and the "James Gang" at street level. Methamphetamines are manufactured locally by an outlaw motorcycle gang and sold to distributors or are imported from Canada. The city's excellent location near a hub of interstate highways provides easy access to all key drug importation centers. Canadian links to the drug traffic are especially important. A remarkable number of large drug rings, many with national distribution networks, use the rural areas surrounding "Morrisburg" as a depot for imported drugs pending distribution, despite the fact that, in many cases, this area is a considerable distance from the home base of the drug network itself. It is interesting to note the number of real estate transactions involving vacation homes in the mountains surrounding "Morrisburg" that have involved outlaw motorcycle gang members or organized criminals from the New York and Philadelphia areas. Presumably they are interested in something more than mere recreational activities on their country estates. It is equally interesting to note the number of investors from Miami who have suddenly discovered the value of "Morrisburg's" declining hotel industry and acquired resort properties at inflated prices.

Like all cities, "Morrisburg" has many criminal organizations whose main business is drugs. However, there are only three organized crime groups of any real size or sophistication involved in drug trafficking: the "Knight" Organization; the "James Gang"; and the "Akbar" brothers. The "Knight" Organization is the largest of the groups and is the only one which directly imports its supplies without utilizing the services of a wholesaler. Its primary business is in supplying other drug trafficking groups, although it has a sophisticated street distribution organization of its own. In addition, the "Knight" Organization wholesales to major organized crime groups in Baltimore, Philadelphia, and other cities. Both the "James Gang" and the "Akbar" brothers are involved in street-level retailing, usually in concert with the prostitution business. They buy some of their supplies from the "Knight" Organization and also from drug networks in other cities. The "James Gang" deals extensively with black organized crime groups in New York and Philadelphia, and the "Akbars" make some purchases from Philadelphia-area traffickers.

One of the most interesting aspects of the "Morrisburg" drug trade is the role of this relatively minor backwater as a source of supply for large metropolitan areas. For example, it is surprising to note that "Morrisburg" serves as a source of supply for the "Greek Mob," a powerful organized crime group operating in the metropolitan Philadelphia-area and engaging in a variety of functions including extortion, loansharking, arson-for-hire, and drug trafficking. "Chuck Theopolis," a member of that group indicated that their primary sources of supply were through New York City and "Morrisburg." He indicated that another major Philadelphia-based drug network, composed primarily of black members and somewhat derisively referred to by law enforcement agencies as "the Black Mafia," also receives a substantial amount of their supplies through "Morrisburg."

"Chuck" claims that the relationship between the "Greek Mob" and "Morrisburg" has a number of advantages. First, and most importantly, the price is lower in "Morrisburg" than in New York or at other major points of supply. In addition to price, the ease of transport also plays a role in the decision to use "Morrisburg" suppliers. Drugs warehoused in "Morrisburg" can be moved by private car, a situation which greatly reduces the chances of detection or hijacking. Because "Morrisburg" is only two hours away, this method of transportation is the safest and most convenient for the Greek drug dealers. Finally, "Chuck" indicates that the "Morrisburg" pipeline is reliable. Merchandise arrives on schedule and commitments are almost always fulfilled by "Morrisburg" traffickers. This protects "Chuck" and his cohorts from what they consider to be the greatest danger to a smoothly operating drug network—interruption of supply. He argues that such interruptions cause confusion, cost money, and often require a restructuring of street-level operations before a normal flow is once again established. The "Greek Mob" apparently finances their drug buys from the proceeds of other illegal enterprises. However,

Figure 4.2 Local Drug Trafficking Organizations Active in "Morrisburg"

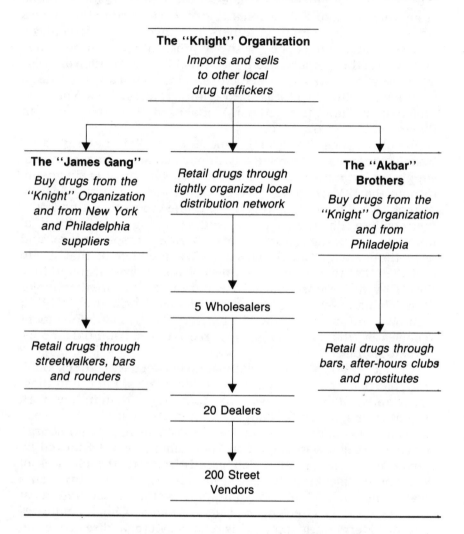

"Chuck" said that occasionally the drug transactions are jointly financed with several bookmakers in the Philadelphia area.

The actual structure and functioning of "Morrisburg" drug networks were studied with considerable assistance from two primary informants, "Robert Knight" and "Kathy." "Knight" is a "Morrisburg" local, currently in hiding in Toronto as a result of an earlier arrest. Despite his fugitive status, he moves freely across the

U.S.-Canadian border, and frequently conducts business in Buffalo, New York and Erie, Pennsylvania.

"Knight" explains that Toronto is an ideal location for drug import and subsequent distribution for five primary reasons:

1) Transportation between "Morrisburg" and Toronto is easy by road. Routes traverse areas where intervention by local police departments is unlikely because those departments are either small or the local towns have no police departments at all.

2) The drug source in Toronto is reliable and steady, providing apparently sufficient quantities of high-grade methamphetamines, heroin, and cocaine.

3) By using Toronto, "Morrisburg" entrepreneurs are able to deal directly with their source of supply, rather than with another layer of individuals in the middle, which would raise prices and reduce the quality of their purchases.

4) Local sources are unreliable, particularly in the case of the motorcycle gangs, which "draw too much heat" and "don't have the kind of political connections" that Toronto sources have.

5) There is apparently a longer history of business relationships between "Morrisburg"-based financiers and Toronto suppliers than exists with other cities in closer proximity.

As "Knight" explains the process, there is a standing order placed with Toronto suppliers which is picked up about every two weeks. Financing for the purchases comes from several sources:

1) Local drug profits, which are usually more than sufficient to cover the cost of a standing order;

2) Local financiers outside the drug network who finance special buys (which entail either special substances, such as Quaaludes, or substances of a higher grade and quality, or increased quantities purchased for export from "Morrisburg"); and,

3) On occasion, up-front funding is supplied by buyers in Baltimore or Philadelphia if they increase their normal purchase quantities or add other substances to their order.

The drugs are transported to "Morrisburg" where 20 to 40 percent are earmarked for local distribution (primarily through the "Akbars" and the "James Gang"); the rest are sold to drug organizations in other cities. Non-"Morrisburg" clients have to arrange to pick up their purchases in "Morrisburg." Drugs distributed locally are put on the street by a complicated system of go-betweens, dealers, and street vendors. "Robert" estimates that

Figure 4.3 The Toronto/"Morrisburg" Connection

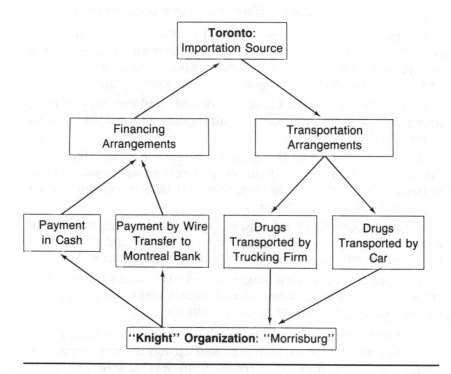

in the "Knight" Organization there are about five intermediaries operating in the "Morrisbrug" area, supplying about twenty dealers, who in turn supply about two hundred street vendors. The profit margin for drugs sold locally varied from abut forty cents on the dollar for methamphetamines, to seventy-five cents on the dollar for heroin, to two dollars on the dollar for cocaine. Wholesale charges to organized crime groups in other cities carry a flat 100 percent markup across the board.

The specifics of "Knight's" story deserve closer attention. His source in Toronto consists of several distributors for a large organized crime group consisting of Corsicans and Arabs. The drugs are prepackaged in a variety of legitimate goods, ranging from dairy products and meat to fabric and ceramics. Payment is made in cash from standing orders (about $1.25 million) on a quarterly basis. Special orders, which "Knight" estimates to run at about $2.5 million a year, are paid for by wire transfers to a Montreal bank.

"Knight" points out that the individuals in "Morrisburg" who transfer this money often transfer much larger sums in that they also handle funds tied up in underground pornography production.

When the purchase has been made, the drugs are transported in several ways. Some of the drugs are moved by a major trucking firm, which also serves the garment industry. At other times drugs are moved by private vehicle across the border at Buffalo, often with motorcycle gang members hired to ride shotgun. A third much less frequently utilized method of transportation involves flights into the local airport. The transportation methods employed are scrambled so that the same methods are not used either back-to-back or in any discernible pattern.

Obviously, one of the most important aspects of this network is financing. As "Knight" said, much of the cash is merely recycled drug profits from the streets of "Morrisburg." However, two other sources are frequently employed. When a purchaser in Philadelphia or Baltimore wishes to invest at a greater level than usual, the money is transferred prior to the purchase through intermediaries. The primary purchasers were identified as a group frequently referred to as the "Black Mafia" in Philadelphia, several Greek gamblers and loansharks, a consortium of Philadelphia-based bookmakers, and individuals often associated with the alleged Cosa Nostra family operating in southeastern Pennsylvania. Additionally, financing is occasionally supplied by local entrepreneurs seeking to turn a quick profit or to reinvest illicit capital. "Dave Perlman" and "Izzy Green" are two such regular investors. None of the financiers deals the drugs directly. Rather, they commission the "Knight" Organization to dispose of the supply for them in return for a sizable profit on the original investment.

Drug Trafficking on the Streets

How do people become drug traffickers—either at the highly successful level of "Robert Knight" or at the more ordinary level of a retail street vendor? Information on this aspect of the drug trade came from "Kathy," a twenty-eight-year-old "Morrisburg" woman with twelve years of experience in the drug network. She has been arrested twice for selling drugs (once methamphetamines and once heroin). "Kathy" began as a very low-level distributor when she was in high school. She maintains a full-time job with a local manufacturing firm and is not a heavy drug user herself, although she does use cocaine on a regular basis.

She got into the drug business because she needed pocket money when she was in school. She said that drug use was quite common in her high school, and she was acquainted with a substantial number of people who used regularly. She knew some individuals who sold drugs at the retail level and was given the opportunity to deal during her sophomore year. Her "job" consisted of getting a quantity of drugs (Quaaludes, amphetamines, and hallucinogens) from a distributor and selling them to "clients." The system was such that she did not have to solicit customers; she had a list of steady buyers whom she supplied on a regular basis. At the end of each week, she turned the money she had collected over to her contact who paid her a 20 percent commission. She states that she was able to make between fifty and one hundred dollars a week during her high school career, and that this line of work was far preferable to the minimum wage after-school jobs that were available to her.

After high school, "Kathy" graduated to the next step in the drug network. Although she does not like the word "pusher," her role fit that description. Once again, she claims that her drug selling job was merely a way to supplement her income and improve her access to luxuries and material goods. The life of a drug dealer was preferable to the other alternative she had considered, which was prostitution. She described her few attempts at being a hooker as psychologically difficult because of her inability to "anesthetize" herself during sexual encounters. After several years as a low-level pusher, she was promoted into a middle-level distributor position. She claims that this was the best of all possible situations because she didn't have to sell drugs, rather her job was to supply them to street-level retail dealers. However, several years ago she was one of several people arrested in a major investigation of drug trafficking in the "Morrisburg" area. Of the more than twenty people arrested in the crackdown, she indicated that only three or four were middle-level operatives, with all the rest working the street. The arrests apparently resulted from assistance given to law enforcement agents by two inside informers who were plea bargaining against previous arrests. Despite the arrests, "Kathy" claims that the drug network was able to continue operations. Primarily this was because the investigation never got to the source of supply nor did it disrupt the flow of money so vital to drug organizations.

As she describes the operations of this drug network, supplies were purchased in Toronto and transported to "Morrisburg." Once in "Morrisburg" they were warehoused, and about one-third of the total supply was consigned to local use; another two-thirds were sold to the black, Greek and Italian drug dealers in Philadelphia. She declined to confirm "Knight's" comments on specific drug sources used by the group, but she did confirm that some of her cohorts made regular trips to Toronto.

"Kathy" is still actively engaged in the drug business and runs a group of some twenty street retailers, including several prostitutes. When pressed on why the group she is associated with did not have closer associations with the motorcycle gangs, particularly in relation to the provision of methamphetamines, she stressed unreliability and the fact that the gangs usually dealt with smaller, less-established groups. The drug organization she is involved with needs a steady and dependable financial network and source of supply.

She maintains that there are many small drug entrepreneurs in the "Morrisburg" area, but only two major organizations. These major organized crime groups often work together, but are distinguished by their sources of supply.

The Organization of Drug Trafficking

Our look at drug trafficking in "Morrisburg" suggests several important points with regard to criminal organization. First, it appears that those drug networks with a clearly developed hierarchy and a functioning division of labor have greater success than less organized drug operations. The "Knight" Organization is set up in such a way as to minimize contact between layers of the operation. Street-level pushers have no information on the activities of wholesalers. Dealers have no knowledge of financing or sources of supply. In addition, on a horizontal axis, people performing similar functions often do not have contact with each other or knowledge of each other. A built-in system of compartmentalization separates operatives. All of this is vital to controlling the one commodity the organization values as much as their drugs—information. By controlling what employees know and how much they know, a highly structured operation like the "Knight" organization can protect its sources of supply and its day-to-day operations. For example, the arrest of one pusher, under the worst of all possible circumstances, can result in subsequent arrests of about nine other pushers and one dealer, leaving 95 percent of the organization's operation intact and functioning. Even if law enforcement officials move up the ladder to arrest a dealer, the best they can achieve are cases against one wholesaler, three other dealers, and forty street-level retailers, leaving 80 percent of the organization unscathed. The "Knight" Organization is structured in a manner that allows for the insulation of key operatives and the protection of most employees through segmentation of the operations.

The "James Gang" and the "Akbars," on the other hand, do not exhibit the same level of organizational sophistication. They conduct business through their bars or on the streets, often through their prostitutes. There is only a minimal hierarchy, with group leaders acting as managers and everyone else in the operation acting as salespersons. An arrest of even a minor pusher can have devastating effects on the whole organization. The obvious question in this case is, if more structure means greater safety, then why haven't these other groups emulated the "Knight" Organization? There are two answers to this question. First, both the "James Gang" and the "Akbars" mix drug trafficking with a number of other illicit businesses, particularly prostitution. The conduct of a prostitution business, and their other business ventures such as after-hours clubs, necessitates a looser, more informal system of control and management. Frequent social contact with prostitutes is the only way to effectively oversee that business. When prostitutes are also used as pushers the social distance between drug selling and organized crime group management is reduced to the barest minimum. The "Knight" Organization, dealing only in drugs, can structure itself in a way that most effectively protects daily operations and investments. Second, the "Knight" Organization has far more resources at their disposal than the "James Gang" or the "Akbars." Financing comes from many sources. Distribution often goes to other organized crime groups rather than directly to the street. The "James Gang" and the "Akbars" generate capital from their bars and their prostitutes, both publicly accessibly sources. They also distribute through their bars and their prostitutes. They lack both the contacts and the money to guarantee safety. In the case of the "James Gang" and the "Akbars," what little capital they have available to use in protecting their enterprises must be spent locally, on local police and local judges. As a result, their activities must be confined to "Morrisburg" proper, preventing expansion and thereby preventing the accumulation of the additional resources necessary to develop a more sophisticated organization. They are caught in a cycle that precludes more successful operations.

The drug business in "Morrisburg" is organized at a higher level of sophistication than one would expect of a city its size. The complexity of the largest drug organization (the "Knight" Organization), and its sources of finance and supply, would rival any found in a major city. Analysis of drug trafficking in "Morrisburg," therefore, provides excellent insights into the drug business:

1) There are multiple drug networks supplying "Morrisburg." They range from the highly structured drug traffickers associated with "Robert Knight," to open dealing in the city's strip associated with the "James Gang" and the "Akbar" brothers, to occasional ventures by even smaller, less organized entrepreneurial groups.

2) Employee loyalty in drug trafficking is achieved by two principle means. First, the economic rewards are considerable. However, the risk is also quite high in terms of jail sentences and the possibility of arrest. Therefore, most drug organizations complement economic incentives with coercive means of control. The threat of violence against disloyal members is quite real. In "Morrisburg" several cases of threats, beatings, and even kidnapings have been associated with the activities of the "James Gang," for example.

It is interesting to note that in drug trafficking the interpersonal and community contacts inherent in the other types of criminal activities we have discussed are often missing. Gamblers, fences, and loansharks usually form organizations around a core of people with similar backgrounds, common values, and long-standing relationships. This kind of social bonding is less evident in drug trafficking. Drug organizations tend to involve younger participants from less stable community backgrounds than other organized crime groups; membership in drug organizations is less predictable and less stable than is the case in other kinds of organized crime. The individuals involved often have more extensive criminal records and a greater dependence on criminal enterprises.

3) Unlike other criminal enterprises, drug trafficking seems to be quite unintegrated (with the exception of highly structured entities like the "Knight" Organization). Drug distribution usually involves a series of arm's-length transactions rather than the integration of importing, wholesaling, and retailing aspects of the business.

Participants in drug trafficking are in constant peril from law enforcement. Conviction leads to heavy penalties. It is relatively easy to have one's entire stock of goods and assets confiscated. Extortion by corrupt police officers and other criminal justice system participants is a constant threat. Legal protection is very expensive. It, therefore, makes great sense that drug traffickers will establish routines that minimize the numbers of individuals with whom they must deal on a regular basis.

4) Unlike other criminal enterprises, particularly gambling and loansharking, no credit relationship exists in the drug trade. Reputation as a means of doing criminal business is less important

in drug trafficking than in other enterprises. "Gentlemen's agreements" are quite rare and actually unnecessary. The buyer tests the product for quality and weighs it for quantity. A reputation for dishonesty or other unpleasant business practices on the part of the supplier need not impair the deal.

5) Success in drug trafficking can be equated with the degree of cooperation crime groups receive from the political and law enforcement bureaucracies.

6) Networks with the most dependable sources of supply and the most varied financial portfolios appear to be the most stable and successful. Every drug trafficker interviewed for this study pointed to the importance of stability of supply to the success of a drug business. Not only does stability enhance planning and capital accumulation, it is a necessity if steady client relations are to be maintained. In addition, stability is an important means of cutting costs. Having to restructure and reorganize a drug network after arrests not only interferes with sales but is expensive in terms of recruitment, rewards for new employees, and establishing adequate protection.

7) Drug trafficking is clearly an important part of organized crime. It just as clearly takes a back seat to more traditional illicit services such as gambling, loansharking, and fencing. As with prostitution, it appears that there is a clear demarcation between the gambling organizations and the drug networks. The "Gianellis" have clearly refused to participate in, or for that matter even to abet, drug trafficking. Rather, it appears that drug trafficking is the province of less established, incipient organized crime groups.

Illicit Sexual Services

As emphasized earlier in this chapter, organized crime groups are in the business of providing illicit goods and services to willing customers who desire those goods and services. Less is known about the role of organized crime in the delivery of illicit sexual services than any of the other activities.

"Morrisburg's" three main organized crime groups (the "Gianellis," the "Akbars," and the "James Gang") all play some role in prostitution and pornography. While these three groups are distinct and separate, there are discernible overlaps. For example, much of the real estate in the vice district is owned by the "Gianellis," even the buildings in which "Akbar" enterprises are located. In a city the size of "Morrisburg," with a vice district of only ten or twelve blocks, it is inevitable that members of these three groups will intermingle and socialize.

The illicit sex industry in "Morrisburg" is open and easy to find. It is far more pervasive than a city this size and economic condition might initially indicate. Sex services run the gamut from prostitution, after-hours clubs catering to solicitation of various sexual preferences, and pornography outlets, to the production of pornographic films. The questions addressed here are: how are these services organized and who profits from them?

Prostitution

It can be argued that the prostitute embraces so wide a range of types and behaviors as to be almost useless as an operational concept. We will, therefore discuss several different types of service delivery.

Streetwalkers

Individual streetwalkers and bar girls can be seen in a variety of locations in "Morrisburg" from the mid-afternoon to the very early hours of the morning. There appear to be several peak times for this business—there is the "businessman's hour" (3:30 p.m. to 5:30 p.m.); the early evening trade (7:30 p.m. to 10:00 p.m.); and the small hours shift (1:00 a.m. to 4:00 a.m.). Most streetwalkers in "Morrisburg" are black although a few are young white women. The conditions of plying one's trade in this manner are often abysmal.

"Terry" is typical of women who work the streets. She is black and engages in streetwalking as a second job (she is a telephone operator by day). On the night she was interviewed, she had taken refuge in an all-night restaurant to escape the rain and cold. She was working the 2:00 a.m. shift before going to work the next morning and was very high on amphetamines when she was interviewed. In general, prices for streetwalkers are low (about $30 for oral sex). The "Dover Hotel" seemed to reserve most of its seventh floor for prostitutes. "Terry" claimed, and other evidence supported her assertion, that streetwalkers operate outside of the major organized crime groups. This fact creates problems for her. While the "Morrisburg" police are clearly "fixed" with regard to gambling, drugs, and other goods and services, they are far less reliable in overlooking streetwalkers. "Terry" has had a series of bad experiences with the police—the "Morrisburg" police department was not honest; they did not stay bought. Despite the

fact that "Terry" paid off at regular intervals, she was still pressed
for sexual services in lieu of arrest.

Organized crime has ongoing relationships with the police department. Thus, streetwalkers play an important scapegoat role in
"Morrisburg." Their vulnerability allows some arrests for
prostitution and thereby relieves pressure on the police to control
crime; streetwalkers are most likely to be sacrificed to law-and-order
crackdowns.

Call Girls

Most call girl activity in the town is run by an agency called
"Couples." "Couples" is operated by several members of a local
motorcycle club whose girlfriends (Mamas) or female motorcycle
club associates (Sheep) mainly comprise the workforce. The notable
fact about "Couples" is that it is part of a business complex run
by a major fence and loanshark who also uses the bikers as
enforcers and collectors. "Couples" appears to be just one of many
ancillary businesses run by this loansharking-fence operation.
Other call girl activity is connected with "Akbar" operations in the
vice district and will be discussed below.

Exotic Dancers

One of the many anachronisms of "Morrisburg" is the ongoing
popularity of exotic dancers or, as they used to be called, go-go girls.
Several major informants came from this group. They live in upstate
New York and ride a circuit throughout New York, Pennsylvania,
New Jersey, and Delaware.

The women earn their living by dancing and by turning tricks
between acts. Depending on their talents and qualifications, they
are paid $75 to $125 a night for dancing and are allowed to collect
all the tips they can manage. For the most part, they specialize in
quickies lasting only a few minutes and costing about $20. These
liaisons take place in a secluded part of the bar or in an adjacent
room. Depending on the excitability and affluence of their audience,
they may earn up to $200 a night in tips. Some of the dancers
interviewed also worked in pornographic films as a sideline. All of
the dancers who were interviewed are drug users, although they
are not addicts, showing a clear preference for uppers and cocaine.
They regarded "Morrisburg" as a wide-open town and were very
helpful in providing access to individuals operating in both vice and
pornography.

In addition to their circuit-work, they provide call girl services
to special customers who want more exotic practices than those

available on the streets. They are referred to these clients by their employer, who also refers them to the filmmakers.

The "Wizard" Network

The full extent of "Morrisburg's" sex industry cannot be appreciated without surveying the establishments operating in the vice district. The 500 block of "Abundance Avenue" contains an intense concentration of organized vice. At 512 "Abundance" is a billiard room run by the "Gianellis," which serves as the headquarters for their numbers and sports betting operations. The "Gianelli" complex includes two adjacent stores and a garment manufacturer. At numbers 524 and 532 are two ostensibly separate bars and lounges. All of these buildings are three stories high, and there is as much activity on the upper floors late into the night as there is in the bars themselves. These three establishments are run by the "Akbars," though they clearly overlap with "Gianelli" activities and real estate holdings.

At 524 "Abundance" was a bar known as the "Maya," now called the "Moonlight Lounge," a fairly plush bar which is all but empty on most nights. Right next door is the "Wizard," both a bar and an after-hours club replete with a spyhole in the door, just like 1920s Chicago. "Joey Akbar" is constantly in evidence at the "Wizard," whether behind the bar or at the door greeting customers (his brother, "Tom," is currently incarcerated for a drug operation). The "Wizard" contains a bar, a dance floor, and a pair of restrooms—which may account for a significant portion of "Morrisburg's" economic life.

Observations conducted at the "Wizard" were extremely interesting. A casual drink or two at "Wizard" allows one to observe men coming in at regular intervals and passing large sums of money over the bar to "Mr. Akbar." "Joey" duly noted the amounts and filed what were obviously betting slips in a cash box under the bar. In addition, "Wizard" is notable for its drug activity. Throughout the evening, one or more of a group of black men, rather garishly dressed, would leave the bar and go either to the men's or ladies' room. They would be followed by a line of customers placing their orders for heroin, "krank," or cocaine. These individuals were clearly dealing for the "James Gang." At other times people ordered $100 cocktails from "Mr. Akbar," who took the money and returned with a mixed drink and a small foil packet passed directly over the bar.

On any given night, "Wizard" was populated by fifteen to twenty women, most from the upper echelons of local prostitution. It is interesting to note that very few of the women were working the bar itself (on average two women worked the bar). However, the other women were, in fact, working. "Wizard" serves as a central switchboard for local prostitutes and call girls. Messages come in, are received, and the women leave for their appointed rendezvous.

Down the street from "Wizard" is an all-night restaurant called the "Yorke Cafe." The sidewalk outside the "Yorke" is streetwalker turf. At night this block is populated with both female prostitutes and boy prostitutes. The male prostitution, just like that of the women, was blatant and fairly ostentatious. An hour sipping coffee in the "Yorke" leaves no doubt that both women and boy prostitutes do a heavy volume of business in "Morrisburg." The scale of open homosexual prostitution came as a surprise in that most other studies indicate that such activities are limited to much larger cities, such as New York and San Francisco.

One of the exotic dancers, "Rachel," provided entree to the world above the three bars, the hidden three floors. Directly above the bars are two large apartments. They are both used by "Morrisburg's" more exclusive prostitutes. The apartments have three bedrooms, all complete with bars, elaborate stereo systems, mirrors, and track lighting. The rooms are soundproof and offer maximum privacy for customers willing to foot the bill. These are the haunts of the "Akbar" prostitutes. This is a traditional, high-class prostitution service, with clients screened in advance, payment made in advance, and sessions running several hours instead of the fifteen-minute quickies available on the streets. "Rachel" says that on a weeknight four or five clients may be entertained, but on weekends business is so heavy that prior reservations are required.

Incidentally, the third floors of these establishments are used for storage, with electronic gambling devices still in their crates lining the walls (very probably "Gianelli"-owned machines).

At the top of these buildings is a kind of spacious attic which can only be reached by a freight elevator in the back. These rooms are long with small cubicles abutting them. In the main room itself are sofas, chairs, a refrigerator and a small sterilizer, such as those commonly found in doctors' offices. This is "Morrisburg's" version of a rather elite "shooting gallery." There are no windows to the street, and the accommodations are used by those who wish to partake of various drugs. The attic shooting gallery provides protection from the police. In addition, "Rachel" says that two bouncers are employed there to keep patrons from becoming unruly, and medical care is readily available if anything goes wrong. Prostitutes are also available if one's high takes that direction.

Of course, there are also other establishments in this vice network. Three blocks away is the "Pub George," which offers a similar range of dancing, prostitution, and drug services. It was clear from talking to the women who worked these establishments that they were closely linked to the local vice organization which directed the women to clients and to syndicate-connected bars and cafes.

Pornography

The pornography trade acquires its main importance from providing a territorial base for other forms of vice scattered throughout major cities. The adult book store provides both temptation and opportunity. Exactly how blatant vice is can be determined by looking at a number of variables, including the economic sophistication of the business networks concerned, the nature of public attitudes—demand and tolerance—and above all, the permissiveness of law enforcement agencies.

As a very rough rule of thumb, a look inside a pornography store provides an easy index of police corruption in an area. Adult book stores can be categorized in the following manner:

1) **Bookstore only**. Pornographic books and magazines are sold. Heterosexual themes predominate, and the material is rather tame. Mild sado-masochism is the limit of perversion on display.

2) **Books and film**. In the back of the store there might be a number of individual booths, anywhere from four to forty, each with two projectors or a television monitor. Contents of the films available are advertised either on the door of the booth or on a central placard. The customer enters the booth, sits, and places quarters (sometimes tokens) in a coin box to purchase a short time of viewing. A whole film might cost $10.

3) **Live shows**. In larger cities, the system of individual booths and the purchase of short viewing time has been applied to live peep shows. The entertainment offered may simply be a naked dancer; effectively, the porn store is simply replacing the old burlesque or strip joint. In variations on this theme, the stripper may approach the viewer and offer extra activities, so there is the potential for prostitution. Bigger cities offer live sex shows on a common stage, viewed from a series of surrounding booths. The male participants may—for a price—be drawn from the audience in the booths. In recent years, the "telephone booth" is common where the viewer pays for a curtain or blind to be raised; a naked woman is in the other part of the booth, separated by a glass partition. Conversation takes place through a telephone—including prostitution arrangements if that is the customer's preference. If law enforcement is not a concern, the woman will simply make an outright offer to visit

the patron's booth to take part in sexual activity.

This by no means exhausts the potential of pornographic establishments. They may sell newspapers or magazines with the descriptions, addresses, and phone numbers of local prostitutes. The film screens themselves may be used for graffiti giving the phone number and predilections of (usually homosexual) clients.

These stores also offer homosexual venues, primarily "glory holes"—a round hole of two to six inches in diameter in the side of one of the film booths, through which various parts of the anatomy may be placed. When two men are sitting in adjacent booths, an invitation to engage in oral sex may be expressed in a number of ways at this hole.

Adult bookstores may vary in the provision of glory holes. Some lack them altogether. In some, glory holes exist in every booth and the assumption must be that these cater to a predominantly homosexual clientele, even where many of the films are of a heterosexual content. This is a practical need: men who would not mind being seen entering a pornographic film store would fear association with a purely gay hangout. It must appear that there is the option of heterosexual activity there. Most stores compromise. Most booths do not have glory holes, but there are complexes of three booths linked together which do have them. In each of these triads, there are at least two films available—one straight, one gay. (There must always be the option of being presumed to be viewing a heterosexual film.) From the central booth, each neighbor is accessible. This happy compromise means that homosexual clients can use the store for sexual activity, while straights will not be bothered by sudden and unwanted incursions from the adjacent patron. Incidentally, the ethos of the establishments seems to be toward transient sexual activity. Clients do not have encounters in booths which lead to further relationships. Rarely do men leave the stores in pairs. Homosexual activity is purely confined to the booths.

"Morrisburg's" porn trade is small by most standards. The city has two adult book-and-film stores. These establishments do not feature the live shows common in larger cities, nor do they supply outlets for the blatant advertising by prostitutes found in larger cities. "Morrisburg" vice exists on traditional lines. One store is part of the "Abundance Avenue" vice district; despite the ready availability of heterosexual films and publications, it clearly has an overwhelmingly homosexual clientele. Every film booth has a glory hole, and the booths feature graffiti advertising names and phone numbers of males interested in sexual liaisons.

The other porn outlet is in a syndicate-owned building about a block off "Abundance Avenue." This store is heavily guarded by two steel doors, and there is no advertising to let customers know the store is in operation. This store is exclusively heterosexual, and the physical layout suggests that other business, probably related to the retail drug trade, is also transacted there.

The real story of pornography in "Morrisburg" is not in the retail outlets. "Morrisburg" is a major production center for strictly illegal pornography. One of the primary informants in this study, "Tiffany," works for an elite call girl ring out of Baltimore and Washington, D.C. Through this link, she often works in porn sessions in "Morrisburg." "Tiffany" specializes in what she calls "hard-to-get" items, in her case extremely violent rape scenarios. She has been trained in stunt techniques and makes it clear that the punches, kicks, and blood are all simulations, except for the occasional unfortunate accident. She says that "Morrisburg" is the site for these productions because: (1) the cost of extras is much less there—while she commands $250 an hour, "bit-players" get as little as $20 an hour; (2) "Morrisburg" is conveniently located for technicians from New York, Philadelphia, and Baltimore, the cities in which both film producers and financiers live; and, (3) "Morrisburg" appears to be a safe city. "Tiffany" claims that none of her productions have been raided in "Morrisburg," whereas she has been arrested in Baltimore and New York.

"Tiffany's" information was confirmed by another source, "Misty," who is one of the circuit-riding dancers. "Misty" has been involved in productions filmed at two downtown "Morrisburg" locations. While these films cover a wide range of plotlines, two specific types seem to be most in demand: (1) the violent scenarios "Tiffany" spoke of; and (2) films involving pre-teen training, in which the plot revolves around the initiation of ten and twelve-year-old boys and girls into sexual activity. These productions are funded by enterprises in New York and Baltimore.

The Underground Market

In addition to the production of pornographic films, "Morrisburg" also has a thriving business in illicit films which cannot be legally sold in retail adult bookstores. An introduction to this subterranean market was provided by "Gil," a middle-aged executive of a large "Morrisburg"-based insurance firm. "Gil" said there were two distributorships that he knew of operating in "Morrisburg" that provided this service: one a retail clothing establishment and the other a video club. The available stock of films and picture sets included such topics as family fun and kiddie porn (in great abundance); rapes; dogs and horses; and the like. The films sell anywhere from $100 to $250. "Gil" also pointed out that another service available at both locations is the purchase of young women. Customers are shown a photo album with a brief biography and allowed to order a liaison with the woman of their choice.

Sex Clubs

"Gil" also belongs to a club that is located outside of the "Morrisburg" city limits. The club caters to members with explicit sexual tastes tending toward the bizarre. The structure itself resembles an old warehouse which might have been converted to use as a bar and banquet hall. Security in the building is quite tight. One must pass through a locked door, guarded by a very large doorman. Then there is a hall about ten feet long with a steel door at the far end. Above the steel door is a camera monitoring guests. After being scanned a buzzer releases the lock on the steel door and one enters a reception room of about twelve by fourteen feet. There is a security man sitting at a television which monitors the door, and at the other side of the room is a desk with a receptionist. The waiting room is comfortably furnished. After checking in with the receptionist and confirming the appointment, the customer is admitted into the club itself.

After being admitted by the receptionist, customers find themselves in a room resembling a bar, with tables, a jukebox and waitresses. For all outward appearances, this is just another after-hours club. Behind the bar and to the right are two doors, both of which are guarded. These doors admit customers into male and female locker rooms, complete with lockers for one's clothes and a shower. Through a door in the back of the locker room is another bar considerably different from the first. This room has a bar located along the back wall. On the left wall are a series of bondage devices including shackles, stocks, ankle chains, and a pommel horse equipped with ropes. In the middle of the room are tables at which people are drinking and engaging in various forms of deviance, from voyeurism to fellatio. On the right wall there is a partition, replete with glory holes. People stand on one side and subway-like straps have been provided for their convenience. On the other side, short, padded stools have been provided. In the far left corner of the room are two hallways leading to five cubicles in each hallway. These cubicles are for more private liaisons. Half of them are provided with two-way mirrors so that spectators may gather and watch, while the other five appear to afford some level of privacy.

The people in attendance at the club were clearly interested in all aspects of its services. Several women assumed the traditional garb of the dominatrix—leather, high heels, whips. Others were simply nude, and two were attired in little girl outfits. There were also five other women fully dressed. The men showed considerably less imagination, with most being simply nude. "Gil" indicated that to his knowledge none of the people in the room were "professionals," although the club did offer prostitution services.

In fact, at the entrance to one of the hallways leading to the cubicles was a desk with three telephones on it. The woman behind the desk indicated that she was able to secure special services, for a price, to those who might be interested. She even had a price sheet which informed the customer that it would take only thirty minutes to arrange the service. The price sheet included some of the following: water sports (female) $150 an hour, (male) $100 an hour; submissive partners $150 an hour; abusive partners $100 an hour; dinner dates $100 an hour.

"Gil" indicated that people come from all over Pennsylvania, New Jersey, and New York to visit this club and that membership fees were $500 a year, conveying no privileges except access. He also indicated that it was his belief that the prostitutes used in the telephone service were local.

The Organization of Illicit Sex

The obvious question is who controls all of this? Certainly the "Akbars" play a major role in both call girl services and bar prostitution, particularly in their own establishments. It is also clear that some of the streetwalkers are connected to the "James Gang" and their drug network. Conventional wisdom holds that the "Gianellis" are a strictly moral and religious clan of gamblers, pillars of the community, who do not venture into prostitution or pornography. However, this kind of division seems unlikely. The buildings comprising "Morrisburg's" vice district appear to be under syndicate ownership, containing properties owned and managed by both the "Gianellis" and the "Akbars." To say the least, the various crime networks seem to have very cordial relationships.

The more exotic services are controlled outside of "Morrisburg." The pornography stores are tied into the national pornography syndicate based in Cleveland, although they are locally managed. The production of pornographic films is funded through financiers in New York and Baltimore, both probably tied into the pornography syndicate.

What can be said with certainty are three things: (1) vice in "Morrisburg" is controlled by local crime networks providing a wide range of services and goods; (2) operations requiring elaborate logistics or financing are organized outside of "Morrisburg" by people with close ties to the national pornography syndicate; and (3) illicit sexual services, whether traditional or more bizarre, are big business, realizing big profits in the illicit economy of "Morrisburg."

Chapter 5

The Organization of Crime

It should be clear from the preceding discussion that "Morrisburg" offers a wide range of illicit goods and services through organized crime groups. It should also be abundantly clear that a wide variety of groups supply these goods and services. While the "Gianellis" may be the largest gambling network in "Morrisburg," they clearly do not possess a monopoly. While the "James Gang," the "Knight" Organization and the "Akbar" Brothers deal with drugs and prostitution, so do other, smaller entrepreneurs.

These crime networks are organized in a manner to provide the logistical support necessary to their business interests. Yet, are there other factors in the organization of "Morrisburg" crime? Are there consistent and unifying themes which we can cite as vital to the organization of crime? The data would suggest that corruption and finance are overarching concerns vital to the successful creation of an organized crime network.

Corruption

It is quite clear to anyone walking the streets of "Morrisburg" that the political fix is in and extends from the cop on the beat to the

101

most senior political officials. Corruption in "Morrisburg" has a long history—clearly detailed as early as the Kefauver Committee's (1951) investigation of police officials and the district attorney's office. Discerning specific instances of corruption in "Morrisburg" is difficult because it is so pervasive and such an intrinsic part of the political life of the area. It appears that gamblers, like the "Gianellis," are considered part of the business elite of the community and, therefore, have access to almost every political figure.

Much of the political influence buying is done directly. Political contributions and funds to meet personal political "expenses" are transferred from the organized crime groups directly to the officials of both political parties. Both the Republicans and the Democrats have designated "bagmen" who receive the "donations" from the crime networks. The major political "fixer" in "Morrisburg" appears to be long-time political fundraiser and restaurateur, "Jimmy Ryan." His tenure as a "Morrisburg" political power extends over forty years and he has shared business interests with the "Gianellis" throughout his career.

The district attorney's office has been publicly, and repeatedly, linked with the gambling syndicate. These links have included both past and present DAs. It is also interesting to note that retired district attorneys reappear with regularity as the leading defense counsel for major gamblers, drug dealers, and hijackers.

Two sitting judges have been the subject of a journalistic inquiry as a result of their public socializing with the "Gianellis." In addition, several public officials, including the same two judges, have been compromised through real estate investments involving "Gianelli" enterprises. No official action has ever been taken against these officials, and most city and county officeholders make no attempt to disguise their business dealings with "Gianelli"-related enterprises. County officeholders have been especially close to gamblers, and some present officeholders are active in attempts to legalize casino gambling in the area.

Police corruption is handled directly and is all but ignored. One case, which became public and resulted in several prosecutions, involves a police investigator being caught in an attempt to tamper with evidence on behalf of the "James Gang" and the "Akbars." The result of both a judicial inquiry and a departmental investigation was a demotion in rank, with no formal prosecution, criminal action, or thought of dismissal entertained by "Morrisburg's" criminal justice elite. Perhaps one reason for the gentle "tap on the wrist" which this officer received was the public testimony at his hearing from other police officers suggesting that bribe taking was a normal activity. Those officers were not even investigated for their sworn testimony about their own corruption.

Organized crime group links with state government officials have traditionally been handled through the Department of Transportation and have included both the selling of jobs and of road repair and highway contracts. Additional links to corruption at the state level are handled through local money movers like "James Haggerty" and "Sidney Fine" (discussed below).

While corruption is bad in "Morrisburg" itself, it is even worse in the communities surrounding the city. Many of the neighboring communities appear to be wholly-owned subsidiaries of the gambling organizations run by the "Orlandos" and/or the "Gianellis."

A first-hand description of official attitudes was provided by a "Morrisburg" police officer, Patrolman "Krause." He is a relatively young (twenty-five years old) patrol officer. He is manifestly unhappy about what he considers to be a police force which is unprofessional, dominated by politics, and built on cronyism. He is one of a small minority of local officers with a college education and with a desire to return to school and then to move on to another job.

In his four years on the force, he has been assigned to patrol duty, often during the night shift. For six months, he was assigned to the night shift in the central city vice district. According to "Krause," the police do not engage in proactive crime control strategies but respond only to complaints and to visual sightings of crimes in progress discovered by routine patrol. He says that it is well known that gambling, prostitution, and drug dealing occur openly in the central city area. The police are tolerant of gambling, seeing it as a social activity which does no harm and hence warrants no interference. Similarly, the police are tolerant of prostitution, except when under political pressure to get it off the streets. "As long as it is in the bars or clubs there is no problem. Occasionally we have to move the girls off the street to improve the downtown's image." He says the police are not at all tolerant of open drug dealing, but they will not violate the "sanctity" of the bars and the clubs. Drug dealing on the street, if it is open and visible, results in arrests.

He readily concedes that many police are paid off, but the payoff system is not as unified as it might seem. For example, in gambling, the "Gianellis" and their associates do not directly pay off the police, but rather "contribute" to the political establishment and to community activities. They are always amenable to large contributions to hospital fund drives, the United Way, etc. In addition, they make sizable political contributions, recently under other people's names, and also make illegal cash contributions to both parties. The "Gianellis" regularly offer "investment opportunities," often in real estate, to political and governmental figures.

Gambling vendors, the people in bars, tobacco shops, and newsstands—those who collect the bets—pay officers on the beat directly. Often this payment is in the form of services (no tab for lunch or dinner, or drinks, or cigarettes, etc.)

"Krause" says that the "Akbars" operate more directly, paying money on a bi-weekly basis to a ranking police officer, who distributes a graduated payoff to other officers. The payoff is primarily to insure that police will stay on the outside of "Akbar" establishments. In addition, the "Akbars" expect that the police will notify them of any inquiries or investigation by other law enforcement agencies.

Prostitutes working the street pay off the police either directly or though their "managers." Krause says there is not a real pimping system in "Morrisburg"; some hookers do have "business managers" who take care of protection. If officers working the strip do not consider the payoff large enough, they may engage in additional shakedowns. These shakedowns are individual, not systematic, although departmental interference is unlikely to occur when a complaint is registered.

The drug trade works a little differently. The "Akbars" pay a high-ranking (captain) police official who looks after their interests. The black drug dealers and their associates also select specific officers to put on the "pad." There is no protection for street operations as a result of these payoffs; they are primarily for information and for silence on the part of knowledgeable officers. In addition, Patrolman "Krause" says that in extraordinary cases, large sums of money may be proffered for tampering with an ongoing case or investigation (for example, leaking information about the prosecution's case or tampering with evidence). He believes that very few police officers are on the drug payroll, and he claims that most find drug trafficking offensive. However, the code of silence is so strong in the police department that no effort is made to stop corrupt officers from assisting the drug networks.

Patrolman "Krause" also claims that fixers are quite active. Fixers represent clients to the police. For varying amounts of money, they get the police to drop charges or to change arrest reports for offenses ranging from drunk driving to narcotics. The fixer system is well established in "Morrisburg." According to "Krause," it is common practice for the arresting officer to agree to a deal. He said that any "respectable citizen or businessman" can offer a bribe without fear of repercussions.

A single thread which runs through most studies of organized crime is corruption. As Stuart Hills (1969: 26) argues:

> [. . .] it is highly doubtful that organized crime could thrive so successfully in America without the cooperation and outright connivance of a portion of our political and law enforcement machinery . . . bribes, delivery of votes, fixes, payoffs, and public officials beholden to the syndicate continues *ad nauseam*, allowing organized crime in many large and small cities to operate in comparative immunity. At various times, organized crime has been the dominant political force in Chicago, New York, Miami, and New Orleans. . . .

"Morrisburg" provides living proof of Hills' thesis. The overt connections between the leaders of the political parties, officeholders of both parties, and the organized crime network is the central theme in "Morrisburg's" organized crime. The system of political payoffs and the active connivance of local business people add the final elements needed to organize crime.

William Chambliss aptly argued that:

> [. . .] the people who run the organizations which supply the vices in American cities are members of the business, political and law enforcement communities—not simply members of a criminal society (1976: 182).

Chambliss could have as easily been writing about "Morrisburg" as about Seattle. Corruption—on a massive scale including politicians, police, and businessmen—is the single essential element in organizing "Morrisburg's" crime groups.

Money

Corruption is one factor in the organizing of crime, but not the only social force which determines structure. In order to fully understand the evolution of "Morrisburg's" organized crime groups and their present functions, it is necessary to identify the relationship of "Morrisburg" to crime networks outside of "Morrisburg." By doing so, we are led to the other basic principle that organizes crime—money. The appropriate point at which to begin an examination of organized crime money and money movers is with the legitimate business activities of these individuals.

According to estimates from the United States Department of Commerce, organized crime groups own about 10,000 legitimate businesses in the United States, which generate an annual profit of about $12 billion (Pennsylvania Crime Commission, 1980). In 1970, the Pennsylvania Crime Commission reported that it had "compiled a roster of over 375 legitimate businesses which were involved . . . with criminal syndicates (Pennsylvania Crime Commission, 1970: 49).

Documenting organized crime involvement in legitimate business is no easy undertaking. Obviously, organized crime groups do not advertise these business holdings. As a result, information on investments by organized crime groups only comes to the attention of investigators in the context of some other inquiry. Once a researcher or a law enforcement agent hears about an organized crime foray into legitimate business, he or she must research the available corporate records to see if that charge is true. What very often happens is that those records only reveal hidden ownership of "straw parties," which makes documentation that much harder. In addition, the task of documenting actual ownership and control is hampered by inadequate corporate reporting laws in many states, which allow businesses to report only their president and treasurer—offices which may have no direct bearing on who really owns the enterprise. Documentation is further impeded by the fact that only a few relationships between organized crime interests and other businesses ever come to the attention of law enforcement.

Despite these obstacles, it is possible to assemble information on legitimate business interests involved with organized crime. Information gleaned from the records of the Pennsylvania Crime Commission, information supplied by informants, and follow-up checks of business filings in the "Morrisburg" area produced a list of over one hundred businesses directly tied to members of organized crime groups. Organized crime groups in "Morrisburg" have extensive holdings in vending companies, the garment industry, and the coal industry. They also have scattered interests in a wide variety of other legitimate investments.

These investments have created an extensive portfolio of legitimate businesses and a complex money-laundering and reinvestment mechanism for "Morrisburg's" organized crime groups which has been in place for some forty years. The sophistication of the business networks used by these organized criminals demonstrates the vitally important role business investments play in the day-to-day operations of organized crime groups.

The "Gianellis"—Gamblers or Businessmen?

All six of the "gambling Gianellis" are heavily involved in a number of "Morrisburg"-based businesses. Combined, they have interests in seven vending machine companies, three retail service stores, and four real estate companies. Their impressive business network creates extensive logistical support for their gambling enterprises and for facilitating money laundering. Their vending industry holdings and retail stores are often used as sites for their gambling operations, and their real estate companies have created a convenient means for the profitable investment of illicit capital.

"Gianelli" business ventures include the following (see also Table 3.1):

1) **"Gianelli Amusements"** has been in operation since 1939. It is presently run by "Steve Gianelli, Jr." and two partners. One of the partners, linked with the "Gianellis," has a record of arrests for gambling stretching back to 1938. The other partner has interests with "Agosto Gianelli" in another vending company.

2) **"Al-Bro Vending"** is operated by "Agosto Gianelli" in concert with a partner outside the family, but within the gambling network.

3) **"Star Amusement Company"** is run by "Tommy Gianelli" with one other partner.

4) **"University Billiards"** is also operated by "Tommy Gianelli" with the same partner who is active in "Star Amusements." "University Billiards" is located in the heart of "Morrisburg's" vice district and serves as the headquarters for the "Gianelli" gambling network.

5) **"XYZ Vending"** distributes cigarette machines and is run by "Steve Gianelli, Jr." with his partner from "Gianelli Amusements." Every cigarette machine in downtown "Morrisburg" carries the label of this company.

6) **"Harry Gianelli Cigarette Company"** supplies the cigarettes used by the vending companies as well as all the smoking supplies to newsstands, luncheonettes, and tobacco shops in the center city area.

7) **"Northern Vending"** was originally incorporated by the "Orlandos." However, the business address of the company is the home address of "Agosto Gianelli," suggesting a close working relationship between the two gambling networks.

8) "Steve Gianelli, Sr." and "Harry Gianelli" are partners in **"Pine Records."** This is a classic example of a business being used as a front for illicit enterprise. The record shop has little stock available and nothing of current interest. Therefore, it is highly unlikely that it supports itself on record sales. However, it does have a workroom in the back with a bank of telephones, a paper shredder,

and accommodations for several "office men," an arrangement which strongly suggests that it is a bookmaking front.

9) **"Michael's Fashions"** is owned by "Michael Gianelli" and is located in a suburban mall outside of "Morrisburg." In addition to selling some clothes and providing minimal fabric repair and cleaning services, "Michael's" also prominently displays a poolselling and bookmaking business. In fact the establishment has been raided by the state police, and "Michael Gianelli" has been arrested for his on-premises gambling activities.

10) **"Robot Car Wash"** is an automatic car washing establishment owned by "Agosto Gianelli" in partnership with two other individuals, both of whom have long records of association with "Gianelli" gambling operations. As an enterprise that takes in quarters, this business fits neatly with the vending businesses owned by the "Gianellis."

11) **"Borgia Apartments"** is a rather mysterious company owned by "Agosto Gianelli" and a long-time gambling associate. As far as could be ascertained, this corporation has no place of business and no land holdings. It has, however, filed the requisite corporate papers to register in the state and shows both income and profit from its operations.

12) **"Tallyrand Apartments"** was incorporated by "Tommy" and "Agosto Gianelli" and another partner in 1964. At various times, the company has listed "Joe Orlando," the bookmaker, as one of its officers. When "Agosto Gianelli" was arrested in 1977 for poolselling and bookmaking, the site of his operation was his apartment in the "Tallyrand" complex.

13) **"Bellevue Apartments"** is the only company owned by the "Gianellis" which is not located in the "Morrisburg" area. It is in New Brunswick, New Jersey, and was incorporated in that state by "Agosto Gianelli."

14) **"Valley Apartments"** is owned by "Agosto Gianelli" and an individual who shares other business interests with him as well as sharing gambling interests.

All of these enterprises dovetail neatly with the "Gianelli" gambling business. In addition, other businesses are pleased to do business with "Gianelli" enterprises, thus extending the legitimate network. For instance, bars and pornography stores obtain their vending and video poker machines from various "Gianelli" companies.

The "Gianellis" have also had wide-ranging business relationships with other organized crime groups and individuals.

In 1962 they extended a $16,500 no-interest loan to a corporation managing the estate of the late gambling magnate "Jacob Schiff." In the early 1970s, they extended another loan of $4,000 to a bar in downtown "Morrisburg" owned by an individual who works with them in a bookmaking operation. Most importantly, the "Gianellis" have a close personal and business relationship with "Morrisburg's" premier money mover, "Michael Haggerty," who will be discussed below.

The "Gianellis" derive their importance in local criminal activities from a very sophisticated network of businesses and corporations that straddle the worlds of legitimate and illegitimate activity. They are classic examples of an organized crime group that gives every appearance of being a very normal and conventional component of the business life of the community in which they reside. They have achieved a highly successful degree of integration of interests and activities, spanning both licit and illicit operations. The harmony between crime and business activity which can be observed in the "Gianelli" operation is striking. This is not a case of an extortionist "muscling" in on a business, nor of successor generations of criminals turning legitimate. Since the 1930s, the "Gianellis" have been among the leading gamblers in "Morrisburg." They represent organized crime as a community institution.

The Garment Industry

Since the 1940s, organized crime has played a key role in the organization of the garment trade in the "Morrisburg" area, a role it continues today. When garment manufacturing moved out of New York City during the Second World War, organized crime moved with it.

The garment industry is an important component of "Morrisburg's" economy, especially in light of the decline of coal as a major energy source. These companies are an important source of jobs, particularly jobs for semi-skilled labor. Most of the "Morrisburg" garment manufacturers are subcontractors for larger firms in New York City. The local companies cut patterns from cloth shipped in from New York and then return the patterns to New York for sewing and finishing. There are over fifty garment manufacturers in the "Morrisburg" area. Of those, thirty-one have direct ties to organized crime groups.

The influx of the garment trade to "Morrisburg" was begun by Harry Strasser who opened a factory in the 1940s with Jack Parisi, a fugitive from a murder warrant in New York, as his production manager (Kefauver, 1951). Parisi had, in fact, been hidden by the "DeSoto" brothers in "Birchwood" since 1939, in a secret room above their garage. In 1948, Albert Anastasia and Strasser opened another dress company in the area, and once again Parisi was installed as manager. Parisi managed this company and several others even after the deaths of Strasser and Anastasia. Strasser's additional holdings consisted of three other garment plants and the largest trucking company transporting garments in the "Morrisburg" area.

The garment trade was attractive to many organized crime organizations. The Gambinos opened a garment company in the area in 1948. Nig Rosen and his brother Louis Stromberg had investments in several "Morrisburg"-based garment plants dating from the same time. In 1958, the son-in-law of Thomas Luchese moved into the women's garment business in "Morrisburg." Harry Strauss and other close associates of Meyer Lansky, Lepke Buchalter, Jake Shapiro, and Bugsy Siegel (the real powers behind organized crime in New York City in the 1940s) also capitalized on the garment opportunities.

In contemporary "Morrisburg," much of the garment trade is controlled by "Joseph Marcantonio" and the successors of "Morris Green," particularly "Harry Weinstein" and "Izzy Green." "Marcantonio" controls seven garment manufacturing companies and his close associates, the "DeSoto" brothers control another. "Weinstein" and "Green" have interests in at least six garment plants. It is probable that their interests are even larger, but they have always taken great care to hide their business interests. It is thus quite difficult to uncover the true extent of their holdings.

In addition to having direct interests in garment manufacturing, organized crime has almost total control of the trucking industry which services the garment manufacturers. One of these carriers is a "Morrisburg" area firm founded by "Morris Green." This company has exclusive contracts with over half of the garment plants in the area. The other plants are serviced by a company which "Murder, Inc." chieftain Albert Anastasia helped to create in the early 1950s. It is currently operated by two individuals who were closely tied to both "Morris Green" and "Joseph Marcantonio."

In addition to controlling trucking services for the garment interests, mob interests control the garment industry unions. The "Morrisburg" area is one of the few garment manufacturing centers in the country not under the control of the International Ladies Garment Workers' Union. In 1946, local organized crime interests including "Jacob Schiff," "Morris Green" and "Joseph Marcantonio" sponsored a local workers' association as an alternative to the I.L.G.W.U. It is this local company (and mob) union which represents "Morrisburg's" garment workers and controls not only their contracts but also their pension funds—a most convenient arrangement for anyone interested in money laundering services.

The complex tangle of companies and interlocking patterns of ownership in the garment industry have important implications for organized crime's financial operations and money-moving operations in the "Morrisburg" area. Not only does the industry allow easy access to legitimate business by anyone with money to invest, but over the years it has developed into a closed industry with organized crime interests as the dominant force.

The Coal Industry

One of "Morrisburg's" most important gangster-entrepreneurs is "Michael Haggerty." "Haggerty" is a former state police officer who became a phenomenally successful insurance salesman (owning over 130,000 shares of stock in a major insurance company). In the early 1980s, "Haggerty" began to move organized crime funds into a variety of investments, many of which were in the coal industry.

"Haggerty's" financial manipulations have taken place within the context of a group of money movers. One of the most important of "Haggerty's" collaborators is "Sidney Fine," an associate of Jimmy Hoffa while Hoffa was head of the Teamsters Union. Since 1960, "Fine" has borrowed over $40 million from the Teamsters' Central States Pension Fund. Other members of this money-moving cartel include "Morrisburg" area banker "John Germano," whose bank serves as a legitimate financial institution heavily used for organized crime business deals, and "Fred Rodea," a local businessman with close connections to alleged Cosa Nostra boss "Joseph Marcantonio."

"Haggerty" and his cohorts first moved into the coal fields in 1973, when "North State Coal," which held over half of the recoverable anthracite reserves in the coal fields, was purchased by another company owned by "Haggerty" and "Fine." An $11.5 million loan to make this purchase was supplied by a real estate investment company based in Florida—regarded by Florida law enforcement agencies as a part of the late Meyer Lansky's financial empire. The stock in the new coal company was divided as follows:

"Haggerty" held a 50 percent interest; "Fine" held a 10 percent interest; and "Fine" held an additional 40 percent interest representing Hoffa's share of the company. Within a matter of months after the acquisition of the coal company, the partners began selling off its assets. They first sold its mining equipment to another local company in which "Haggerty," "Germano," and the "DeSoto" brothers had joint ownership. The coal reserves were sold to another company owned by "Haggerty." The company's mineral rights were sold to another "Haggerty"-owned company, which purchased the rights through a loan from "Germano" and his bank. After having sold off most of the assets of "North State Coal," "Haggerty" contracted with yet another coal company, which was owned by this cartel to mine the remaining coal reserves. Insurance policies for the coal companies involved in this scheme were written by a "Germano"-owned insurance underwriting company. The net result of all of these financial manipulations was a bankruptcy petition filed by "North State Coal." The outcome of the bankruptcy proceedings was to assign the company's mortgage to a realty company owned by "Germano." The ultimate outcome of all financial manipulations was a total profit of about $9 million to the individuals and companies involved in the scheme, and a total cost of $10 million to the state of Pennsylvania in insurance settlements, backfilling costs, and unpaid taxes.

In addition, "Haggerty" and "Rodea" control several other major coal companies in the area, and also are major investors in a racetrack outside of "Morrisburg." The racetrack has been the scene of several major race-fixing scandals over the last two decades. "Haggerty" holdings in the racetrack were valued at $1 million. "Haggerty" also has other interesting investments including a partnership with "Joseph Dottore," a local industrialist who has been identified by law enforcement agencies as a close associate of "Marcantonio," in "Jacob Schiff & Sons," a scrap metal business formerly owned by the late crime boss.

By the end of the 1980s, "Haggerty" had accumulated holdings in fourteen more coal companies; four real estate companies (at least two of which were Florida-based companies close to the late Meyer Lansky's business interests); and three manufacturing concerns.

"Haggerty's" investment efforts on behalf of organized crime, particularly in the coal industry, were enormously important. First, he enabled organized crime groups to acquire significant interests in the anthracite coal industry. Not only do organized crime groups now have lateral control throughout the anthracite coal fields, but they also have vertical control through their interests in industries which provide support services to the coal industry. Second, the

Pennsylvania Crime Commission has developed evidence that companies controlled by organized crime are engaged in a pattern of forced bankruptcies and fraudulent coal sales. Third, because of loopholes in the tax laws and Security and Exchange Commission (SEC) regulations, organized crime groups have been able to realize massive tax savings through their ownership of coal companies and have been able to sell worthless interests in those companies to investors looking for a tax dodge.

Despite the convenience and lucrative nature of both the garment industry and coal interests, they are insignificant compared to legitimate bank operations as a subsidiary of organized crime.

Organized Crime's Full Service Bank

"John Germano," who played a key role in the coal acquisitions described above, is also the president of a "Morrisburg"-area bank with $68 million in assets. Mr. "Germano" is not a newcomer to the world of organized crime. He was convicted twice in the 1930s and 1940s of price fixing in the coal industry and has been consistently linked by law enforcement agencies to a series of organized crime groups. Ironically, "Germano's" companies have over $200 million in state and federal government contracts, all awarded after his convictions.

"Germano's" political contacts have played a key role in his success. For example, in 1977 after a criminal conviction, he was able to rely on a letter of support from the governor of Pennsylvania which was presented to the court at the time of his sentencing. Also in that case, one of the unindicted co-conspirators was a state representative.

Court records produced in the coal company acquisitions listed "Germano's" business interests. In those documents, he was identified as having legal or equitable interests in thirty-seven coal companies, seven companies providing support for the coal industry; five manufacturing concerns; four real estate companies; two transportation companies; three insurance companies; and all three cable television companies servicing the "Morrisburg" area. In regard to the cable television companies, other owners include "Joseph Dottore" and "Fred Rodea."

Follow the Money

As we have seen, organized criminals have played an important role in the economic life of "Morrisburg" since the 1930s. Initial investments in the garment industry have now blossomed into a series of complex financial arrangements which cover banking, communications, transportation, garment manufacturing, and coal mining. These relationships are important because they facilitate the work of organized crime groups, cleaning their money and profitably reinvesting their capital. They are also important to the community. We would not be far wrong if it were to be argued that organized crime is the single largest investor in the economic health and security of "Morrisburg."

Both the legal and illegal economies of "Morrisburg" have developed in such a way that it is very difficult to distinguish between business and crime. A local judge characterized "Haggerty" as follows:

> "Haggerty," for example, deals in millions of dollars. He works
> with bankers, he works with other businessmen. He's a crook.
> Lots of other people are crooks too. Whether they're criminals
> is another matter.

The judge characterizes "Sidney Fine," "Haggerty's" business partner and close friend, in a similar way. According to the judge, "Fine" "acts as an investment counselor for local people, takes their money and invests it in other places."

Crime, politics, and finance all clearly form part of a peculiar milieu. They are not separate activities, they are not distinct from one another—they are only different areas of a single economic spectrum.

Chapter 6

What Is Organized Crime?

While the preceding discussion of organized crime in "Morrisburg" may be interesting as a description of criminal activity, it must be analyzed in terms of structure and function to contribute to our understanding of the complex phenomenon we call organized crime. What is organized crime? Finding definitive answers to that question is beyond the scope of one slim volume. As was pointed out earlier, the paucity of primary data about organized crime makes any attempt to reach definitive conclusions problematic at best. What local case studies can contribute, however, is a sense of direction for future inquiries. Only when the organized crime database has been expanded by many more research efforts directed at the actual workings of organized crime groups or the activities of organized crime in a specific area can we begin the task of theoretical formulation and explanation. For now, the study of organized crime must confine itself to the production of models or paradigms which will direct this additional research. On the basis of information gathered in "Morrisburg" and in the handful of other primary studies in existence, we can begin to raise issues which may redefine our admittedly nascent understanding of organized crime.

Several primary considerations must govern our understanding of organized crime. From these primary considerations, a series of somewhat speculative propositions may be derived. In the discussion that follows, it will be argued that the available data strongly suggest three overarching propositions in describing organized crime:

1) Organized crime groups are loosely structured, flexible, and highly adaptable to environmental impacts. Organized crime is, in fact, a loose system of relationships, what sociologists might call a "social network," engaged in the delivery of illicit goods and services.

2) Organized crime is a business and has many similarities to businesses in the legal market. However, because organized crime groups operate in the illegal market, they are subject to a series of constraints which limit and define organizational structure, size, and mode of operation.

3) While the illegal market determines many aspects of the actual structure, scope, and style of organized crime groups, the coordination and management of relations between and among groups engaged in illicit entrepreneurship is another vital element in understanding organized crime. The next chapter discusses this essential organizational component.

For purposes of this discussion, we shall define organized crime, following Block and Chambliss (1981), as the management and coordination of illegal enterprises connected with vice (gambling, prostitution, high-interest personal loans, pornography, and drug trafficking), and racketeering (labor and business extortion). This definition delineates both the market in which organized crime groups operate and places an important emphasis on the management and coordination aspects of criminal organization. It is not so constricting as to tie us to a specific, previously developed model, nor so broad as to be meaningless in providing a means to distinguish organized criminality from other types of criminality.

The data from "Morrisburg" and other case studies of organized crime, discussed within the context of the definition above, allow us to assess the validity and implications of the propositions listed above. All three propositions overlap and interrelate but are not necessarily dependent on one another. The social context within which organized crime groups form and operate is an excellent place to begin our analysis.

Organized Crime as a Set of Social Relationships

Organized crime is, at its most basic level, a product of over-lapping and interrelated social relationships. Joseph Albini has suggested that organized crime actually consists of a number of what he calls "syndicates" in a "loose system of power relationships" (1971: 229). Organized crime is not a rigidly organized, highly bureaucratized, monopolistic entity. Rather, vice and crime are organized at the local level by "cabals" or networks made up of businessmen, bureaucrats, police officers, and other community figures (Chambliss, 1978).

For the most part, organized crime groups tend to be loosely structured, flexible, and highly adaptable. In fact, it can be argued that the real power and effectiveness of organized crime is found in these amorphous qualities. Rather than resembling a formal, corporate structure, organized crime more closely resembles a social exchange network in the community. How that very informal system of social exchange becomes organized crime is quite easy to visualize. Every person in society is part of a social network, which is defined as "the chains of persons with whom a given person is in contact" (Boissevain, 1974: 24; cited in Abadinsky, 1985). Because people have contact with many other people, who in turn have contacts with even more people, relationships can be extended to far more people than the individual actually knows on a personal or direct basis, the proverbial "friends of friends" (Abadinsky, 1985; Boissevain, 1974). Additionally, Boissevain points out that, "Every individual provides a point at which networks interact. But not everyone displays the same interest in and talent for cultivating relationships with strategic persons for profit" (1974: 147). The organized criminal has both the interest and the talent. Organized criminals have strategic contacts with people who control resources and also have resources of their own (Boissevain, 1974). The organized criminal bridges communication gaps between police and other criminals, between business people and labor racketeers, between the world of legitimate business and illicit entrepreneurship. This unique position has been identified by both Boissevain and Henner Hess (who studies the Sicilian Mafia) as *partito*—a surrounding circle of dyadic relationships whereby individuals have little or no relations with each other except through a central person, in this case an organized crime figure (Hess, 1973; Abadinsky, 1985).

The organized criminal "provides economic aid and protection against both the legal and illegal transactions of authority" (Wolf, 1966: 16–17). The customer, client, or whatever we wish to call him or her returns the favor with political support, loyalty, or other intangible assets. The organized criminal, in this formulation, is a power broker between clients, customers, and the larger society (Wolf, 1966).

Organized criminals may play this power broker role in a specific geographical area (a street, a neighborhood, a city) or in a specific industry (gambling, drugs, pornography). They have at their disposal a network of connections (for example, with police and other public officials) and a network of specialized operatives (such as fences, enforcers, technicians). An organized criminal is really an information center, a resource for others to draw on for specialized criminal activities, a coordinator for organized criminal activities:

> [Organized criminals] do not belong to an organization. Instead the structure of their relationships is predicated by the particular activity engaged in at any given time and the nature of patron-client, friendship, and other forms of relationships motivating the participants. Rather than being a criminal secret society, a criminal syndicate consists of a system of loosely structured relationships functioning primarily because each participant is interested in furthering his own welfare (Albini, 1971: 288).

There is considerable empirical evidence to support this argument. For example, Peter Reuter (1983) conducted an extensive examination of bookmaking, numbers gambling, and loansharking in New York City. He found that illegal markets "tend to be populated with small and ephemeral enterprises," which entrepreneurs begin and subsequently abandon largely due to economic considerations. Reuter also found that these enterprises were not centrally controlled (Reuter, 1983: 176):

> [Illicit enterprises] are not monopolies in the classic sense of subject to control by some external organization. . . . Numerous economic forces arising from the illegality of the product tend to fragment the market (1983: 176).

Finally, Reuter found that the use of intimidation and violence was much less common than is usually claimed. Further empirical evidence to support this characterization of organized crime was presented by Alan Block. In 1979, Block conducted a historical analysis of the illicit cocaine trade in New York during the early 1900s. He compiled information on nearly two thousand criminals in the New York City area, the large majority of whom were of Jewish descent. His findings clearly demonstrated that the cocaine industry was not run by a single, centralized criminal conspiracy:

> It was organized and coordinated not by any particular organization, but by criminal entrepreneurs who formed, re-formed, split and came together again as opportunity arose and when they were able . . .

Second, this analysis places the narcotics trade during the second decade of the twentieth century with the broader context of a multiplicity of illegal enterprises engaged in by organized criminals. It suggests that such criminals were in reality criminal justice entrepreneurs acutely responsive to a broad panoply of activities which often bridged the gap between illegal enterprises and positions within New York's criminal justice bureaucracies. It also details the manner in which criminal careers were structured—not within a particular organization but through an increasing web of small but efficient organizations (1979a: 44–51).

Block characterizes organized crime as an enterprise engaged in by small, flexible organizations of criminals, which respond to opportunity and environmental factors.

In addition, while Jews seem to have played a large role in the cocaine trade, there were also Italians, Greeks, Irish, and blacks who did not always work within ethnically defined organizations:

> Whether or not the Jewish underworld revealed by [these data] was a large or small part of New York's underworld, it did exist and was significant. Also notable is the evidence of interethnic cooperation which clearly suggests that at times parochialism was overcome by New York's criminals (1979: 95).

Block's findings support the view of organized crime as entrepreneurial behavior that happens to be illegal and supports the idea that organized crime is a fluid and loosely organized entity.

This looseness of structure combined with organizational flexibility extends to questions of participation in organized crime groups. Organized crime groups tend to be task-oriented and structured in such a way that many roles and positions are interchangeable. This means that an organized crime group will involve only those individuals needed to conduct business effectively and efficiently. They are neither groups with inflexible membership requirements (like a fraternal organization), nor groups with clearly designated, permanent job duties (like corporations or other highly centralized, formalized, and specialized organizations). The "Morrisburg" gambling network, for example, is complex in terms of the several business fronts it uses, but its actual structure is simple and straightforward, with a large number of interchangeable roles and positions. The skills required for the various roles are fairly rudimentary. A pickup man can also function as a writer. Anyone in the organization who can drive can do pickups. Those with rudimentary skills in addition and subtraction can work in the office and record the daily betting action. At the lowest levels of the gambling operation, most operatives are part-time employees, whose only function is to take bets from customers and turn them over to the organization. In this sense, writers are not even organization employees, only affiliates. In most organized crime activities the skills needed to perform a task are basic, and, therefore, tasks can easily be reassigned among members. The "Knight" drug organization exhibits the same flexibility in personnel assignments. Over the years, its leaders have frequently been imprisoned. This has not significantly impacted on the operations of the group however, because lower-level employees have been able to step into the vacated roles with ease. The skills required at the various levels of the drug network are very similar. The only discernible differences between the leaders of the group and street-level employees are years of experience in organized crime and the amount of capital available to invest in the enterprise.

In addition to having interchangeable roles in relation to a specific enterprise, most organized crime groups also have overlapping roles in other criminal enterprises. Employees of the K & A Gang in Philadelphia shared and exchanged the roles of thief, drug dealer, gambler, and money-mover (Potter and Jenkins, 1985). Philadelphia's other gambling enterprises also show similar role exchanges, with the Nichols numbers bank having members who are both gamblers and fences, and the Hampton numbers bank having members who are both gamblers and drug dealers (Pennsylvania Crime Commission, 1986). Very similar arrangements were noted and detailed by Chambliss (1978) for Seattle and Gardiner (1970) for Reading, Pennsylvania.

It is important to realize that organized crime groups are not limited by a rigid, inflexible hierarchical structure. There is no precisely defined system of bosses, underbosses, capos, and soldiers. Such a system would be self-defeating (Smith, 1975; Albini, 1971). It is the flexibility and fluidity of an organized crime group's structure that enables it to adapt to changing environmental demands. It is the nature of the illegal market that superfluous, honorary, or nonfunctional roles would seriously endanger the group's activities by involving too many people in illicit enterprise. Organized crime groups are relatively simple and are defined by the specific financial, logistical, and personnel requirements particular to the activities being undertaken at any given time. The structure of organized crime relationships is predicated by the specific activities in which the group is currently engaged.

This consideration relates to our discussion about the role of ethnic backgrounds in organized crime. Participation in an organized crime group is dictated by the particular activities and needs of that group. Some organized crime groups, depending on the scale of operations, require more complex staffing and well-defined financial operations than others. However, organized crime groups tend to function in a similar manner regardless of the backgrounds or ethnicity of group members.

Many, if not most organized crime groups, are made up of or have substantial interactions between and among individuals of a variety of ethnic backgrounds (Jenkins and Potter, 1987; Block, 1979b). The K & A Gang is a classic example of a multi-ethnic (Irish, Jewish, and Italian) organized crime group. In "Morrisburg," the gambling network, despite being Italian in leadership, has members of Irish, Slavic, and WASP descent; it also shares turf with other groups made up of Middle Easterners and blacks. The Hampton crime group in Philadelphia, while primarily black and operating in an almost exclusively black area of the city, has James Creagh, an Irishman, as one of its principal members.

The impact of ethnicity in organized crime is limited to those same impacts we would expect to see as the result of urban social demography (a gambling organization in the black community would be predominantly black; in the Italian community, predominantly Italian, etc.). Ethnicity has frequently been cited as a determinant of organized crime group membership, but it is often misconstrued. What is usually meant, and what makes considerably more sense, is that community and social affiliation are directly related to participation in an organized crime group. These social networks come into play in the formation of organized crime groups in exactly the same way they would in a fraternal organization or a volunteer fire department in the same community. We would expect a volunteer fire department in an Italian neighborhood to be predominantly Italian and composed of people with wide-ranging associations with each other. We would not claim that this is indicative of Italian ethnicity as a requirement for being a fireman. Ethnicity has no greater impact on participation in organized crime groups than on any other aspect of community life. While it is important as a social variable, it is not a defining organizational variable for organized crime.

It is the flexibility in structure and in personnel recruitment and use that leads to one of the greatest strengths of organized crime. Organized crime groups are characterized by continuance over time, without regard to the individual fate or mortality of group members. Organized crime groups are not dependent upon the continued participation of any single individual. Leaders can be assassinated, incarcerated, or even die of natural causes without catastrophic results to the organized crime network itself. As Albini remarks:

> If a powerful syndicate figure is incarcerated, all that has really
> been severed is his position as a patron to his clients. If it so
> happens that another individual is in a position to assume this
> role, the clients may continue in this enterprise (1971: 285).

The Rosen Mob in Philadelphia persisted despite the narcotics arrest
of Nig Rosen in 1959 and his subsequent retirement from crime
(Jenkins and Potter, 1985). Even the Philadelphia Bruno Family,
a far weaker and less organized group, was able to continue
operations without significant interruption following Angelo
Bruno's assassination. The same pattern can be seen in other cities
and other organized crime groups. The Seattle crime cabal showed
remarkable persistence despite major arrests (Chambliss, 1978);
Abe Minker's gambling syndicate continued in business after his
death (Gardiner, 1970); the Pennsylvania pornography network
survived the assassination of John Krasner, the jailing of Allen
Morrow and the decision by Thomas Sherwood to flee
"harassment" in Philadelphia (Potter, 1986). The arrest or death
of key organized crime group members does not imperil the
continued operations of the organization. The fact is that almost
every organized crime group tends to have more than one powerful
individual in a leadership position, making no single individual
irreplaceable.

Finally, in addition to considerable flexibility in task assignments,
recruitment and disengagement, and leadership roles, organized
crime groups also exhibit considerable variability in both their
geographic scope and in the variety of goods and services provided.
For the most part, empirical research on organized crime has
pointed to locality relevance as a characteristic of the vast majority
of organized crime groups (Potter and Jenkins, 1985; Reuter, 1983;
Anderson, 1979; Chambliss, 1978; Ianni, 1974, 1972a; Laswell and
McKenna, 1972). The overwhelming majority of organized crime
groups are organized in a specific city, or even a neighborhood
within that city. However, there are exceptions. In drug importation
we often find organized crime groups that distribute over fairly large
areas, and occasionally we find bookmaking ventures that involve
several cities. A classic example of a very extensive organized crime
group was the "Combination" or "Seven Group," which formed in
the 1920s to control and facilitate the importation of whiskey into
the United States. This group was national in scope and power,
stretching from Boston through New York and Philadelphia, out to
Cleveland and later Detroit (Abadinsky, 1985; Potter and Jenkins,
1985; Block and Chambliss, 1981). Similarly, organized crime
groups which have developed with legalized casino gambling in

Nevada and New Jersey (and with illegal but officially welcomed casinos in Arkansas, Kentucky, and Florida) are national and even international in their range, with large numbers of investors from all over the country and a very complex financial system involving offshore banks and foreign corporations. However, the groups which cover large areas are clearly the exception, usually arising to meet the exigencies of some specific historical or social curiosity, such as Prohibition, the legalization of pornography, or the adoption of legalized gambling. Most organized crime groups are those specializing in localized bookmaking, numbers, and loansharking, which extend only to the limits of a major city or a section of that city. Most groups tend to be local in their area of operations and in their sphere of influence.

Organized crime groups do not, however, necessarily limit the scope of the goods and services they provide. It is not surprising to find a group involved in both narcotics distribution and cigarette smuggling—occupations which require similar skills and often (at least in the case of cocaine) emanate from similar geographic points and follow similar smuggling routes. A gambling operation will almost surely provide ancillary loansharking services. In most major cities retail pornography operations have considerable overlap with prostitution rings (Potter, 1986). In Philadelphia, the K & A Gang had professional burglary as their primary enterprise, but they also had considerable interests in drug trafficking and gambling (Potter and Jenkins, 1985).

Most organized crime groups, even small, local groups, invariably operate within a broad context of a multiplicity of enterprises. Very seldom do we find specialization in only one illegal enterprise. Philadelphia's largest black narcotics organization engaged in auto theft (Potter and Jenkins, 1985). Seattle's gamblers were involved with pornography and labor racketeering (Chambliss, 1978). "Morrisburg's" drug dealers provide prostitution services; fences serve as loansharks; and gamblers are heavily involved in a variety of business crimes.

In many ways, organized crime thus resembles other social interactions which occur in the community. Like those other social relations, organized crime relations often tend to be informal, changing, and predicated upon need and opportunity. Rigidity of structure, centralized power, and a precisely defined division-of-labor resulting in clear occupational roles would be deleterious to the effective organizing of crime. At the very least, organized crime represents a social network, a loose interplay of relationships among individuals in the community who come together to pursue a goal. In this case, the goal is to make money through illicit enterprises.

It is the fact that organized crime activities are illegal and take place in an illicit market that serves to further delineate structure and function in organized crime groups, adding the impacts of the market to the realities of social relations.

Organized Crime as a Business

Organized crime is a business and has many similarities to businesses in the legal market. We mentioned earlier that organized crime is subject to a series of constraints which further limit and define structure, size, and mode of operation. Operating in the illegal market creates these constraints.

Before discussing the exigencies of the illicit market, it is helpful to look at organized crime, in context, as a business. Organized crime is simply an extension of normal business operations into the illegal market (Smith, 1980). As Smith tells us, organized crime comes from "the same fundamental assumptions that govern entrepreneurship in the legitimate marketplace; a necessity to maintain and extend one's share of the market" (Smith, 1980). In fact, organized crime operates along a "spectrum of legitimacy" (Smith, 1980). This means that a pharmacist and a drug pusher are engaged in precisely the same activity, except that they work on different ends of this spectrum. One operates legally and the other is engaged in illicit enterprise. The fundamental function of both—providing drugs to a particular set of consumers—is the same. Organized crime is simply entrepreneurial activity that happens to be illegal.

Drug trafficking, loansharking, gambling, prostitution, and other illegal enterprises come into existence because the legitimate marketplace leaves a large number of customers unserved. As a result, understanding organized crime is difficult if attention is focused either on organizational leaders or specific criminal organizations themselves. A better approach is to address organizational behavior in the illegal market.

The business of organized crime, for the most part, involves those goods and services that are in public demand, but are also illegal (Reuter, 1983; Schur and Bedau, 1974; Geis, 1972). The fact that these acts (primarily gambling, prostitution, pornography, loansharking, and drug trafficking) are illegal creates a number of opportunities for organized crime groups to realize significant economic gain; a number of social consequences that allow organizations to flourish; and a number of constraints on those criminal organizations.

Organized crime groups, whether engaged in gambling, loansharking, drug trafficking, or prostitution exist for the explicit purpose of making money. Rubinstein and Reuter have detailed the role of organized crime groups in gambling and loansharking (1978a, 1978b), two activities which provide a service to customers at a profit. Chambliss (1978) detailed the role of organized crime in gambling, pornography, prostitution, and labor racketeering in Seattle and noted the close relationship it has with legitimate businesses which act as less profitable fronts for criminal activity. In a case study of Philadelphia (Potter and Jenkins, 1985), organized crime groups were shown to have varied portfolios of illicit services, dedicated to the pursuit of considerable profits.

Organized crime groups have as their primary objective the provision of illicit goods and services to customers who desire them and have demonstrated a willingness to pay for them (Vold and Bernard, 1986). The profitability in this relationship can be attributed to what Stuart Hills (1971) has called a protective "crime tariff." The crime tariff—essentially a surcharge on illicit goods and services which calculates proper remuneration for risks taken by organized crime groups and the additional profit that can be realized from limited supply in an illegal market—enables organized crime groups to secure an illicit monopoly in the marketplace on the provision of the good or service in question. Because the product is illegal, there will be no competition from legitimate competitors. The illegality of the product, combined with public demand, assure profitability. For example, heroin is a relatively inexpensive drug to produce and market. If it were marketed by legitimate pharmaceutical companies, its cost would be less than 10 percent of the price charged in the illegal market (Hills, 1971). A more subtle example is legal versus illegal gambling. Legal casino gambling and state-run lotteries are regulated in terms of credit extended, odds given, and a myriad of other factors that impact on profitability. Organized crime groups, operating in the illegal market, can extend credit to whomever they wish, can set odds at a level that will stimulate profits, and can operate under house rules written to stimulate greater income from illegal games. Loansharks can set their interest rates as high as the market will bear, rather than being subject to legal restrictions on interest. The illegality of the product, in and of itself, virtually guarantees profitability. The crime tariff not only defines the market, but also keeps the price of the product artificially high.

In addition, the illegal market serves to regulate competition. Because the product is illegal, legitimate companies and investors, with considerable available capital and highly structured delivery organizations, are not likely to invest in the illegal market. A major airline company is unlikely to try to shore up its economic health by entering into a formal contractual arrangement with Colombian cocaine dealers to smuggle drugs into the United States. The high risk of such a venture and the continual exposure to law enforcement, makes such an ongoing organized crime role by the airline less attractive. A major bank is unlikely to try to increase its profits by establishing betting windows at branch offices, unless such a service becomes legal. Legitimate corporations, while often committing crime and sometimes collaborating with organized crime groups in specific ventures, are unlikely to take on the continuing provision of illegal goods as part of their business because the risk and potential cost is too high. Legitimate corporations are regulated and are subject to both civil and criminal sanctions. They are regulated in such a way that their legitimate operations and profits would be imperiled, if not totally lost, if they overtly entered into the illegal market. This keeps considerable capital out of the illegal market. The illegal market is left for organized groups who do not have to report to regulatory agencies, who do not have to submit to regular audits of company books, who do not have to meet SEC regulations. As a result, the illegal market is less organized than the legitimate market, but it is also a place where entrepreneurship is easier and access is readily available. Of course, there is competition in the illegal market, but it is competition that is less intense and unregulated in comparison to legitimate enterprises.

The opportunities afforded by the illegal market and the crime tariff are clearest in drug trafficking. In "Morrisburg" the local drug network is able to set the retail price for heroin, methamphetamines, and even cocaine for an entire metropolitan area simply by operating a highly efficient and cost-effective importation network through Toronto. By their own estimates, this drug network realizes an overall profit of 100 percent in the resale of drugs to more localized, smaller, distribution groups. A similar pattern can be seen when comparing the wealth of U.S. and British gambling operations. In the United States, gambling syndicates were able to accumulate considerable capital and power because of the illegality of the service they provided. The "Gianellis" have been able to become the dominant force in "Morrisburg" gambling because they face no serious competition from upperworld competitors. They are well aware of the fact that the service they provide is in heavy demand; they are also aware of the fact that some minimal risk taking on their part will allow them to capture that demand. The "Gianellis" are able to exact an additional profit in return for the risks they have taken. While legal bookmaking ventures in New York City, for example, must operate within tight constraints, the "Gianellis" can adjust the "rules of the game" to enhance profitability whenever they feel the need. In contrast to the situation in "Morrisburg" and much of the United States, more permissive gambling laws in Britain prevented the creation of a large-scale illegal gambling industry, and thus served to limit the profitability of the enterprise and the amount of intensive capital available for reinvestment in other activities (Jenkins and Potter, 1989).

The fact that the goods and services of organized crime are illegal offers opportunities for attractive investment in the illegal market. However, the illegal market, because it is unregulated and because it is relatively unstructured, also serves to limit the kinds of organizations that can operate in the illegal environment. The opportunities created must be balanced against the fact that the mere existence of the enterprise is a criminal offense and subject to sanctions, a problem not encountered in the legitimate marketplace.

One of the most obvious constraints imposed by the illegal market is the need to keep business activities clandestine and carry out daily business with discretion. For example, methamphetamines are produced in dozens of clandestine labs located in rural or suburban areas near major cities. The illegality of the product requires secrecy in production and circumspection in distribution. On the other hand, most major pharmaceutical companies produce diet pills and other prescription drugs of similar pharmacological content that are quite legal. Their products can be produced in the open, in legitimate factories, by skilled technicians employed in legitimate jobs. They can be sold openly by sales representatives and purchased at any retail drugstore. Alcohol presents another classic example of illegality affecting the logistics of a market. During Prohibition, alcohol had to be brewed in secret, transported by armed caravans, and sold in speakeasies, which screened their customers. With the repeal of Prohibition, alcohol could once again be produced in large manufacturing complexes, openly transported, and sold with minimal regulation. The legality or illegality of a product defines how conspicuous an enterprise can be. That means that illicit enterprises must incur additional costs to operate in secret and have a more difficult time reaching potential consumers (they clearly cannot advertise or distribute samples).

Illegality changes the character and organization of the market. In particular, it has three compelling consequences for illegal markets that are not found in legal markets (Reuter, 1983). First, the illegal organization cannot rely on contracts and agreements which are enforceable in court; second, the illegal enterprise incurs a significant risk of asset seizure if the enterprise is identified and closed down by law enforcement agencies; and third, all the participants in an illegal enterprise face the risk of arrest and imprisonment for being involved in the enterprise itself. Obviously, these risks vary in relation to the actual product. Heroin dealers face far more scrutiny and more severe consequences related to discovery than do marijuana dealers. The likelihood of discovery and arrest is much higher for an organization of streetwalkers than for a business dealing in elite call girls, but all such enterprises face some risks.

The primary organizational consequence of product illegality is the need to control information about illegal activities (Reuter, 1983). The risk of exposure must be minimized. Such considerations influence decisions on how activities are structured, on who can be employed in those activities, and on who will be selected as patrons of the enterprise. Each of these considerations play a key role in just how conspicuous an illegal enterprise will become.

As stated in chapter 1, employees in illegal enterprises may be the greatest threat to organized crime operations (Reuter, 1983). Employees make the best possible witnesses against organized crime operations during criminal prosecutions. It is, therefore, in the best interests of an organized crime group to limit the number of people who have comprehensive knowledge about the group's operations and then to limit the amount of information available to the various employees. Most organized crime groups try to insulate themselves from street-level operatives. This requires that at the actual level of product delivery, the organized crime group participant only knows about his or her own job.

Organized crime enterprises that have the highest risk tend to be the most highly segmented. Segmentation reduces contact between organized crime bosses and street-level employees. The best example of this segmentation is found in the heroin industry where production, importation, and distribution are almost always kept as discrete functions handled by different organizations. This ensures that the arrest of a pusher will not imperil the supplier; the arrest of a supplier will not imperil an importer; and the arrest of an importer will not imperil laboratories producing the drug. The "Knight" Organization operating in "Morrisburg" is a classic example of this kind of compartmentalization and segmentation. Street-level pushers have limited contact with each other and contact only with the dealer with whom they arrange supplies. The same situation occurs with regard to dealers who have access to only one wholesaler, and so on up the organizational ladder. In addition, importation and distribution are quite distinct functions with different organized crime groups taking primary responsibility for each aspect of the trade. A similar kind of segmentation is noticeable in gambling, where runners report to pickup men, who report to office men, who report to the banker. The "Gianellis" have raised this kind of organizational circumspection to an art form, going so far as to separate their "writers" from the organization itself by employing them on a commission basis. The only person about whom a writer could give incriminating information is the pickup man, usually a vending machine company employee. To work up through the maze of companies and the layers of the gambling organization would require the commitment of immense resources and a great deal of willpower by law enforcement agencies.

In addition to minimizing the proliferation of knowledge, organized crime groups also try to offer incentives for loyalty and discretion. The obvious means for achieving loyalty is through economic reward. Reuter (1983), for example, points out that gambling operations pay well above market wages. In "Morrisburg," the remuneration received from participation in gambling for full-time employees makes the difference between a comfortable living and subsistence. The gambling network provides income supplements to retirees, small storekeepers, housewives, and the otherwise unemployed or underemployed. Individuals working for the "Gianellis" are well aware that their illicit income from gambling is what elevates their economic status beyond mere subsistence. Such a strategy not only increases loyalty to the organization, but it provides an incentive for the employee to keep his or her beneficent employer out of jail. It should also be pointed out that there exists a degree of loyalty based upon social association and commitment in most organized crime groups. Organized crime groups tend to form in specific communities and recruitment tends to take place among people familiar to each other. Therefore, a kind of social and community bonding and familiarity occurs which means that organized criminals operating in a group usually come from similar backgrounds, usually have known each other for some time, and share a very common outlook on the world. Two very different examples of this process are evident in "Morrisburg." First, the "James Gang" consists primarily of members of "Morrisburg's" embattled and very small black community. This fact, in and of itself, creates an insular, defended community type of loyalty. Since the members are all from a small geographic area of the city (about sixteen square blocks), they grew up knowing each other and having primary social relationships with each other. Group fidelity is thus heightened. The second case is the "Gianelli" network, which has carefully groomed its associates from individuals with whom business, social, and familial contacts have existed. Extended families, long-standing associations in the Catholic church and community groups, and highly integrated business arrangements make it highly unlikely that one member of the group will do harm to another as a result of a criminal investigation. It is this process of community recruitment of friends and acquaintances that often gives the appearance of ethnic determinism to some organized crime groups, primarily because the community being served has a strong ethnic composition. More accurately, this process is the result of long-term socialization in both the social and criminal communities.

While rewards are no doubt the most common means of encouraging employee loyalty, an alternative strategy is available for particularly difficult cases. That strategy is intimidation. Intimidation simply involves an organizational reputation for inflicting injury on disloyal participants. This is clearly not a preferred strategy (Reuter, 1983). First of all, it raises costs. The employer must incur some cost in attaining the capability to carry out intimidation. The employer, therefore, must hire "enforcers" or "kneebreakers" and display them to a degree sufficient to establish a reputation for violence. This, in turn, increases other costs. Employees would have to be compensated for the stress of working under a system of constant intimidation and danger. Given a choice between loyalty guaranteed by incentives and loyalty coerced by violence, the average person is going to opt for incentives. Another danger of a strategy of intimidation is that it serves to make the operation more conspicuous. Police can overlook numbers betting, but people bleeding in alleys are far more difficult to ignore. Investigation is almost inevitable and that is what most illegal organizations wish to avoid at all costs. The use of violence is almost entirely absent from the "Morrisburg" organized crime scene. Only two groups, both at the bottom of the organized crime hierarchy, the "Perlmans" and the "James Gang," have been implicated in any publicly acknowledged acts of violence in the past two decades. The "Gianellis" appear to forgo this option altogether, using economic sanctions as a means of assuring compliance and, if necessary, simply ceasing service in difficult cases.

The problem of monitoring employee performance and employee loyalty is one of several constraints in the illegal market which tend to mitigate toward locality-relevant operations. As previously emphasized, illegal enterprises do not usually opt for expansion across large areas. Increased exposure is simply too great a risk for most organized crime groups. Geographic expansion is also limited by the increased danger resulting from transportation and communication across distances. Telephones are notoriously dangerous; therefore, personal communication is essential. The idea of traveling six or seven hours to relay a simple message is not attractive to most illegal enterprises. Transporting drugs or betting slips across long distances means that organized crime participants will be exposed to the danger of detection for significant periods of time, thereby increasing risk and incurring additional costs to compensate employees. Gamblers often use rice paper to record bets because it can be disposed of in water in a matter of seconds. Therefore, it makes little sense to create a logistical arrangement in which records are being carried over long distances and significant time spans. Finally, the larger the geographic area covered by an illegal enterprise, the greater the number of law enforcement agencies involved. Arranging protection with one or two agencies is merely a cost of doing business. Trying to accomplish this with eight or ten agencies is not only risky but very costly.

The "Gianellis" represent the classic case of limiting illegal enterprise to reduce risk. They have available the capital necessary to expand, they have readily accessible markets in neighboring areas, and they would face no serious opposition from other gambling networks, most of which are quite weak when compared to the "Gianellis." They could easily break out of the confines of "Morrisburg" and its suburbs and dominate gambling across a very large area. Yet they choose not to, despite the potentially staggering increase in profits they could realize. They have achieved a level of operation in which they have well-established political contacts for protection, a smoothly operating laundering service for the conversion of funds, and a manageable sales force. From their point of view, expansion, while potentially profitable, would disturb the safe and rather tranquil business climate they have created.

In a very real way, illegality, while offering tremendous opportunities for organized crime, also constrains the organization of crime itself. This certainly helps to explain why most organized crime groups operate in a small and limited area. It also helps to explain why organized crime groups are reluctant to gobble up new, lucrative markets. Effective and efficient organization guarantees a continuation of significant profits; greed and overexpansion may well spell the end of the enterprise all together. Successful organized crime operations are willing to accept these limits and still manage to generate considerable income for participants. Greed may be the greatest danger an organized criminal has to face.

The exigencies of the illicit market, particularly the dangers of illegal enterprise, play a key role in modifying the structure of illicit enterprise. Large groups of people, working over vast distances, in a highly visible way, are anathema to the successful organization of crime. The workings of the illegal market help to explain how organized crime evolves from a network of social relations into a business enterprise. The coordination and management of criminal enterprises are further modified by the impact of other environments with which organized crime must deal on a daily basis: specifically, the upperworld commercial and business environments; the political and legal environments; and the community-context, the social environment within which organized crime must live and work.

Organized Crime and Its Environments

While the illegal market determines many aspects of the actual structure, scope, and style of organized crime groups, it is the coordination and management of relations between and among groups engaged in illicit entrepreneurship which is vital to an understanding of organized crime. How crime is organized is determined largely by political, legal, economic, and social factors. Understanding how these environmental factors come together to provide opportunities for the organization of crime and also to constrain that organization is critical to understanding organized crime as a social process.

We will discuss four environments of organized crime, but there are two primary factors which occur in each of the four environments. The first is access to official power—the crime cabal and those public officials with whom it must cooperate. The second is money, the shared need for finance, capital, and money-laundering facilities.

Organized crime groups find it imperative to preserve friendships with law enforcement agencies and official government bodies. Both the police and the bureaucracy have the discretion to permit the continuation of vice activity—that is, they can choose to ignore the existence of an illegal gambling operation or street-level drug dealing. Discretion is exercised at a price, and purveyors of vice are successful only if they remain in official favor. The syndication and organization of crime is, therefore, promoted by the need to centralize and coordinate payoffs. It is this regulatory function that unites criminals and others into a cabal.

While some scholars of American organized crime have emphasized the crucial role of money movers, illicit financiers and bankers, attention has really been focused only on the most celebrated, men like Meyer Lansky, John Pullman, and Allen Dorfman. However, each city or local area has its own local clique of money suppliers who are not necessarily affiliated with any specific organized crime group but rather bridge the financial gaps between and among those groups (Potter and Jenkins, 1985; Lernoux, 1984; Cook and Carmichael, 1980; Fried, 1980; Anderson, 1979; Kwitny, 1979; Chambliss, 1978). These money movers, whose activities we explored in chapter 5, have sometimes received less than their due, but the fact is that money is a crucial organizational tool. It finances drug operations, capitalizes investments in real estate necessary for a pornography or prostitution venture, and brings professionals together to carry on a successful robbery or hijacking ring.

Alan Block (1979b) has suggested that in studying organized crime, we are really dealing with two different realities. The street-level organization of crime involves a large number of people in a social world. This is the fragmented, often competitive and antagonistic day-to-day world of providing illicit goods and services. The purveyors of vice engage in business relationships, interpersonal relationships, and other social interactions at the micro-level. These relationships are both unstable and highly volatile, constantly changing and, as Peter Reuter (1983) would say, "disorganized crime." These relationships represent the conduct of the specific crime in question. However, the organization of crime requires that we look at a social system—the environment in which purveyors of illicit goods and services operate, the social parameters which define the limits of regulation (corruption), the exigencies of the illegal market (money), and the coordination of crime. It is in this social system that we will discover the opportunities and constraints facing the organization of crime which emanate from finance, politics, and the administration of justice. In order to fully understand what organized crime is, we must look to the larger social system:

It is no accident that whenever the presence of vice and organizations that provide the vices is exposed to public view by politicians, exposure is always couched in terms of organized crime. The question of corruption is conveniently left in the shadows. Similarly, it is no accident that organized crime is inevitably seen as consisting of an organization of criminals with names like Valachi, Genovese, and Joe Bonnano. Yet the data . . . makes it abundantly clear that this analysis is fundamentally misleading.

[. . .] The real significance of syndicates has been overlooked; for instead of seeing these social entities as intimately tied to and in symbiosis with the legal and political bureaucracies of the state, social scientists have emphasized the criminality of only a portion of those involved. Such a view contributes very little to our knowledge of crime and even less to attempts at crime control (Chambliss, 1978: 4).

The "Gray" Market Underworld and Upperworld Commerce

As Dwight Smith has pointed out, organized crime exhibits many of the same characteristics that could be applied to many similar legal businesses (Smith, 1978). As is the case with any business enterprise, organized crime groups seek to make profitable and safe investments. As a result, organized crime networks invariably move into legitimate enterprises (i.e., vending, bars, night clubs, food products, the garment industry, banking and finance, trucking, etc.) To a large degree this ambition to find legitimate investment for organized crime capital is dictated by the constraints imposed upon organized crime enterprises by the illicit market. We have seen how geographical expansion is risky and how the need to control information mitigates against the inclusion of too many employees in organized crime operations (Reuter, 1983). Expanding and reinvesting in additional illicit enterprises is often judged to be foolhardy. The next choice is legitimate business. The close interrelationships between legitimate and illicit businesses have been documented time and again in every local study of organized crime groups.

Organized crime represents a series of reciprocal relationships and services uniting criminals, clients, and public officials. Organized crime has as its most important function the task of providing a bridge between the covert world of crime and the overt world of legitimate business, finance, and politics. It is this reciprocal relationship, the uniting of what Alan Block calls the underworld and the upperworld, which is the primary task of a crime network.

In Philadelphia, the liquor syndicate of the 1930s openly did business at the Union National Bank, using a series of bogus accounts and laundering their money through real estate transactions arranged by the upperworld banking system. In addition, the liquor syndicate had an ongoing contract with the Reading Railroad to transport their illegal products (Potter and Jenkins, 1985). In present-day Philadelphia, at least one gambling organization uses a local bank's loan officer, rather than a loanshark, to assist in cleaning up outstanding debts (Potter and Jenkins, 1985). In "Morrisburg," the gambling network is run in concert with two dozen local businesses which provide not only money-laundering services but ready-made reinvestment opportunities for gambling capital.

The interface with legitimate business serves several vital functions for organized crime groups (Anderson, 1979):

1) It provides a means to conceal illegal activities. In "Morrisburg," employees of a series of legitimate vending companies serve as the pickup men for the gambling organizations. In addition, a variety of jewelry stores, second-hand shops, and Army-Navy stores serve as fronts for fencing organizations. Chambliss (1978) uncovered a similar situation with regard to gambling operations in Seattle.

2) It provides a means to launder profits from criminal activities. In Philadelphia, illicit money was laundered through a variety of mechanisms including a legitimate bank, a beer distributorship, and a series of bars and nightclubs (Potter and Jenkins, 1985). Such money-laundering operations range from the very simple, such as the vending machine/real estate nexus in "Morrisburg" and the nightclub business in Philadelphia (Anderson, 1979), to the extremely complex arrangements manifest in the Exchange Bank of Geneva, Switzerland, and various subsidiaries of Meyer Lansky (Lernoux, 1984; Fried, 1980). One of the most complex laundering/business arrangements was the pornography network of Reuben Sturman, which in its Pennsylvania-based activities alone used a system of seven corporations, one layered on top of the other, to conceal the ultimate distribution of pornography profits (Potter, 1986; Pennsylvania Crime Commission, 1980).

3) It provides a source of legitimate and reportable income. The Pennsylvania Crime Commission (1984) has reported that the use of bars and restaurants as a legitimate reporting mechanism for

illicit profits is a common occurrence. In "Morrisburg," the gambling syndicate was able to report all of its income as profits realized in its vending and real estate transactions.

4) It serves to further the already high degree of integration between organized criminals and "respectable" members of the business community. Chambliss (1978) reported that the distinction between crime and business in Seattle was almost impossible to discern. The same conclusion can be reached elsewhere. For example, in "Morrisburg," local dinettes, newspaper stands, bars, and tobacco shops serve as collection points for betting action directed to the gambling network; a dry cleaning establishment served as a distribution point for underground pornographic films; a "gold exchange" served as a front for a fencing and loansharking operation; and a downtown hotel served as the home base for in-the-street prostitution. "Morrisburg" fences reported that most of their business involved selling stolen goods to retail establishments.

5) It provides stable and relatively safe investment opportunities. Organized crime operations entail some degree of risk in the accumulation of illicit capital. Therefore, such networks very often look for safe investments, in which they have relatively high confidence, as a means of legitimately depositing their profits. In both Philadelphia and "Morrisburg" there is a long-standing pattern of investment in the garment industry (Potter and Jenkins, 1985; Pennsylvania Crime Commission, 1980). In "Morrisburg," as well as Seattle and Reading, a pattern of real estate investments by organized crime groups can readily be discerned (Chambliss, 1978; Gardiner, 1970).

The line of demarcation between illegitimate and legitimate business is often difficult to discern at all, primarily because organized crime groups are so well integrated into the economic life of the legitimate business community. In "Morrisburg," the gamblers are considered part of the business and community elite, participating in community fundraising drives and having a wide-range of legitimate business partners. Chambliss indicated that the two groups were one and the same in Seattle, and Gardiner reported, at the very least, close cooperation in Reading.

Organized crime provides useful and functionally necessary services to the business community. This does not imply that all members of the business community deal with organized crime, nor that all organized crime activities are "good for business." What it does mean is that in a significant number of specific situations people in legitimate businesses avail themselves of the services of organized crime, for example:

1) Organized crime networks provide stolen goods for resale by businesses. This is particularly true in the case of ongoing relationships between fences and retail establishments.

2) In legitimate business, people often use the racketeering services of organized crime groups to harass competitors or to secure favorable contracts with employees (Potter and Jenkins, 1985; Block and Chambliss, 1981; Pennsylvania Crime Commission, 1980; Chambliss, 1978). This relationship can be seen in a number of historical and contemporary examples. The garment industry made use of organized crime services to ward off unionization by the "radical" International Ladies Garment Workers' Union in "Morrisburg." Construction companies in Philadelphia made use of both the Teamsters' and Roofers' unions to harass competitors. For years relative labor peace in the "Morrisburg" mines was secured through the intervention of organized crime groups. In the 1940s, Detroit automobile companies used organized crime to suppress efforts to unionize the auto industry and to supply strikebreakers (Pearce, 1976). Chambliss reported that in Seattle members of the local business community gladly chose the corrupt Teamsters Union of Dave Beck over Harry Bridges' Longshoremen's Union, a more radical alternative, and Block and Chambliss (1981) detail symbiotic relationships between New York's garment manufacturers and the labor racketeers of the 1930s and 1940s.

Of course, labor racketeering also provides an opportunity for organized crime to gain control of unions with the collusion and assistance of management. Such control facilitates organized crime's ability to engage in extortion and to manipulate the welfare and pension funds of the workers, as evidenced by hundreds of millions of dollars "loaned" to organized crime's casino acquisition efforts in Las Vegas. The Teamsters Union is the prime example of such a relationship, but organized crime control of union health care plans in the Philadelphia area is also an important example (Pennsylvania Crime Commission, 1983).

3) Businessmen often utilize the financial services of organized crime in joint investments or in times of economic hardship. Every local study of organized crime reported specific instances of people in legitimate business being openly engaged in partnerships with known organized crime figures, particularly in trucking, construction, mining, and banking.

This consensual relationship between business and organized crime has the advantage of stimulating quick capital accumulation for both parties. The need for quick capital is not always met by illicit activities but occasionally requires an ability to secure "legitimate" capital as an ancillary source of financing. The profits from "Morrisburg" drug networks, for example, are a ready source of funds to lend for investment purposes. The interest on this legitimate capital may later be turned into wholesale drug purchases. Legitimate business holdings by the "Morrisburg" gambling organization have all but obviated the need for lay-off services by maintaining a large and ready cash reserve for gambling networks.

We have seen that the relationship between organized crime and business is both functional and necessary to the continued existence and efficient operation of organized crime. The degree of integration between organized crime and business is summed up by Richard Quinney:

> Organized crime and legitimate businesses may mutually assist one another, as in regulating prices of commodities or enforcing labor contracts. Interdependence between the underworld of crime and the upperworld of business ensures that both systems will be maintained. Mutual assistance accompanied by the profit motive assures immunity.

> Organized crime has grown into a huge business in the United States and is an integral part of the political economy. Enormous amounts of illegitimate money are passed annually into socially acceptable endeavors. An elaborate corporate and financial structure is now tied to organized crime (Quinney, 1975: 145).

Criminal activities alone are not sufficient for explaining organized crime. The specific instances of illegal enterprises do not occur in a vacuum. The environment in which activities occur serves to organize crime. The business and commercial communities clearly have an impact on the question of how many opportunities for legitimate collaboration and expansion organized crime groups have. We have explored how this environment is closely tied in with the illicit market as an organizing influence on crime. Other environments are more subtle in their effects. Remember that we have emphasized the social relationships and overlapping social networks which help to define participation in organized crime groups. Just as commerce is directly related to the market influences organized crime feels, the community is directly related to this basic, defining network of social relations.

Organized Crime and the Community

In order to operate efficiently and effectively, organized crime needs social acceptance in the community. It achieves that acceptance, and in some cases outright support, for two reasons. First, organized crime performs important service functions for the community. Second, organized crime is a functional means of adaptation in a highly stratified society. We will explore these relationships between organized crime and the community in some detail starting with the "latent functions" of organized crime.

Most analyses of organized crime fail to consider the latent functions (Merton, 1967) performed by organized crime groups in the community. The fact is that organized crime, particularly in depressed or declining communities, often provides what the legitimate world cannot or will not. For example, organized crime provides jobs. Laswell and McKenna found that in the Bedford-Stuyvesant community of New York City, the numbers business was the single largest employer (1971). William Foote Whyte (1961) also found that the numbers game provided employment for many local men who were unskilled and who would not otherwise be able to secure gainful employment. In "Morrisburg," the "Gianelli" gambling operation provides full-time employment for at least fifty individuals, and part-time supplemental employment for hundreds of others. For men and women who are existing on subsistence pensions from the railroads or coal mines, or who are struggling to keep small stores afloat in a depressed community, the gambling business is a vital supplement to their legitimate income. Not only do they see nothing wrong with gambling, but they become more or less dependent on it as a means of income support. In addition, the other vices also provide employment. Prostitution, questions of morality and exploitation aside, employs women who desperately need to supplement their legitimate incomes. Remember "Terry's" story in which she had to be a streetwalker to support her family because Ma Bell simply didn't pay enough. Pornography provides jobs. Even the drug networks provide at least part-time employment to considerable numbers of "Morrisburg" residents. In addition, there are some legitimate jobs generated by the vice industry: waitresses and barmaids, bartenders, clerks in porn stores, vending machine technicians, etc. It is not just that organized crime careers save people from destitution, these jobs also often employ people who may well be a threat to the community. Consider those young men who, because of their limited skills and education, cannot find other gainful employment. It is not too great a leap to assume that these people might turn to robbery, burglary, or other more substantial criminal threats to the community if they were not offered the option of working in vice. In a very real way, organized crime may reduce the threat of conventional criminality in towns such as "Morrisburg."

Jobs are only one contribution organized crime groups make to the community. Another is money. For example, Whyte reported that in Boston the gamblers were "known as free spenders and liberal patrons of local enterprises" (1961: 142). Whyte argues that local shopkeepers are often dependent on the money they receive from selling numbers and taking bets. In addition, people who come into the store or luncheonette for the purpose of betting may just turn into customers (Whyte, 1961). In fact, as was reported earlier, Charles Silberman has argued that gambling profits make it possible for small storekeepers to compete with supermarkets and chain stores (1978). This may seem a minor point, but if you are a struggling store owner in a depressed community like "Morrisburg," or Harlem, or Jersey City, the spending money generated to your customers by organized crime may well make the difference between being in business and out of business altogether.

Organized crime frequently provides investment capital that would not be readily available otherwise. In "Morrisburg," the gambling syndicate not only props up many small businesses and provides a great deal of marginal employment, but it has also played a key role in encouraging outside business interests to locate there in an attempt to revitalize a sagging economy. Organized crime was primarily responsible for the growth of the garment industry in the "Morrisburg" area (albeit that wages and working conditions are not optimal). In 1980, the Pennsylvania Crime Commission estimated that about two thousand women were employed in the mob-owned garment plants surrounding "Morrisburg."

Organized crime also provides other less tangible rewards in the community. For example, gamblers are particularly good sources of information on everything from available housing to where merchandise (sometimes of questionable origin) can be secured at discount prices (Cartey, 1970). There is some merit to the argument that organized crime provides some level of protection from street crime. It is certainly true that in the "Morrisburg" study, the Philadelphia study (Potter and Jenkins, 1985), and the Bedford-Stuyvesant study (Laswell and McKenna, 1971) a pattern of reduced crime was noticeable in neighborhoods with strong organized crime associations.

These latent functions of organized crime go a long way toward explaining the persistence and durability of organized crime and toward explaining community ambivalence toward efforts to root out organized crime. Where the mob provides more social functions than the government, it is safe to expect that the government will receive little support in its suppression efforts.

While relatively tangible economic rewards emanating from the presence of organized crime groups are important, equally significant is the role organized crime may play in providing a mechanism through which people can adapt to the demands of a stratified society. While a detailed analysis of this point is beyond the scope of the present discussion, a brief summary of the major sociological concepts in the area may help to explain why organized crime is not necessarily regarded as an inherent evil in every American community.

Daniel Bell argued almost thirty years ago that crime is an American way of life. Bell, quite correctly, points out that the founders of American industry, the early pioneers of American capitalism, were not graduates of the Wharton School of Business, but rather attained their fortunes by "shady speculation and a not inconsiderable amount of violence" (1964: 13). Bell, Ianni (1974), and others have argued that crime, and particularly organized crime, provides a means for social mobility in communities where more legitimate paths are blocked or difficult.

Still, why do people choose that option? In order to explore this, we must briefly discuss some very basic social ideas. Robert Merton (1938) argued that in American society there often develops an emphasis on "specific goals." This emphasis becomes disproportionately important, "virtually exclusive," and ignores the issue of what means are appropriate for achieving those specific goals. Merton described this situation by using a term developed by Emile Durkheim, (1947) *anomie* (state of confusion, social instability which results from a breakdown of standards and values), in his attempts to describe those social conditions which predispose individuals toward deviance. Simply put, this idea states that if we conform to the normative order, and make certain sacrifices to do so, we must be compensated by socialized rewards (Merton, 1938). When those expected rewards are not forthcoming, deviant acts, outside of the normative order become attractive. As Merton says: "Aberrant conduct, therefore, may be viewed as a symptom of dissociation between culturally defined aspirations and social structured means" (1938: 674). Merton argues that "the extreme emphasis upon the accumulation of wealth as a symbol of success" leads to a disregard for considerations about how that success is attained. "Fraud, vice, corruption, and crime," under these circumstances, are increasingly common means of achieving that "culturally-induced success goal" (Merton, 1938, 675–676).

When we think about the situation in "Morrisburg," this explanation makes some sense. This is a town of hard-working, pious, religiously-oriented people. They have seen their work, their heritage of success, collapse around them. First the mines, then the railroads, and now most forms of basic manufacturing have closed down, leaving the city and its residents with limited options of achieving Merton's success-goal. Society still enshrines success but provides only limited opportunities for reaching it, among which is crime.

Merton argues that when individuals select a path to success outside of normatively prescribed channels, they are engaged in innovation: "the use of conventionally proscribed but frequently effective means of attaining at least the simulacrum of culturally defined success" (1938: 678). Taylor, Walton, and Young provide a concise summary of this concept:

> The "American Dream" urges all citizens to succeed whilst distributing the opportunity to succeed unequally: the result of this social and moral climate, inevitably, is innovation by the citizenry—the adoption of illegitimate means to pursue and obtain success (1973: 97).

It is important to remember that in a town like "Morrisburg," there is at least some history of the use of illegitimate means to achieve goals. It was less than a century ago that the grandfathers and fathers of today's residents were engaged in illegal efforts to organize unions. Many residents started their working careers in illegal sweat shops and as child laborers. It is not unusual for a working-class "Morrisburg" family to have a rather proud history of illegitimate adaptation.

While those behaviors may have been illegal at the time, crime is a more extreme innovation. Why do some people turn to crime, let alone organized crime, when faced by this disturbing dilemma, and others turn to activist roles in politics, real estate, banking, or some other sanctioned activity? What conditions encourage a criminal direction? Albert Cohen has pointed to the role of reference groups in adaptation to anomic conditions. Cohen argues that when we see those around us who have attained "success" by innovating, we experience a "sense of strain" which helps shape future normative conformity (1956: 6). When we identify with these reference groups, we may well be influenced by their actions and their means of success attainment. Edwin Sutherland (1973) suggests that criminal behavior is learned in interaction with other persons, and our propensity for innovating through criminality is dependent on the strength or intensity of those criminal associations. He called this *differential association*. Sutherland suggests that criminal behavior occurs when there is "an excess of definitions favorable to violation of law over definitions unfavorable to violation of law" (1973: 5).

So, generally speaking, the sociological argument goes something like this. The socioeconomic stratification of society relegates some people to an environment wherein they experience a sense of strain and differential association. In the environments that have traditionally spawned organized crime, this feeling is intense. Deprivation, limited access to legitimate alternatives, and readily available, innovative success models (pimps, gamblers, drug dealers) create a susceptibility to criminal behavior (Sutherland, 1973). Cloward and Ohlin summarize this proposition as follows:

> [L]ower-class male adolescents experience desperation born of the certainty that their position in the economic structure is relatively fixed and immutable—a desperation made all the more poignant by their exposure to a cultural ideology in which failure to orient oneself upward is regarded as a moral defect and failure to become mobile as proof of it (1960: 106–107, cited in Abadinsky, 1985).

That innovation should result is both natural and very American. Cloward and Ohlin also point out that illegitimate means of success like legitimate ones, are not equally distributed throughout the community: "Having decided that he can't make it legitimately, he cannot simply choose among an array of illegitimate means, all equally available to him" (1960: 145). They conclude:

> Only those neighborhoods in which crime flourishes as a stable indigenous institution are fertile criminal learning environments for the young. Because these environments afford integration of different age-levels of offender, selected young people are exposed to "differential association" through which tutelage is provided and criminal values and skills are acquired. To be prepared for the role may not, however, ensure that individuals will ever discharge it. One important limitation is that more youngsters are recruited into these patterns of differential association than the adult criminal structure can possibly absorb. Since there is a surplus of contenders for these positions, criteria and mechanisms of selection must be evolved. Hence a certain proportion of those who aspire may not be permitted to engage in the behavior for which they have prepared themselves (1960: 148, cited in Abadinsky, 1985).

It is at this critical juncture that the opportunity for recruitment to criminality and eventually organized criminality occurs. It is also at this point that the community itself plays a key role in the selection process, providing the early socialization toward organized crime through a process of cultural transmission and a sense of criminal history.

Several studies of criminal gangs point to cultural transmission of criminal behavior through generations living in the same ecological niches. Shaw and McKay, in their 1942 study of Chicago gangs suggested that a kind of criminal apprenticeship takes place in the community. They found a consistent pattern where younger boys participated in "offenses in the company of . . . older boys, and so on, backward in time in an unbroken continuity" (1972: 175). They suggest that young, would-be criminals have contact with older, more-skilled delinquents, who have contact with older criminals, and that this process not only provides training but also allows for evaluation of an individual's potential for criminal success by more experienced actors (1972).

It is in this period of development that Walter Miller (1958) has argued that the qualities useful to organized crime are inculcated in apprentice criminals. Miller points particularly to "toughness" and "smartness" (getting money by one's wits) as values to be developed (1958). In addition, Miller believes that the "capacity for subordinating individual desires to general group interests as well as the capacity for intimate and persisting interaction" (1958: 14) develops in this crime community.

Added to this developmental process is what Gerald Suttles has called "a strong sense of history" (1968: 111). Suttles points out that his research in Chicago indicated that almost every gang member traced his genealogy back to an earlier gang. He believes that this sense of history, even though it is almost invariably based on inaccurate data, provides an even stronger sense of criminal heritage.

While the study of organized crime in "Morrisburg" did not have as its objective an evaluation of the socialization process described above and did not collect data to either confirm or deny the hypotheses presented here, it is important to reflect on the socializing functions of the community as they relate to organized crime. Clearly many of the conditions described here are present in "Morrisburg" and have been for well over a century. There is a strong sense of "criminal"/community history. Family members who have been involved in organized crime and/or in early bootlegging operations are regarded with reverence. Social cynicism is clearly expressed in conversations with criminal actors—as well as the belief that they really do nothing substantially different from their counterparts in legitimate business and politics. There is a well-defined system of neighborhood demarcation, both ethnically and socioeconomically. Many neighborhoods, particularly those in which today's organized crime figures are located, would have been "slums" by the standards of the early researchers from the Chicago

School. There is a clear and pervasive sense of economic and social desperation in a town which has declined from affluence, importance and greatness. None of this proves any of the theories cited above, but it all serves to lend credence to the idea that there is a socialization process, a social bonding process, that plays a key role in recruitment to organized crime groups and in ensuring a sense of loyalty and belonging among organized criminals. It certainly provides a better and more rational model of their socialization process than stories of blood oaths, medieval ceremonies, and men kissing each other on the cheeks.

Community is a very broad term, encompassing almost every aspect of our social and political lives. In the preceding discussion, that concept has been limited to dealing with the community functions of socialization and social participation. However, it is equally true that the community also performs a political function and a social control function. The way a community performs these functions is obviously tempered by the social processes which have just been described. However, both social control and politics, despite being functions subsumed in the community, have vital implications for organized crime.

Organized Crime and the Criminal Justice System

Because organized crime is engaged in illegal acts on a continuous basis, some accommodation must be made with the criminal justice system. This process of compromising law enforcement involves a wide range of considerations with direct impact on organizational structure and function. This is not simply a matter of corruption and graft. The nature of the accommodations developed between criminal syndicates and forces of social control can be traced to the nature of the law itself (McCaghy and Cernkovich, 1987).

The nature of the laws against the illicit goods and services provided by organized crime makes selective and discriminatory enforcement of such laws inevitable (McCaghy and Cernkovich, 1987). The use of discretion in dealing with these offenses by the criminal justice system offers an opportunity for organized crime to influence the process of justice itself. The legal environment creates opportunities for organized crime in many ways.

We know that the primary business of organized crime is providing willing customers with goods and services which are illegal. As was pointed out earlier, this is a consensual arrangement in which one party wishes to purchase and another wishes to profit by supplying. The very nature of these crimes makes law enforcement a very difficult and troublesome task for several reasons (see, McCaghy and Cernkovich, 1987; Schur and Bedau, 1974).

First, laws against consensual crimes are relatively unenforceable. These criminal acts, by their very nature, involve cooperation between seller and buyer. No one involved in the transaction perceives of himself or herself as a victim, and consequently no one files a complaint with the police. Without a complainant, the police have a great deal of difficulty ferreting out offenders and frequently resort to illegal or highly questionable activities to make an arrest.

Second, when the laws are enforced they are enforced on a highly selective and discriminatory basis which favors organized crime groups over individual entrepreneurs. Offenders who are actually apprehended tend to be those easiest to catch. It is simply a matter of common sense that the better organized a group is, the less the chance of getting caught. The corollary to this is, of course, that organization is far preferable to individual entrepreneurship in terms of risk of arrest and prosecution. It is the highly visible streetwalker, not the call girl who works for an organized sex ring, who is most likely to come to police attention. It is the street dealer hawking drugs who is subject to arrest, not the distributor who is insulated by an organization.

Third, the high demand for these illegal goods and services creates capital sufficient to offer substantial inducements to police, prosecutors, mayors, judges, and other criminal justice system functionaries to be less than vigilant in their enforcement of those laws.

Finally, the simple fact that a significant portion of the population desires gambling, drugs, prostitution, and pornography but is legally denied their desires makes the creation of organizations to meet that unfulfilled demand inevitable. It is a fallacy that organized crime produces the desire for vice. Organized crime doesn't force people to gamble, snort cocaine, or read pornography. It merely fills an already existing social gap. The law has made organized crime inevitable because it denies people legal sources for those desired goods and services. The criminalization of strongly demanded but legally proscribed goods and services makes organized crime an attractive entrepreneurial option.

Selective enforcement and the exercise of discretion usually serve to strengthen one or more organized crime groups at the expense of smaller organizations or individual entrepreneurs. In "Morrisburg," for example, the "Gianelli" gambling organization is virtually immune from law enforcement and prosecutorial efforts, thereby ensuring continued dominance in the gambling market.

In North Philadelphia, for almost two decades, Caesar Nelson's numbers bank enjoyed full protection assuring continued and uninterrupted profits at the expense of smaller operators (Potter and Jenkins, 1985). Similarly, in Philadelphia, call girl rings that are part of the "system" are guaranteed hassle-free existences, where independents either face arrest or payoff schedules in excess of those of the better organized operators (Potter and Jenkins, 1985)

Selective enforcement also serves a vital function for the legal bureaucracy itself. By reducing competition in the provision of these illicit goods and services, the criminal justice system limits organizational strain and reduces the prospects for violence. The dangerous effects of a breakdown in this system can clearly be seen in the mob war that raged in Philadelphia during the 1980s (Potter and Jenkins, 1985; Pennsylvania Crime Commission, 1984). On the other hand, "Morrisburg" has had only rare occurrences of organized crime violence, which are contained and quickly extinguished before any real damage is done. The relationship between organized crime and criminal justice agencies serves the social control goal of maintaining public order and public tranquillity in a community.

The adoption of a functional "tolerance policy" by the law enforcement bureaucracies reduces the strain emanating from the contradictions inherent in the law itself. Social control bureaucracies are confronted with the vexing problem of enforcing the laws on gambling, prostitution, drugs, etc., about which little social consensus may be discerned. Some groups' values are offended by these behaviors and these groups may engage in "moral entrepreneurship" (Gusfield, 1963) to seek a cessation of these behaviors. The community's ruling elite seeking to expand its coalition of support may work in concert with social control bureaucracies seeking to expand their budgetary/personnel resources and their enforcement power to pass laws proscribing offensive behaviors (Harring, 1977; Hindus, 1977; Chambliss, 1976b; 1964; Becker, 1963). However, because the powerful in any community often wish to partake of these goods and services, and more importantly because they often profit directly from their involvement in the provision of these goods and services, there is pressure placed upon the law enforcement bureaucracy to allow these activities to take place. The adoption of a tolerance policy allows the criminal justice bureaucracy to accommodate both those persons in the community who wish to partake of these goods and services, while continuing to give the impression of enforcing the law.

In addition, a tolerance policy or "crime committing license"

(Hills, 1971) facilitates control of these illicit activities by confining them to certain parts of the community (usually far away from the homes of the economically and politically powerful). In these geographic zones the actions of vice purveyors and customers can be more carefully monitored and controlled, thereby preventing incidents that might incite inquiry or investigation. In "Morrisburg" the vice district is neatly contained in about six city blocks, heavily patrolled by the police who maintain order without interfering in the illicit business conducted in front of them.

Finally, members of the criminal justice bureaucracy benefit from organized crime activities directly through the provision of graft and payoffs. Widespread corruption has been documented by Gardiner in Reading, Chambliss in Seattle, the Pennsylvania Crime Commission (1974) in Philadelphia, the Knapp Commission in New York, and by interviews conducted with organized crime figures and public officials in "Morrisburg" and Philadelphia (Potter and Jenkins, 1985).

The relationships between organized criminals and the police represent the ultimate example of the social integration of organized crime. Here we have two supposed antagonists, at polar ends of the criminal justice continuum, engaged in a most profitable and functional collaborative effort. However, while much attention has been directed in the literature at police and judicial corruption, the fact remains that it is the political system, the legitimate agencies of community governance, that make it all possible.

Organized Crime and Politics

Previous discussions have stressed the fact that organized crime must be viewed as an integral part of society's political, economic, and social structure. In fact, it is a basic characteristic of all organized crime that it must, of necessity, emphasize collusion between the criminal, the police, and the politicians. As Chambliss (1976a: 182) has argued in his study of Seattle, the cabal "that manages the vice is composed of important businessmen, law enforcement officers, political leaders, and a member of a major trade union."

Political corruption is critical to the survival of organized crime. In fact, organized crime could not operate at all without the direct complicity and connivance of the political machinery in its area of operation (Hills, 1971). Studies of organized crime at the turn of the century commented on the close symbiosis between the machine and ward leader and organized criminals at the turn of the century (Peterson, 1983; Block and Chambliss, 1981). Investigations have consistently demonstrated the close relationship between political organizations and organized crime. The 1937 grand jury in Philadelphia exposed collusion between the gambling syndicate and both the mayor and the district attorney (Potter and Jenkins, 1984). The entire Seattle crime cabal was held together by political collusion (Chambliss, 1978), as was the Reading gambling syndicate (Gardiner, 1967). In Pennsylvania, any major organized crime trial of the 1940s or 1950s could be certain to include a list of public officials (judges, city councilmen, legislators) appearing as character witnesses for the defense (Pennsylvania Crime Commission, 1970). In "Morrisburg," in 1951, "Jacob Schiff" and his cohorts were warned of impending subpoenas to appear before the Kefauver Committee by the district attorney. In contemporary "Morrisburg" the political party chairmen have served as bagmen for the gambling syndicate. Investigation after investigation has disclosed a consistent pattern of corruption by government officials acting on behalf of organized crime groups.

Once again, this is a symbiotic relationship. In return for official favors, organized crime is able to provide campaign moneys, private graft, investment opportunities, and direct assistance in certain kinds of bargaining and negotiations to public officials. In "Morrisburg," the gambling network hands out both above-the-board, legitimate political contributions to political parties, and under-the-table cash, which is primarily used as "street money" to encourage efforts to bring out voters. In addition, it is alleged that the gambling organization has had business relationships with two sitting judges and other county officials, particularly in a series of real estate transactions. "Morrisburg" gamblers and other organized crime participants have also played a major role in encouraging outside business interests to locate there, thereby assisting, indirectly, governmental and civic efforts.

As long ago as the 1960s, it was estimated that $2 billion annually was given by organized crime figures to public officials each year in the form of campaign contributions (King, 1969). Allowing for inflation, that figure may have tripled or quadrupled by the 1990s. Historian Mark Haller summed up the situation well in saying, "It is not so much that gambling syndicates influenced local political organizations, rather gambling syndicates were the local political organizations" (Haller, 1979: 88). While Haller was writing about the great machines of the past, his words are also descriptive of the situation today. William Chambliss points to the role of organized crime as a very important source of political corruption at all levels of government. In commenting on organized crime in Seattle, Chambliss said:

> Money is the oil of our present-day machinery, and elected public officials are the pistons that keep the machine operating. Those who come up with the oil, whatever its source, are in a position to make the machinery run the way they want it to. Crime is an excellent producer of capitalism's oil. Those who want to affect the direction of the machine's output find that money produced by crime is as effective in helping them get where they can go as is the money produced in any other way. Those who produce the money from crime thus become the people most likely to control the machine. Crime is not a by-product of an otherwise effectively working political economy. Crime is, in fact, a cornerstone on which the political and economic relations of democratic-capitalist societies are constructed.
>
> In every city of the United States, and in many other countries as well, criminal organizations sell sex and drugs, provide an opportunity to gamble, to watch pornographic films, or to obtain a loan, an abortion, or a special favor. Their profits are a mainstay of the electoral process in America and their business is an important (if unrecorded) part of the gross national product. The business of organized crime in the United States may gross as much as one hundred billion dollars annually—or as little as forty billion—either way the profits are immense, and the proportion of the gross national product represented by money flowing from crime cannot be gainsaid. Few nations in the world have economies that compare with the economic output of criminal activities in the United States (Chambliss, 1978: 1–2).

A basic characteristic of organized crime is that it depends on the corruption of government officials for survival and continued profitability. Bribery, campaign contributions, delivery of votes, and other favors are used to influence legislators, city council members, mayors, judges, district attorneys, and others. It is not possible to place organized crime in a social context outside of its relationships with the political system—nor to understand it without comprehending the full extent of its involvement in the political machinery of this nation.

Most explanations of organized crime focus directly on the structure, organization, activities, and conduct of organized crime groups on a micro-level, relegating the impact of environmental forces to a secondary or modifying position. The reason for directing so much attention to the environments of organized crime in this discussion is to refocus attention on the operations of illegal enterprises in a social system. Like any other enterprise, organized crime must operate in a general social environment, which includes relations with political institutions, with businesses that deal in legal goods and services, and with regulators and social control agents. It is this complex web of relationships that provides the most compelling context for understanding the persistence of organized crime and its success as an economic and social force in American society.

Chapter 8

The Structure and Environment of Crime Organizations*

The enterprises of organized crime groups are shaped by the same environmental and technological forces as are the enterprises of legitimate businesses. Viewed from a rational systems perspective (Perrow, 1972; Thompson, 1967; Gouldner, 1959), all organizations, whether licit or illicit, seek to exploit opportunities for profit making offered by some niche in the environment. In the case of organized crime, the organization exists for the explicit purpose of making a profit from market activity that involves the distribution of illicit goods and services (Vold and Bernard, 1986; Block and Chambliss, 1981; Smith, 1978; Albini, 1971). With the exception of the legal status of the product being offered, organized crime operates its illicit enterprises in a manner congruent with legitimate businesses. It is only their respective locations on what

*This chapter was co-authored by Mittie D. Southerland, Professor of Police Studies at Eastern Kentucky University. She earned her MS at Eastern Kentucky University in 1973 and her Ph.D. at the University of Kentucky 1984. A former criminal justice planner and juvenile counselor, her expertise is in the areas of administration, management, and supervision with particular emphasis on organizational environments and change in the police setting. Dr. Southerland is coauthor of *Police Administration: Design, Organization, Management, and Control Processes* (MGraw-Hill, 1991) and has also published in the areas of organizational leadership and communication, rape, juvenile justice and criminal justice education.

Dwight Smith, Jr. has called a "spectrum of legitimacy" that differentiates criminal and legitimate enterprises (Smith, 1980). In exploiting the available opportunities for profit, criminal enterprises adapt in both structure and function to the opportunities offered by a particular niche. Not surprisingly, then, we would expect to find a wide variety of structural forms resulting from this adaptive process.

In looking at organized crime from a rational systems perspective, we would expect that not all structural forms are equally well adapted to their environments (Perrow, 1972). There will be a winnowing out of less successful structural forms under pressures from competing organizations seeking to exploit the potential for profit in the same market niche. In general, organization theory tells us that we will see a limited number of structural forms adapted to any given environmental niche (Katz and Kahn, 1978; Perrow, 1972; Thompson, 1967). Some organizational forms will be more effective than others in a particular environment and will therefore survive the competition, prosper, and be imitated by others seeking to exploit that niche. Some organizational forms will not be viable, or will be unable to adapt to changes in the organizational environment, and will wither away and cease to exist. The key issue then becomes what are the components of successful structural forms that allow survival and continuity in the illicit market.

This chapter will try to translate this general organizational framework into a set of propositions related to the illicit market activities of organized crime. Developing these theoretical propositions should serve two purposes:

1) The framework should provide a basis for systematizing our knowledge about organized crime and, more specifically, about the criminal enterprises of organized crime. We may find that much of the organizational literature based on legitimate businesses and government bureaucracies applies equally well to organized criminal enterprises. More likely, we will find that some of these concepts need to be redefined and refined to be applicable to the illicit market environment. For example, we might anticipate the need to readapt concepts such as "effectiveness" and "interorganizational competition" in the illicit market.

2) Second, from a practical view of controlling organized crime and its illicit activities, two major benefits can be anticipated. If it is indeed true that the organizational structure of criminal enterprise is adapted to the exigencies of technology and environment, then the specifics of this adaptation process should suggest points of vulnerability in those organizational structures

that would be most amenable to law enforcement intervention. Further, if this basic proposition is true, then it should become clear that no single, universal enforcement strategy can be expected to be effective in all interventions against organized crime. Different environments will pose different opportunities for law enforcement intervention.

Defining Criminal Enterprise and Organized Crime

In chapter 6, we gave a succinct definition of organized crime. It is not necessary to incorporate and reconcile all the attributes of organized crime mentioned in the scholarly literature into a simple definition. Rather, it is only important that we come up with a working definition that emphasizes those attributes of organized crime centering on criminal entrepreneurship and illicit enterprise. Again, the key characteristics of a criminal enterprise include:

1) **The production and/or distribution of goods and services** for the purpose of making a profit in the illicit market (Reuter, 1983). Such criminal enterprises would include gambling organizations, drug distribution networks, an organization which produces and distributes pornography, or a loansharking operation.

2) **A consumer population** that provides a stable and constant demand for the good or service in question. Examples of consumer populations abound. The 11 percent of the U.S. population that gambles illegally is one example (Commission on the Review of the National Policy Toward Gambling, 1976). The estimated twenty-five million Americans who have used cocaine constitutes another good example (Miller and Cisin, 1983).

3) **Some core aspect of the enterprise is illegal.** That core aspect can be product or the service itself, for example, illegal drugs or gambling, or its mode of distribution may be illegal, such as the high-interest loans made by loansharks. What is important is that this core aspect must be the major source of profit, the economic livelihood of the enterprise, not just an ancillary illegal sideline of an otherwise legal enterprise.

These criteria serve to delimit the types of enterprises and organizations to be considered. For example, they rule out gangs of thieves brought together for a particular "score," or ephemeral organizations that have been created for a one-time illegal activity.

The Concept of Structure

The term structure, as used in this discussion, will correspond to the general usage of the word in organizational theory. While structure is commonly thought of as just entailing the structure of *positions* in an organization and a description of the organization's hierarchy, span of control, and the like, our use of the term will be far broader. While structure does include a consideration of positions, it also includes:

1) **Procedures** detail how things are done, the actual steps that are followed to complete a task (Perrow, 1972; Blau, 1956). In manufacturing, procedures would tell us what to do when the number of product defects coming off the assembly-line exceed an acceptable level. In organized crime, procedures involve issues such as, how to know when the level of wagers placed on a certain horse, a particular football game, or a given number has become sufficiently high to layoff those bets to a layoff banker. In the case of a drug enterprise, procedures might entail making determinations of the appropriate level of purity of a kilo of cocaine at which it can be cut once, twice, etc.

2) **Policies** tell us what to do under certain specified circumstances, how to act and react to specified conditions (Ansoff and Brandenburg, 1971). For example, certain affirmative action policies might inform a business that, all things being equal, preference in hiring should be given to women and minorities. In the criminal enterprises of organized crime, policies may entail such things as the appropriate payoff schedule for usurious loans (shall it be weekly? monthly?); the criteria to be used by bookmakers in extending credit to gamblers; or the criteria used for acceptance of a new client by a call girl ring.

3) **Programs** are those repetitive agendas found in organizations for realizing a stated purpose (Perrow, 1967). A major company might require formal leadership training programs for all its management-level personnel. In criminal enterprises, similar programs might include the apprenticeship period of a call girl or the experience gained as a numbers runner prior to promotion to the role of pickup man.

Formal structures shape and constrain behavior in all organizations, be they legitimate or illicit. They also are responses to organizational needs created by the technology and environment of the enterprise(s) the organization is engaged in as part of its profit-making activities.

Structuring Dimensions

The organizational literature identifies three basic structuring dimensions. They are referred to as dimensions because they are not causal factors in determining a particular structure but are types of organization found to varying degrees in different enterprises. In complex structures, for example, one expects to find multiple levels of hierarchy and narrow spans of control as a structural dimension of complexity. The **need** for that complexity, however, is a response to environmental demands impacting on the organization. The three structuring dimensions are **formalization/standardization**, **complexity/specialization**, and **centralization**.

Formalization/Standardization

The concept of formalization or standardization as a structuring dimension is characterized by the explicitness of operating rules and procedures in the organization (Pugh et al., 1968). It is primarily related to procedures as structure in that it defines what is to be done and when, who is to do it, and how it is to be done. It also defines any limitations on the exercise of authority and the specification of functional authority by organizational staff.

A numbers gambling syndicate serves as a good example. In such an illicit operation common procedures are invariably followed. Numbers bets are written on the street, in bars, at newsstands, in tobacco shops, in luncheonettes, and the like. Customers come into the establishment, make their bets, pay their money, and have their transaction recorded. At specified times during the business day pickup men come to collect the bets from the writers. The bets are then taken to a central office or bank where they are totaled and recorded. After the winning number for the day has been determined, the office men identify the winners and send their winnings back to the writers through the pickup men. In a small numbers syndicate this represents the totality of the organization. A single banker oversees the whole organization and exercises total authority—authority gained by virtue of the fact that it is his or her money in play. In larger numbers syndicates the procedure is the same, it is simply replicated many times. In larger syndicates there are many neighborhood "banks" which follow the additional step of reporting their daily take to a central bank, which provides overall financial backing to the whole operation. In very large numbers organizations, there may be yet another level added involving the use of a layoff bank. The layoff bank covers extraordinarily high betting action on a particular number, providing a kind of insurance against a large "hit," in return for an ongoing percentage of the numbers organization's profits (Pennsylvania Crime Commission, 1987; Simon and Witte, 1982; Rubinstein and Reuter, 1978a; Fund for the City of New York, 1972).

A couple of specific cases clarify the concept. For three decades Caesar Nelson ran a massive numbers gambling organization in North Philadelphia. Nelson's annual wagering volume was estimated to be about $40 million, or $160,000 a day. In order to achieve this volume he had about 2,000 writers on the streets, making for a very large organization. Those 2,000 writers turned their betting action into separate neighborhood numbers banks, which in turn passed the daily take to Nelson's central bank. By operating in this way, Nelson was able to run an extensive gambling organization from which he, as the principal financial backer, was buffered. No actual bets ever went beyond the smaller banks. Transactions involving Nelson were strictly large cash transfers. Only daily tally sheets were included—never the betting slips themselves (Potter and Jenkins, 1985; Pennsylvania Crime Commission, 1980; 1974; 1970).

Another, even more complex operation involves the "Gianelli" gambling organization in "Morrisburg," as described earlier. Their organization handles not only numbers bets, but sports and horse bets as well. Gambling action is written in a myriad of local businesses. A series of vending machine companies, owned by members of the "Gianelli" syndicate, pick up the bets several times a day. These bets are distributed to a series of banks, each run by different combinations of syndicate members acting in partnership. The profits are then directly deposited (more appropriately laundered) by transactions with a series of real estate corporations owned by participants in the gambling syndicate, including apartment complexes and land development companies (Pennsylvania Crime Commission, 1980).

The key point, however, is that even in these two highly complex, very large, high volume gambling operations, utilizing thousands of writers, the procedures for conducting business are the same as in any other gambling syndicate. The way business is conducted is exactly the same for small numbers banks handling only a few thousand dollars in action. The nature of the service being provided has dictated an efficient means of doing business, which can be found with only minor variations in all gambling syndicates, everywhere in the United States.

A similar point could be made for narcotics wholesaling and call girl operations. There are a limited number of ways to wholesale drugs to retail street distributors. With very minor alterations, all heroin wholesalers use the same procedures (Wisotsky, 1986; Simon and Witte, 1982). The same is true of call girl rings. The procedures utilized are the same whether one is running a stable of six full-time, professional call girls, or three dozen part-time semi-pros. The initial contact is made by telephone, a means of verification of the client's identity is established (a credit card number, hotel room, etc.), the fee is established for supplying an "escort," the escort checks back with the agency by phone as soon as she arrives in the customer's room, negotiations for sexual services occur following specified rules of conduct (the customer names the act or the price, or preferably both), and the service is provided as expeditiously as possible. The procedures are invariable without regard to the size, scope, or complexity of the operation (Potter, 1986; Simon and Witte, 1982; James, 1977).

Complexity/Specialization

Complexity and/or specialization as a structuring dimension is characterized by the extent of the division of labor in an organization and the attendant task specialization of organizational participants and subunits of the organization (Hage and Aiken, 1970). Specialized organizations are differentiated both horizontally and vertically. Horizontally they are differentiated into functional task units (i.e., production, marketing); vertically they are differentiated as multiple levels of management and distinctions between staff and line operations.

Positions in criminal enterprises are determined by three variables: function, experience, and degree of risk. By way of example, let us consider one of the most rudimentary forms of criminal organization first, loansharking syndicates. In a loansharking syndicate, even at its most complex, vertical differentiation is determined by available capital. At the top is the "financier," that individual who supplies money to the loansharks who in turn "put it on the street." The expectation is that in a specified time the money will be returned with an appropriate profit (Reuter, 1983). In the 1960s in Philadelphia, three major loanshark financiers were active: Willie Weisberg, Frank Jaskiewicz, and Angelo Bruno. They dominated the organization of loansharking because they controlled the flow of money. They supplied capital to the loansharks and expected a 25 percent return on their investments a year later. These loanshark "bankers," for want of a better term, then supplied money to smaller entrepreneurs on the streets who made loans to gamblers, members of the business community, and others at usurious rates of interest (Pennsylvania Crime Commission, 1970; Potter and Jenkins, 1985). It was at street-level, essentially the bottom of the organizational pyramid, that the problems of contacts, collections, collateral, and negotiation occurred. The accrued profits simply flowed back up the money trail. It should be realized that most loansharking operations are even simpler than this arrangement, but the point is that the supply of capital financing dictates the structure and definition of positions in the syndicates (Jenkins and Potter, 1986; Rubinstein and Reuter, 1978b).

A similar arrangement can be found in call girl operations. The manager of the enterprise is the individual with sufficient investment capital to establish an office, buy advertising, put in phones, and pay protection. The call girls themselves are similar to commission salespersons who, based upon their expertise (and probably, their physical attributes) sell the organization's services for a profit. Most call girl operations work very simply. The agency collects a fee (usually $75 to $150) for supplying an escort to a customer. The call girl gets a portion of that fee (33 percent was the usual commission paid in Philadelphia in the 1980s). She is then free to negotiate a tip for her services to enhance that commission. At its most complex, there are three positions in such an organization: a financial backer, a business or sales manager, and a sales staff (Potter, 1986; Potter and Jenkins, 1985; Simon and Witte, 1982; James, 1977).

A similar arrangement attains in drug distribution syndicates. The drug wholesaler purchases the drug from an importer. This requires that the person or persons at the top of the wholesale organization have sufficient liquid capital to make discount buys. Invariably the importer and the wholesaler represent different organizations or syndicates. The arrangement between the importer and the wholesaler may require the creation of an additional position if the wholesaler, in an attempt to hold down cost, agrees to incur the risk of moving the contraband from its point of entry to his or her sales area. In this case "mules" will have to be employed to move the drug to the distribution points. These mules or runners are paid by the trip, often as much as $5000 to $10,000 for a run from Philadelphia to New York, or Florida to Kentucky. Once the drugs have arrived in the area where they will be distributed, the wholesaler will again use his or her mules to deliver them to the retailing organizations which have purchased them. The retailers either pay cash up front (by far the most preferred method of doing business) or take the commodity on consignment, agreeing to pay after retail sales are completed. The latter arrangement is obviously far riskier and often requires that mules also serve as collectors and be appropriately compensated for the added responsibility (Simon and Witte, 1982; Wisotsky, 1976).

In gambling organizations, money is once again a crucial organizational factor. The banker is the individual who has put up the liquid capital needed to establish the business. The officemen, lieutenants, and the like are salaried employees. The pickup men and writers are the rough equivalent of commission salespersons (Pennsylvania Crime Commission, 1987; Jenkins and Potter, 1986; Reuter, 1983; Simon and Witte, 1982).

Centralization

Centralization as a structuring dimension is characterized by the level of authority required for decision making on a given issue and the extent of horizontal and vertical delegation of authority in the organization (Mansfield, 1973; Hage and Aiken, 1970). Also integral to the idea of centralization are the communication patterns involved and the degree of discretionary decision making allowed in unusual and exceptional circumstances. It is important to realize here that the "paper structure" of an organization is no guide to this dimension. For example, police organizations appear to be highly centralized on paper but have no choice but to allow a maximum of individual discretion to first-line workers—patrol officers.

Criminal organizations operate in much the same manner as police departments, with one exception. There is a previously agreed upon level of return expected from first-line employees in criminal organizations. First-line employees have considerable discretion in negotiating business arrangements that will allow them to meet expectations, but very limited discretion with regard to changing that initial agreement on level of return. For example, in a gambling syndicate, a writer may decide whom he or she will take bets from, but the writer has no power to change the odds, the point spread, or the method of moving his or her action to a central bank. If a luncheonette owner wishes to offer a free cup of coffee to an individual betting with him, that is his prerogative, but it is a marketing cost that cannot be passed along to the organization. Similarly, a call girl may negotiate the price of a particular service with each customer on an individual basis. She may negotiate the time she will spend with the customer, the clothes she will wear, the demeanor she will adopt, and the acts she will perform. She may not negotiate the portion of the initial referral fee paid to the agency. Discounts come from her end of the business. It is also expected that she will follow the steps necessary to protect the organization from law enforcement penetration. She will secure identification, she will not name both the act and the price in negotiations, and if suspicious she will challenge the customer to reveal his law enforcement connections, if any. Failure to do so will abrogate the responsibility of the agency to supply her with protection, legal services, and money for fines (Potter and Jenkins, 1985; Simon and Witte, 1982; James, 1977).

Size

While size is usually not identified as a structuring dimension, it obviously has a significant relationship to the others. Yet, size is a function of environmental conditions too. Indeed, we have reviewed good reasons to believe that there is an advantage to criminal enterprise that accrues to small size, one that is related to the security of an organization in a hostile environment.

This point is made in Peter Reuter's study of gambling and loansharking in New York City (1983). Reuter argues that the single most precious asset a criminal enterprise has is information about its activities, information that can lead directly to the arrest of participants and the seizure of enterprise assets. He argues that criminal organizations do three things to protect themselves from information leakage. First, they restrict the number of people with comprehensive knowledge about the organization's business and they restrict information given to lower-level employees to that which they need to know to do their jobs. Second, they restrict the number of total employees in the organization, thereby obviating much of the problem. Third, they restrict the geographical size of the enterprise to make person-to-person communication easier and more efficient, avoiding written instructions and telephones as much as possible.

With this background we now turn to a discussion of the relationship between environment and structure in criminal enterprise.

The Environment:
Exploiting Opportunities for Organized Crime

In general terms, the organizational literature identifies two basic dimensions of environment that shape structure: uncertainty and munificence (Thompson, 1967). Another dimension, which we will call hostility/riskiness, has also been alluded to in the literature, but has been developed in only a rudimentary form (Hage and Aiken, 1970; Thompson, 1967; Emery and Trist, 1965; Parsons, 1960). The hostility/riskiness dimension is so important to any discussion of organized crime and criminal organizations that we will begin with it.

Hostility/Riskiness

Any environment in which a serious error may result in the crippling of the organization are termed hostile. For example, a utility company which uses nuclear power to generate electricity is subject not only to the loss of their facility, but to potentially crippling liability in the event of a nuclear accident. Hospitals and medical consortiums are continually at risk of enormous malpractice settlements which carry the potential to cripple the organization. Tobacco and asbestos manufacturers are in a similar position. Indeed, the position of Johns-Manville (asbestos) is rather like that of a criminal enterprise, in that documents describing early knowledge of the problem of asbestosis became pivotal in findings of culpability against the company (Brodeur, 1985). All criminal enterprise exists in a relatively hostile environment, although differences of degree are evident depending upon the goods and services provided. For example, the environment of a neighborhood numbers bank is decidedly less hostile than that of a retail heroin sales syndicate.

The environment of organized crime is conditioned by legal considerations in three crucial ways (Reuter, 1983). First, the entire criminal enterprise is continually at risk. Participants are subject to arrest, prosecution, and imprisonment, if sufficient proof (and interest on the part of the state) is developed. But far more importantly, the entire organization and its capital are at risk in that there are no bankruptcy laws to protect owner interests in organized crime and there are forfeiture laws which allow the government to seize "ill-gotten gains." Second, there are no contractual guarantees available through a system of law and property rights to organized crime syndicates. If agreements are broken or unsatisfactorily fulfilled, available remedies are threat, intimidation, and possibly violence. Finally, in organized crime there is good reason to avoid the extensive documentation found in legitimate businesses. Such documentation is dangerous and serves little useful purpose.

The complexity of the technology in use is usually inversely related to hostility (Thompson, 1967). For example, nuclear power is very complex technology. Since the environment is generally hostile to nuclear power, organizations increasingly reject that technology. Why invest in expensive technology when the risk of hostility is so high? To the extent that complex technology (a) is difficult to conceal and (b) requires extensive operating documentation, we would expect not to find it in hostile environments (Wieland, 1969; Bell, 1967; Miller, 1960).

Empirical studies of criminal enterprise tend to support this proposition. Bookmaking is among the enterprises with the most extensive documentation. Records of betting action must be held at least temporarily; in some cases, more permanent records reflecting the accounts of patrons must be maintained. In addition, bookmaking usually entails more equipment than other enterprises. Telephones, usually in large number are required for a large book. In rare cases, although recently seen with greater frequency, personal computers have been used to store records and run programs calculating bets and payoffs. In days past, the wire services and the attendant equipment were required, now replaced by televisions tuned to all cable sports channels. A sports and/or horse book of any size is not as mobile and easy to conceal as other forms of enterprise. However, on the other hand, while bookmaking exists in a hostile environment, it is an environment considerably less hostile than, let us say, a crack house. There is widespread public toleration and acquiescence toward bookmaking. In some areas of the country, it flourishes: New York, Pennsylvania, California, Florida, Kentucky, New Jersey—all states which allow some kind of wagering on a legal basis and have some legitimate enterprises dependent on gambling. Police, in general, consider gambling laws not sufficiently important to enforce with any real vigor. As a result, the bookie can take greater chances in his or her business than other criminal entrepreneurs because he or she is unlikely to be the target of public moral outrage or proactive police campaigns (Simon and Witte, 1982; Department of Justice, 1977; Light, 1977; Commission on the Review of the National Police Toward Gambling, 1976; Fund for the City of New York, 1972; Gardiner, 1967).

The cocaine, crack, and heroin wholesaler, on the other hand, must go to great lengths to conceal his or her criminal activity. The organization must be highly mobile, often without a permanent business address. Communication must be in person or through pager systems which allow messages to be exchanged from public telephones. The organization must provide a buffer between those wholesaling large quantities of drugs and the highly visible street dealers. No evidentiary trail that will link the pusher and the supplier can be tolerated. There can be no payroll checks, inventories, or even telephone and address books (Mastrofski and Potter, 1986; Wisotsky, 1986; Simon and Witte, 1982).

Organized crime gauges just how active the hostility towards their enterprises may become in a variety of ways. It is common for gamblers and other purveyors of vice simply not to operate in communities where there is little public toleration of their businesses (Chambliss, 1971; Hills, 1971; Gardiner, 1970; 1967). (This is further reinforcement of our contention that organized crime exists in response to public demand for its goods and services.) In addition, criminal entrepreneurs recognize that because they are selling goods and services to customers, some part of their business is going to occur out in the open. Bribing political, law enforcement, and community leaders is often a high priority and necessary expense of criminal enterprise. Gamblers provide investment opportunities for politicians, campaign funds, and direct payoffs. In most cities, at least some kind of law enforcement "pad" continues to exist. In the 1970s and 1980s in Philadelphia it was revealed that massage parlor owners, escort service operators, after-hours club proprietors, and gamblers were regularly paying off the vice squad in the central police district both to avoid arrest and to guarantee prior warnings of impending crackdowns (Potter and Jenkins, 1985; Pennsylvania Crime Commission, 1983; 1980; 1974). This is a necessary component of illicit enterprises. The most blatant case is, of course, call girl services, many of whom advertise quite openly in adult publications, newspapers, and even the yellow pages of the telephone book. Such a public display of illicit business requires the existence of an ongoing understanding with the law enforcement community (Mastrofski and Potter, 1986; Potter, 1986; Jenkins and Potter, 1986).

In addition to the considerations of size inherent in the preceding discussion, large size in the absence of formal, legal contractual arrangements would place an extraordinary demand on the governance system of a criminal organization. It is extremely difficult for illicit entrepreneurs to monitor workers' performances over large areas or with a large number of employees. The answer, of course, is to stay small or keep street-level operatives segmented from the rest of the organization. Numbers writers, pushers, and prostitutes are paid on a commission basis and are segregated from the decision-making hierarchy.

Lack of formal arrangements such as extensive documentation of rules and procedures, of lines of authority, of channels of communication, and even of agreements with customers will be the rule in hostile environments. This is not the same thing, however, as saying that no such arrangements can exist in hostile environments. What it does say is that if such arrangements do exist, then they will be informal, undocumented, and subject to varying interpretation under different circumstances. In short, such arrangements will be subject to the very difficulties that usually prompt organizations to formalize them in the first place. It is a rather striking thing to say, but most criminal enterprise is dependent on the honor and veracity of the parties involved. If a customer is offered "good" cocaine by a dealer, he or she must evaluate the situation and the character of the supplier and then decide if the dealer's appraisal of the quality of the drug can be trusted. There are no refunds, money back guarantees, nor appearances in small claims court to right a wrong in a drug transaction. At higher levels of illicit commerce this is also true. There were few, if any, written documents reflecting the investment deals between Meyer Lansky and those organized criminals whose money he laundered and invested. Lansky's success (and his longevity) emanated from his reputation, the fact that he "always made money for his partners." If he had failed there would be no recourse to the FDIC or SEC, there would be no savings and loan bailout. His experience, reputation, and the endorsement of others constituted the only guarantee the investor had (Mastrofski and Potter, 1986; Messick, 1973).

Hostility, in and of itself, tells us little about the complexity of organizations. But to the extent that there is a relationship between hostility and technological simplicity, the same relationship will hold for criminal enterprise and organizational complexity. So, in organized crime, as in the world of legitimate business, the less complex the technology, the less the organizational complexity (i.e., specialization, departmentalization).

Most organized crime enterprises utilize simple technologies. The main exception is the highly risky production of methamphetamines and similar drugs in clandestine laboratories, an enterprise with a very high failure rate (Pennsylvania Crime Commission, 1980). Tasks in criminal organizations are interchangeable and require little sophisticated skill or education. Specialization is unnecessary and counterproductive in that it restricts the freedom of the enterprise to get work done on an efficient basis by using all available manpower in the process. Departmentalization makes little sense at all in illicit enterprise. The operations are simply not complex enough to segregate production knowledge or to require a chain of command to oversee the quantity and quality of production. Departmentalization would be creating organizational subunits on the basis of ceremony not necessity.

The relationship between hostility and centrality can be deduced from the preceding argument. First, decentralization relies heavily on formalization, on established rules and procedures documenting the type of actions that can be taken without the approval of supervisors, and on the existence of extensive performance documentation. Decentralization does not mean simply saying "do as you please" in all matters. Therefore, decentralization is problematical in organized crime. In addition, the advantages of decentralization do not accrue to small size, a characteristic related to hostility. Yet on the other hand there are reasons why centrality may not be desirable in hostile environments. Frequent communication with a given organizational participant places that individual at increased risk of detection and consequently would be avoided. Large, decentralized organizations seem insupportable in hostile environments. For somewhat different reasons—namely, risk—so are large centralized organizations. What seems most likely are small organizations with *de facto* decentralization based on mutual understandings and agreements upon a relatively few operating procedures.

It is for this reason that almost all criminal enterprises depend on the recruitment of people who are known to each other, who have had experience (both socially and in business) with each other, and who have a large number of mutual contacts in the community they are serving (Block, 1979a; Ianni, 1974; 1972a; Albini, 1971; Chambliss, 1971; Gardiner, 1970). Perhaps, it is this overlapping set of social and criminal associations which occasionally gives the appearance of a much larger organization operating under the control of a handful of leaders with many criminal associates. However, this is a fundamentally misleading point of view. Empirical studies of organized criminal enterprises in Seattle (Chambliss, 1971), Detroit (Albini, 1971), Philadelphia (Jenkins and Potter, 1986), Reading (Gardiner, 1970), New York (Reuter, 1983; Rubinstein, Reuter, and Wynn, 1983; Block, 1979a; 1979b; Rubinstein and Reuter, 1977; Ianni, 1974; 1972b), and Chicago (Haller, 1971; Landesco, 1968) have all found that organized crime is populated by a large number of actors who come together in an organization, leave that organization, form and re-form organizations, and enter into a series of partnerships, in a constantly shifting panorama of criminal activity and organizational configurations. These actors are not part of a single organization, but rather represent overlapping roles and relationships in a constantly changing census of crime enterprises. Albini referred to this as a series of patron-client relations. Haller has argued that it is a series of informal but pervasive partnerships. He, in fact, depicts the Capone Mob as not a single organization, but a series of senior partners (Nitti, Guzik, and Capone) and junior partners in an ever-changing series of partnerships in illicit goods and services. No matter how we characterize it, the fact remains that every empirical study has shown no central control of criminal enterprise in any city ever studied. Rather, they have all shown a large number of crime networks and criminal conspiracies coming into existence, retreating from the market, and reforming in new configurations over and over again. The consistent picture is one of small, fragmented, fluid organizations engaged in criminal entrepreneurship.

Uncertainty

Environmental uncertainty is the dimension most often cited in discussions of contingency theories of organization design, where it is frequently referred to under the labels of unpredictability or turbulence (Hall, 1972; Gibb, 1968; Mann 1965; Fleishman and Harris, 1962). Components of the uncertainty dimension are: 1) instability, the rate of change of key factors and relationships in the environment; 2) diversity, the relative variety of entities in the environment with which an organization must interact; and 3) interconnectedness, the degree of mutual linkage among those entities. To the extent that an environment is diverse, interconnected, and unstable, it is unpredictable—an environment in which the outcomes of action become uncertain. The relationship between uncertainty and structure is usually conceptualized in terms of the information-processing needs of an organization. In highly uncertain, unpredictable environments, an organization must be able to develop and process information rapidly in order to survive. Structure and procedures are adapted to this need.

With reference to organized crime, uncertainty, unlike hostility, seems to encompass a broad range of possibilities. A local numbers running operation, especially if it operates in a politically "safe" neighborhood, exists in a relatively certain, predictable environment. A heroin dealing operation is just the opposite. However, there do seem to be limits in the extent to which organized crime is willing to enter highly uncertain environments, for the risk consequences of unpredictability may become intolerably high. The fact is that some criminal enterprises are more stable than others. Gamblers have a mathematically guaranteed, although modest return on their investment, usually calculated at between 5 percent and 10 percent (Reuter, 1983; Commission on the Review of the National Policy Toward Gambling, 1976). Drug traffickers on the other hand are in a high-risk business where returns can be hundreds of times greater than investments, but the chances of disaster are also very high (Wisotsky, 1986). Gambling operations work the same way year after year; drug operations change weekly in terms of product, suppliers, price, and distributors.

This arrangement is reflected in the frequent disdain in which drug traffickers are held by gamblers. Interviews with gamblers in a number of studies have shown that they are unwilling to increase uncertainty by even associating with drug dealers, far less, going into the business themselves (Potter and Jenkins, 1985). The same impression is gleaned from discussions with men and women who run call girl services as opposed to street-level prostitution operations, very similar enterprises when considering the ultimate product. Escort service and call girl operators regard streetwalking as risky and dangerous and view the women who engage in it as unacceptable employees. For them, selling sex in a controlled environment with appropriate social amenities is an entirely different type of business (James, 1977).

Aside from the fact that the choice of what environmental niche to exploit limits the choices of available technologies to employ, there seem to be no simple relationships between uncertainty/certainty and technology/size.

Environmental uncertainty is directly associated with structural complexity. Organizations adapt to uncertainty through structural elaboration of specialized positions, procedures, and the like that enable them to deal rapidly and effectively with unforeseen events. So, other things being equal, the most highly elaborated structures in organized crime will exploit the most uncertain environments.

The empirical evidence, once again, bears out this proposition. The heroin industry may be the most highly elaborated of all criminal enterprises. For the most part, separate organizations engage in production, importation, wholesaling and retailing, thereby separating the component phases of the industry entirely (Wisotsky, 1986). In addition, each of these component organizations utilizes a highly sophisticated system of buffers and cutouts to make it difficult to trace an enterprise back to the operator or financier. The heroin market is subject to such intense pressures, both from law enforcement and from the dynamics of the market itself, that this arrangement is almost inevitable. Call girl operations, on the other hand, tend to be very simple and exist in a market with low uncertainty because of both public toleration and law enforcement acquiescence or corruption.

For similar reasons, both formality and centrality bear a negative relationship to uncertainty. Both formal procedures and top-down decision making limit the flexibility of the organization in dealing with unforeseen events. "Standard operating procedures" are useless, or worse, under rapidly changing conditions. Decisions need to be made rapidly at the organizational levels most knowledgeable concerning the problem at hand. Thus, from the information-processing standpoint, structures must be informal and authority decentralized in uncertain environments.

Density

The third dimension is a combination of two factors: the *number* of organizations that seek to exploit a given environmental niche and the availability of *resources* in that niche. What this means is that maximum density might be reached with relatively few organizations in a resource-poor environment or, conversely, with many organizations in a munificent environment. In looking at organized crime there are two important points to be made concerning density. First, the "crime tariff" (an economic effect boosting prices through non-market restrictions on supply) acts to ensure a high level of environmental munificence (Hills, 1971). Because the crime tariff rewards organized crime for risk, its profits—as compared to actual production costs—are highly inflated. The enterprise can make a good return without increasing the supply of the good or service in the market. Therefore, demand is never satisfied. Second, enforcement efforts, ineffective though they may be at controlling the overall trade, do cull out a certain number of organizations, most particularly the smallest and least established. Therefore, for reasons other than economic, the density of the environment is relatively thin. There are two direct consequences of this reality. Economic efficiency should not be a *desideratum* for survival in low-density environments, and criminal enterprise generally takes place in low-density environments.

Since efficiency appears not to be a driving force in the environment of organized crime, technologies will generally be relatively simple. Note that this refers to the *means of production* employed by the organization, not to equipment it might employ, for example, to avoid surveillance.

A primary proposition about the density dimension is that hypotheses established on the basis of research on legal businesses may not hold true for organized crime which takes place in low density environments. There are several reasons for this. The basic assumption of contingency theory is that market organizations compete on the basis of the effectiveness of their operations, and that effectiveness is in part a consequence of appropriate structural adaptation. Maladapted organizations are driven out of the marketplace by more effective ones. When a new environmental niche opens, organizations initially may have a variety of forms. However, as density increases, the shakeout begins and only the better adapted survive. As we have seen, density in organized crime never reaches the critical level where economic efficiency becomes a determining factor in survival. Therefore, the applicability of at least the efficiency-driven hypotheses seems questionable.

Organizational Theory and Organized Crime

While there is an enormous and growing body of literature providing empirical data on the organization of legitimate business, there is a dearth of similar data on criminal enterprise. There are only a handful of empirical studies which look at the business of organized crime. We have already determined that one of the causes is the nature of criminal enterprise. Being illegal, information on its activities are not readily available for use in analyses. In addition, the existing body of data on criminal enterprise has been contaminated with misimpressions and outright inaccuracies emanating from a myriad of journalistic accounts and government reports which have suffered from a lack of credibility and from a fascination with a conspiracy model of criminal behavior.

Nevertheless, we have discussed some seminal efforts at exploring the organization of criminal enterprise through empirical investigation. From these studies there have emerged two consistent themes which can form the basis for further research and exploration. These themes are:

1) Groups engaged in criminal enterprise are loosely structured, flexible, and highly adaptable to environmental impacts.

These enterprises respond readily to the growth or decline of a market for a particular illicit good or service or to the availability of new distributors and manufacturers. For example, when cocaine became an attractive drug of choice in the early 1970s, many drug distribution syndicates responded by adding cocaine to marijuana shipments, or by replacing marijuana with cocaine. Block's study of the cocaine trade in New York (1979b) depicts the trade as operated by "small, flexible organizations of criminals which arise due to opportunity and environmental factors." In recent years, the glut of cocaine on the market in the United States and the concomitant fall in retail price have led to market experimentation by distribution groups with dilaudid (a heroin substitute) and heroin, in an attempt to stimulate new market demand which will be more profitable than cocaine trafficking. Similar adaptations can be seen in the sex industry, where, with the threat of HIV infection, the emphasis has shifted from selling "straight" sex to the selling of "fantasies," "adult conversation," and the like, leaving more routine services to the cheaper, less profitable street market. In yet another example, in Kentucky, with the institutionalization of inter-track wagering, bookmakers have made a marked shift from horse racing to sporting events.

2) Organized crime is a business and has many similarities to businesses in the legal market. However, because organized crime conducts its business in the illegal marketplace it is subject to a series of constraints which limit and define organizational structure, size, and mode of operation.

The empirical evidence strongly suggests that the pattern of association in organized crime resembles what has variously been called a network, a partnership, or a patron-client relationship. Albini, in his study of criminal enterprise in Detroit (1971), found illicit business dominated by criminal patrons who exchanged information, connections with government officials, and access to a network of operatives for economic and political support for their enterprises. He found that these networks of association constantly changed; the roles of patrons and clients fluctuated. Haller (1971) found that criminal enterprise was organized on the basis of a series of separate small-scale business partnerships, involving "senior partners" (those with money and political power) and an ever-changing list of junior partners. Chambliss (1971) found an amalgam of crime networks conducting criminal enterprise in Seattle with shifting memberships and no central control.

These associations continue as long as they are effective and efficient. They do not, however, suggest a vast hierarchy with central control. Reuter (1983) found gambling and loansharking industries in New York populated by small operators, with no organization having a monopoly or market hegemony and no central control or coordination. Reuter found competition, treachery, communications breakdowns, and other forms of disorganization to be characteristic of the criminal enterprises he studied. Studies of criminal enterprises in Philadelphia (Potter and Jenkins, 1985) found dozens of active enterprises with overlapping interests and participants and no central direction or organization.

These studies emphasize that most criminal enterprise does not engage in highly structured production and distribution of goods. Rather, it results from a never-ending series of ad hoc projects and deals carried out through small, short-term agreements.

We propose two basic assumptions about the structure and conduct of organized crime's illicit enterprises based on the research that has been conducted:

1) All criminal enterprises exist in relatively hostile environments primarily as a function of their illegality. As a result of their functioning in a hostile environment, complex technology will be avoided; organizations will stay small in size; formality (i.e., formal rules, procedures, chains-of-command) will be lacking; there will be little organizational complexity; and the organizations will be based on mutual understandings and a relatively discrete and concise set of operating procedures.

2) All criminal enterprise exists in relatively uncertain environments, both as a function of the illicit market and of the uncertain and changing nature of law enforcement policies and public attitudes. As a result, we find that criminal enterprises will increase the danger of structural elaboration as the degree of uncertainty increases. However, the uncertainty of the environment requires that organizational structures be informal with decision-making authority decentralized.

In reaching these conclusions we have combined an analysis of the literature on organizational structure and empirical evidence on organized crime which differ markedly from the popular image of organized crime—and indeed from the model of criminal enterprise used by law enforcement agencies. That model suggests that criminal enterprise is controlled by a single criminal group (Cosa Nostra) or at least by a body of large criminal conspiracies (*Yakuza*, the Triads, the Colombian Cartels, the Cuban Mafia, etc.), which exercise a tightly organized system of control that directs the efficient production of goods and services by organizational members. Inherent in this approach are the assumptions that: (1) such a conspiracy or conspiracies exist, maintain a criminal monopoly in the marketplace, and follow a fixed, detailed operating strategy; and (2) these criminal conspiracies are controlled by bosses at the very top of their hierarchies, with a chain of command that passes orders related to specific criminal tasks down to workers.

Mark Moore suggests that this is not an unreasonable illusion (1986). He argues that viewed from a distance, criminal enterprises might give the impression of producing a very high volume of illicit activity. This prevalence seems to result from a high degree of organization. The distance of the observers allows them to see a single organization, or several very large organizations. However, he suggests, that same structure viewed from the inside would look like a series of partnerships organized around specific criminal projects.

Both the empirical evidence on organized crime and the logic of organization theory strongly dispute a conspiracy model and support Moore's assertions. First, the empirical evidence strongly suggests that the internal structure of criminal enterprises is extremely fluid, with little control or direction from a central authority. In addition, the logic of the situation demonstrates how unlikely a tightly organized criminal conspiracy is in actual operation. A monopolistic syndicate would have to provide constant instruction and information to street-level vice purveyors, thereby imperiling the continued existence of the organization itself. Such a syndicate would have to monitor employee performance, keep careful records, and engage in considerable discussion about specific plans—situations which would imperil the very existence of the organization. **If** such a conspiracy existed, removing its head, its leadership, would cripple the enterprise. Experience demonstrates that this has not happened despite extensive successful prosecutions of alleged syndicate leaders.

So we are left with a model of criminal enterprise that suggests that these organizations are not centralized, formalized, or departmentalized. Such a view has profound implications both for scholarship and for law enforcement. It suggests that scholars interested in unraveling the mysteries of the persistence and prevalence of organized crime should look to market forces at work in criminal entrepreneurship and away from individuals who have attained some degree of notoriety in the field. It also suggests that law enforcement policy should be aimed at disrupting the organizational environment of the enterprise rather than at jailing mythical corporate masterminds believed to be manipulating criminal enterprise from afar.

The model suggested in this analysis is based on a simple truth. Criminal enterprises come into existence, profit, and flourish because there is a strong public demand for the goods and services these enterprises offer. There is a market dynamic at work which is independent of the criminality of any specific individual or group. It is inevitable that organizations will arise to meet these demands and reap these profits. The impetus behind organized crime is not a criminal conspiracy but simple market opportunity. This is also what can constrain organized crime's structure, form, and social perniciousness. As such, it is the market and its environment which are the most appropriate points of intervention in controlling organized crime.

Controlling Organized Crime

Describing organized crime and attempting to explain those factors that ensure its continued success tells us much about our society, our political system, and our economy. It also tells us much about what is required to control organized crime and those pernicious side effects that large-scale illegal and extra-legal behavior spawns. The way we conceptualize and understand organized crime dictates the means selected to control organized crime. While detailed and specific policy alternatives are beyond the scope of this work, a general critique of present policies and some seminal ideas for new policy departures based on a better understanding of organized crime can be articulated. In looking at how we might control organized crime, we will apply the model of organized crime developed in the "Morrisburg" research to a critique of present law enforcement efforts, and then turn our attention to other, innovative policies directed at market demand, corruption, money laundering, improved intelligence, and the strategic selection of law enforcement targets.

Headhunting

The alien conspiracy model has dictated an enforcement strategy based on its precepts. Since Prohibition, the federal effort against organized crime has involved identifying and prosecuting group members for **any** available offense. Many times these charges are unrelated to illicit entrepreneurship and are often for comparatively minor infractions. This strategy is predicated on the assumption that the actual conspiracy is too complex and well-organized to be proved in court. This rationale is based on the myth of organized crime. As we have seen, the actual structure of organized crime operations is not as complex as the myth assumes. The myth of conspiracy becomes an excuse for a lack of success in controlling organized crime. In the headhunting strategy, success is calculated in the form of a body count. Arrests, indictments, and convictions are used to justify budgets and ask for new enforcement powers. Because the conspiracy model places a high premium on position in the hierarchy, the assumption has been that the farther up that hierarchy an arrest goes, the more disruptive it is to the business of organized crime. The most prized catch is the boss of a Mafia family. If the alien conspiracy theory is correct, and these groups are tightly structured and disciplined, the incapacitation of a boss should be debilitating to the organization.

Since the myth postulates an insulated hierarchy, a culture of violence, a code of silence, and the fidelity of clannish conspirators, successful headhunting requires a massive arsenal of law enforcement powers—powers that must be continually augmented and expanded. New laws and new criminal categories ("drug kingpin" or "racketeer," for example) must be created so that heavy sentences and fines can be imposed on those convicted. Simply convicting them of the crimes with which they are charged would not be a sufficient deterrent, additional penalties must be included. The Racketeer Influenced Corrupt Organization act in 1970 was predicated precisely on this philosophy. RICO provided for special grand juries to look for evidence, created a more potent immunity law, eased requirements for proving perjury, provided for protective custody of government witnesses, weakened the defense's capacity to cross-examine and exclude illegally obtained evidence, expanded federal jurisdiction to cover conspiracy to obstruct state law, and increased prison sentences (Chambliss and Block, 1981). It is a curious but seldom noted fact that the Nixon administration, which was responsible for the passage of RICO, chose to ignore organized crime and used the provisions of the act to prosecute anti-Vietnam war protesters (Chambliss and Block, 1981). In addition, RICO has civil provisions that allow the government to pursue what the Justice Department has called a "scorched earth" approach to organized crime—seizing assets and "leaving the mobster with nothing but a return address in federal prison" (Kahler, 1986).

As is the case with many law enforcement programs, rigorous assessments of the headhunting strategy are not available (President's Commission on Organized Crime, 1986). When organized criminals are successfully prosecuted, this is used as evidence that the strategy is working. When convictions are not forthcoming or when the penalties imposed seem mild, law enforcement complains that "its hands are tied"—that it lacks sufficient resources or legal authority to implement the headhunting strategy.

Despite the fact that comprehensive statistics are not kept on how many organized criminals have been put away, some fragmentary data are available to suggest the scope of the headhunting effort. A 1986 *Fortune* article listed the "top fifty" Mafia bosses (based on interviews with law enforcement officials). The article showed that fifteen of the fifty were in jail, ten were indicted or on trial, and one was a fugitive (Rowan, 1986). This included eight of the top ten. Since the publication of that article, the remaining twenty-four "free" crime leaders have been indicted or jailed. If we look specifically at the fabled five families of New York, we find that all of the top leaders of the Colombo, Bonnano, and Lucchese groups have been incapacitated, along with half of the Genovese group's leaders. From 1981–1985 seventeen of the twenty-four alleged Mafia bosses across the country were indicted or convicted (President's Commission on Organized Crime, 1986). In 1984 alone, organized crime indictments totaled 2,194, almost exclusively alleged Mafia group members.

Conviction rates and sentences have been increasing. The General Accounting Office (GAO) estimated that the conviction rate rose from 56 percent to 76 percent in the period 1972 to 1980 (Albanese, 1985). The GAO also noted a concomitant increase in jail terms handed down for convictions.

The problem with all of this is that the government has failed to produce any evidence that these prosecutions have resulted in a diminution of organized crime's illicit ventures. The federal government simply has no measures of the amount of harm caused by organized crime with which to measure such an impact (President's Commission on Organized Crime, 1986). Other indicators seem to suggest that organized crime is alive and quite healthy despite the prosecutorial efforts.

For example, prosecutions of a major gambling syndicate in Philadelphia in the early 1980s had the result of spawning at least two dozen other criminal networks in the same neighborhood as replacements for the targeted crime groups (Pennsylvania Crime Commission, 1986; 1985). Major enforcement efforts directed at "syndicate heads" in Seattle and "Wincanton" resulted in minimal restructuring of street-level operations with no discernible impact on the provision of illicit goods and services (Chambliss, 1978; Gardiner, 1970). Major prosecutions in New York directed at labor racketeering and drug trafficking have had the effect of weeding out inefficient and highly visible operators, leaving more viable organized crime groups in their wake (Chambliss and Block, 1981). Recent prosecutions aimed at the pornography syndicate have resulted in the creation of at least six new, major organized crime groups and the revival of one group that had been closed down a decade ago by successful prosecution (Potter, 1986). Studies of the organization of vice have demonstrated consistently that prosecutions have only negligible impacts on the provision of illicit goods and services and the operation of organized crime groups (Reuter, 1983; Reuter, Rubinstein and Wynn, 1983; Albini, 1971).

The reason that no impact on organized crime can be demonstrated as a result of the headhunting approach is that the model underlying that approach is wrong. Organized crime groups learned long ago that to be successful in a threatening legal environment they must be prepared to adapt their structures and practices. The irony of the situation is that the more successful federal prosecutors become in incarcerating organized crime leaders, the more the industry responds by decentralizing and maintaining temporary and ephemeral working relationships. Because the headhunting approach never disables more than a small proportion of the total number of organized crime entrepreneurs at any given time, it actually strengthens and rewards some organized crime groups by weeding out their inefficient competitors.

It should also be pointed out that headhunting often involves targeting the easiest cases. Successful prosecutions of highly visible and public, but not overly influential, crime figures is good press but will have very little impact. The selection of "Little Nicky" Scarfo, the alleged boss of Philadelphia's Cosa Nostra "family," for special federal treatment has left the field open for far more powerful and dangerous crime figures. While Scarfo has been designated as the head of organized crime in Philadelphia by federal investigators and the press as part of a preconceived notion of conspiracy which justifies the headhunting approach, his actual role and influence are highly suspect. The differences between Scarfo and his associates who were prosecuted (with mixed success) and those who have been left more or less alone are important to understanding the failure of the federal enforcement effort. Scarfo is a small-time hood who lacks political influence and has a minuscule share of the illicit market (considerably less than the 25 percent of the gambling market which was credited to his vastly more competent predecessor Angelo Bruno) (Potter and Jenkins, 1985). In addition, Scarfo's vision of criminal enterprise (among other things) is decidedly limited, highlighted by such capers as an extortion scheme directed at hot dog vendors in Atlantic City (Demaris, 1986). However, also active in Philadelphia during the same time as "Mafia Boss" Scarfo were individuals identified by a variety of sources as controlling a great deal of political clout and a large share of the illicit market. At least one gambler had run a $35 million a year numbers bank virtually unmolested for three decades. A major attorney, identified several times in print as the emissary of Meyer Lansky and later Alvin Malnik, continued to grant favors from his plush offices as allegedly the sole license-granting authority for illicit activities in Atlantic City (Demaris, 1986). A local realtor, whose cocktail parties for judicial candidates are among the premier events of the political season, continued to be the primary landlord for the pornography syndicate (Potter, 1986). Not to belabor the point, there are at least two dozen other operatives of similar stature who operated with relative immunity, while the federal government pursued "Little Nicky" with a vengeance far in excess of his importance or his capacity for future importance (Demaris, 1986; Potter and Jenkins, 1985). It is the relative immunity of major figures in organized crime (such as money launderers, corrupt public officials, and other individuals who serve as bridges between the underworld and the upperworld) that so clearly demonstrates the deficiencies in the model of organized crime on which headhunting strategies are based.

One other issue needs to be discussed before moving on, and that is the fact that headhunting does not always result in successful prosecutions. For example, on October 9, 1985, Jack Nardi, Jr., a Teamsters Union official had charges against him dismissed. In May, 1986, all six defendants in the celebrated trial of "Matty the Horse" Ianniello were acquitted in a RICO prosecution in New York. The defendants were charged with trying to defraud Con Edison. A jury of New Yorkers found that either laudable or impossible and acquitted the defendants. On March 13, 1987, John Gotti and six alleged accomplices were acquitted on charges that they ran the Mafia. In this case, as prosecutors admitted, the jury simply refused to believe turncoat criminals who had been given very lenient sentences in return for testimony. And on December 12, 1987, "Little Nicky" Scarfo and four of his alleged "family" members were acquitted in a drug case. The summation from the jury was simple, "the jury looked at this case that they put on and it stunk"

(*Organized Crime Digest*, 1987a, 1986b, 1985). The point of this litany of defeats is not to suggest federal prosecutors are incompetent but merely to demonstrate that the alien conspiracy theory's credibility is weakening with juries around the country.

The idea that vigorous prosecution and stiff criminal penalties will win the war against organized crime is at variance not only with current research on organized crime but with historic precedent as well. Literally thousands of cases in which organized crime figures have been arrested, convicted, and imprisoned in the last fifty years could be cited here. The fundamental question remains, so what? There is no evidence that these successful prosecutions have in any way negatively impacted or altered the activities of organized entrepreneurial groups in illicit markets.

Rethinking Organized Crime Policy

As should be all too obvious from the discussion of organized crime in "Morrisburg," organized crime groups operate in a complex web of interrelated and tangled environments. Organized crime groups are impacted by the opportunities and constraints of their own illegal market and by market activities that bridge the gap between the illegal and legal market. Activities carried out in the illegal marketplace must by necessity be quite different from those of legitimate commerce. Organized crime groups must deal with a political environment, with the legal system, with legitimate, upperworld commerce, and with the social environment of the community in which they operate. Most attempts to analyze organized crime focus almost exclusively on **criminal** aspects of organized crime. However, it is the **organized** aspects of organized crime which offer the most useful data for formulating future policy. Traditionally, analyses of organized crime have concentrated attention on the deviance of organized crime rather than on the institutionalized and normative aspects of organized crime. Chambliss, in his study of Seattle has suggested that this emphasis has "obscured perception of the degree to which the structure of America's law and politics creates and perpetuates syndicates that supply the vices in our major cities."

Research on organized crime suggests that in order to understand organized crime we must understand its social context. That social context is defined by two recurring themes, two consistent threads running through the organization of crime: official corruption and the conditions of the political economy. These studies suggest that organized crime is simply an integral part of the social, political, and economic system. The evidence is compelling that organized crime should not be conceptualized as a dysfunction in society or as an alien force impinging upon society. Rather, organized crime is part and parcel of the overarching social system. To once again cite Chambliss' analysis of the situation in Seattle:

> Working for, and with, this cabal of respectable community members is a staff which coordinates the daily activities of prostitution, gambling, bookmaking, the sale and distribution of drugs, and other vices. Representatives from each of these groups, comprising the political and economic power centers of the community, meet regularly to distribute profits, discuss problems, and make the necessary organizational and policy decisions essential to the maintenance of a profitable, trouble-free business (Chambliss, 1978: 6).

This point of view has compelling implications for policy and for future research. The question of what we do about organized crime is largely predicated on how we conceptualize organized crime. The arguments advanced here would suggest that policy makers have been attacking the wrong targets.

Dwight Smith (1978) observes that traditionally law enforcement strategy "has rested on the belief that acts of crime are the sole responsibility of the perpetrator, and that as a consequence of removing him from society, the criminal acts would disappear" (162). However, the model suggested here asserts that the existence of illicit drug dealers, loansharks, gamblers, and other illegal entrepreneurs is due to the fact that a number of potential customers for these services are unserved by the legitimate marketplace. In this view, the control of organized crime can be achieved only with a greater understanding of organizational behavior, by "learning how to reduce the domain of the illicit [entrepreneur] . . . and a wider appreciation of the entire market spectrum and a deeper analysis of the dynamics that nurture its illicit aspects" (Smith 1978: 175–176). Smith argues that an understanding of the "task environment" of particular enterprises will promote a better and more comprehensive understanding of how such illicit enterprises emerge, survive, and make a profit from crime. A similar suggestion comes from Reuter, Rubinstein, and Wynn (1983), who argue that investigators of organized crime need to be trained in "the detection of corporate crime, tax evasion and the effect of government regulations, especially licensing, on the motivation of criminals to enter and remain in an industry" (30).

In rethinking organized crime, we must begin by conceptualizing it as a business. Doing so will direct us to efforts that will improve our understanding of the causes of organized crime activities and behaviors and the organization of illicit enterprises. This conceptualization directs our attention toward elimination of arbitrary distinctions between legal and illegal goods and services, particularly gambling, lending, drug distribution, and sexual services.

In this model of organized crime we focus on issues of corporate deviance and political corruption. Any control strategy that fails to recognize the importance of organized crime's political and economic links is doomed to fail. Rather than directing control efforts in an enforcement direction aimed at specific individuals or groups, this model points to the importance of regulation and oversight in both the economic and political spheres. Tighter restrictions on campaign financing and corporate registration, better monitoring of conflicts of interest, more comprehensive financial disclosure, and tighter reporting requirements for businesses would be among steps directed by the model. It is clear that better control of corporate and political deviance would narrow the window of opportunity for organized crime and, therefore, make it more amenable to control.

The way we conceptualize and understand organized crime dictates the means selected to control organized crime. Several new departures in organized crime control policy would seem to be dictated by what we know about organized crime. In specific policies directed at the market and market demand, corruption, money laundering, improved intelligence, and the strategic selection of law enforcement targets need to be addressed.

Handling Market Demand

The largest and most profitable organized crime enterprises are those that provide illicit goods and services to a significant segment of the public eager to obtain them. The most important of these are the victimless crimes of drug trafficking, gambling, prostitution, and loansharking. One approach to limiting demand for these goods and services is to punish the consumer, but this is both practically and politically unpalatable on any significant scale. Another approach is to persuade consumers noncoercively to avoid these products and services. Intensive "educational" efforts at the national level, such as Nancy Reagan's "Just Say No" campaign and local efforts in grade schools and high schools have not resulted in substantial reductions in drug abuse (Levine, Musheno, and Palumbo, 1986; Eitzen, 1983).

Another approach is available. Decriminalization has long been proposed as a method of dealing with these crimes (Albanese, 1984; Luksetich and White, 1982; Abadinsky, 1981; Smith, 1980; Anderson, 1979; Albini, 1971). Removing the criminal label from these activities by legalizing—and regulating—them would probably not eliminate organized crime's involvement. The nation's post-Prohibition experience does suggest that it would be drastically reduced. Realistically, the prospects for decriminalization on a large scale are not good for the near future. However, there is substantial support in large metropolitan areas for police and courts to move away from enforcement of victimless crime laws. Forty-two percent of national survey respondents in communities of over one million in population supported this in 1983. This suggests that some law enforcement agencies might find substantial community support for tacit or even explicit administrative rule making regarding vice enforcement priorities—particularly with regard to setting boundaries for designated high tolerance parts of the city.

Fighting Corruption

It is an axiom of virtually every theory of organized crime that it cannot flourish without a favorable political and professional environment—one where there are systematic abuses of the public trust. Decriminalization of victimless crimes would contribute significantly to improving the corruption problem, but it would not directly affect such enterprises as racketeering and fencing operations. Corruption can be deterred if sufficient resources are committed to monitoring those in sensitive positions of public trust and convicting those who violate the public trust. Instead of collecting urine samples from law enforcement officers and other public employees, governments might more profitably require them to file annual financial statements and submit copies of tax returns. To insure that public corruption cases are vigorously but fairly pursued, state and federal governments could create permanent offices of public integrity with prosecutorial power and status independent of the regular prosecutorial function. Although passage of a law by itself does not insure compliance, Congress could explicitly and unconditionally forbid U.S. intelligence agencies from participating in illegal drug trafficking, which—if obeyed—would substantially reduce the influx of heroin and cocaine to America (see, Mills, 1986; Lernoux, 1984; Block and Chambliss, 1981; Kruger, 1980).

Government agencies can be structured to make corruption more difficult—at least on a large scale. Current practice has the reverse and unintended effect of facilitating corruption. For example, the creation of central vice squads—originally designed to consolidate efforts to control this sensitive function—makes the establishment of corrupt relations between police and organized criminals much easier, as the repeated experiences of departments like New York City, Chicago, and Philadelphia show. Where vice enforcement is centralized, corrupt officers face fewer obstacles in collaborating with and manipulating criminals, particularly powerful ones. Centralized special enforcement units are also cost effective from the crime organization's perspective; once the vice squad establishes its turf, fewer officers need be put on the pad, so both the financial costs and the risks of exposure are minimized for organized crime.

Cleaning Up Money Laundries

The rise in criminal entrepreneurs' drug trafficking income has illuminated the critical role by financial institutions in laundering illicit income. Several exposés are now available which show how dependent organized crime groups are on bankers, stockbrokers, accountants, lawyers, realtors, and others close to the financial community (Demaris, 1986; Mills, 1986; Moldea, 1986; Lernoux, 1984). A brief, although hardly comprehensive, list of policies to make the detection of money laundering less difficult is suggested here. First, more detailed reporting should be required on **all** corporate filings, so that investigators can more easily follow "money trails." State and federal rules vary here, but minimal standards should include listing: 1) all officers and all corporate offices they hold, and 2) complete data on investment capital—including all sources in "chain" investments, foreign corporations, and offshore banks. The enforcement of reporting laws on bank transactions involving large sums of money should be beefed up. Full reporting of trust accounts should be required, including listings of who has access, the sources of income, allocations, and withdrawals. Foreign currency transactions—where money leaves the country—should be limited. Funds that do leave the country should be traced if there are questions about its origins. Finally, there should be more effective monitoring and disciplining of licensed professionals involved in financial transactions—including a nationwide NCIC-type data base available to professional licensing, regulatory, and law enforcement agencies.

Improving Intelligence on Organized Crime

Obtaining useful intelligence on organized crime is admittedly difficult, but law enforcement agencies can vastly improve their understanding of organized crime by refusing to use the precepts of the alien conspiracy model to guide their search for and interpretation of information. First, law enforcement can divest itself of its obsession with organized crime as an ethnic group phenomenon. Although federal authorities are now beginning to acknowledge that the Mafia has no monopoly in criminal enterprises, they insist upon retaining ethnicity as the defining feature of gangs. Having squandered their intelligence efforts on Cosa Nostra groups for years, they are now faced with choosing from their lengthy menu of other ethnically defined groups. This failed strategy should be replaced by one that focuses on developing an accurate picture of organized industries, not separate gangs—one that follows the processes of distribution, supply, manufacturing, and financing—regardless of who is involved (Mastrofski and Potter, 1986). This new approach means that intelligence analysts should be less concerned with forcing data into predetermined organization charts reflecting their preconceived vision of corporate bureaucracies. They should be more concerned with assessing the market, production, and social conditions that shape patterns of organized criminals' interactions.

Strategic Selection of Enforcement Targets

Law enforcement agencies probably overuse traditional tactics in fighting crime. Extensive electronic surveillance of top gang leaders has produced reams of irrelevant data about the intimate details of such things as old Italians' exasperation with younger Italians (McFadden, 1987), but this has yielded relatively little useful intelligence. Using plea bargains and granting immunity may be helpful in obtaining convictions, but such testimony—when really central to a case—is often not corroborated and consequently is at least of questionable validity from an intelligence viewpoint. The well-worn federal practice of selecting a Joe Valachi, a Jimmy "the Weasel" Fratianno, or a Vincent Teresa as a prime informant, and then managing and refining the testimony, and replaying it case after case, produces only a series of self-fulfilling prophecies. Alan Block has characterized investigatory practices into organized crime as "fundamentally creepy." In fact, it was precisely this kind of federally sponsored orchestration which seems to have swayed the jury in the initial cases brought against alleged New York Mafia head John Gotti. The testimony from one of the government's primary informants in those trials indicated that: 1) he was a very low-level crook (he referred to himself as a "coffee boy for a messenger boy"); 2) he had been housed in special facilities with other witnesses in the trial and had been subjected to intensive coaching on his testimony by government attorneys; and 3) the government provided him with drugs, which he not only used but passed on to other witnesses. The Gotti case reeked of orchestration rather than impartial investigation and prosecution.

It seems likely that—despite the public's strong distaste for these law enforcement practices—American police will continue to pursue them. With this in mind, it seems appropriate that the police at least exert greater care in selecting targets. Rather than targeting the presumed bosses for surveillance, they should look at those elements of the illicit enterprise that are most susceptible to law enforcement or regulatory intervention. The emphasis should not be on individuals but industries, with particular attention paid to strategies that will complement the existing impetus in the illicit market toward modest geographic scale and limited enterprise and to the denial of market monopolies to organized crime.

Understanding Organized Crime

The way we conceptualize and understand organized crime dictates the means selected to control organized crime and the focus of inquiries directed at organized crime. An integrative view of organized crime will change our way of studying that phenomenon and planning strategies to control that phenomenon. The view of organized crime presented here should direct us to new and bold departures in both policy and practice, summarized below:

1) We should eliminate the arbitrary distinctions between legal and illegal gambling, lending, sex, and drugs. Legalization or decriminalization of some consensual crimes would reduce the market domain of organized crime.

2) "Headhunting" should be rejected as a strategy of organized crime control. Instead, our knowledge of market dynamics and organizational theory should be applied to the development of means to impede criminal organization in the marketplace.

3) There should be a drastically enhanced emphasis on the regulation and prosecution of political and business deviance. The environmental opportunities for organized crime can only be

restricted by attacking those institutions that make the organization of crime possible.

4) Greatly increased attention should be paid to the financial and money laundering activities of organized crime, and considerably less emphasis placed on the prosecution of vice.

5) Finally, scholars should direct their attention to learning more about organized crime's interactions with political, social, and economic institutions. We need to worry less about secret ceremonies and family lineage and more about the circulation of money. Research efforts should be directed at the establishment of reliable baseline data by continuing with projects directed at developing accurate and comprehensive case studies. Research should precede policy formulation.

Organized crime is not a Cosa Nostra "family," a Cuban gang, or a Jewish hijacker. Organized crime is a pervasive series of criminal networks that have flourished in the United States for well over a century. It exists because there is a public demand for its services. If the public did not wish to bet, there would be no bookies. If the public did not wish to purchase illegal drugs, there would be no pushers. If the public did not desire the opportunity to purchase sex, there would be no pornography outlets and no prostitutes. If the political and law enforcement establishment did not tolerate and very possibly profit from organized crime, there would be no vice districts. Organized crime is a business conceived in our desires for products and services, protected by our politicians and police, and made to flourish by our overt cooperation with crime organizations. Just like Mr. Rockefeller's railroads, Mr. Astor's fur traders, and Mr. Fisk's steel mills, organized crime flourishes because it provides services essential to American social, economic, and political life. It is not alien, it is not foreign, it is not a conspiracy against the fabric of society. It is, in fact, very much part of that fabric.

Sources

Abadinsky, Howard. 1981. *The Mafia in America: An Oral History*. New York: Praeger.

_____. 1981.*Organized Crime*. Boston: Allyn and Bacon.

_____. 1985. *Organized Crime*. Chicago: Nelson-Hall.

Adler, Patricia (1985).

Albanese, Jay. 1982. What Lockheed and La Cosa Nostra have in common: The effect of ideology on criminal justice policy. *Crime and Delinquency* 28: 211–232.

_____. 1984. *Justice, Privacy, and Crime Control*. Latham, MD: University Press of America.

_____. 1985. *Organized Crime in America*. Cincinnati: Anderson.

Albini, Joseph L. 1971. *The American Mafia: Genesis of a Legend*. New York: Appleton-Century-Crofts.

Albini, Joseph L. and J. B. Bronislaw. 1978. Witches, mental illness, and social reality: A study in the power of mythical beliefs. *International Journal of Criminology and Penology* 6: 285–294.

Anderson, Annelise Graebner. 1979. *The Business of Organized Crime: A Cosa Nostra Family*. Stanford, CA: Hoover Institution Press.

Ansoff, H. Igor and Robert G. Brandenburg. 1971. A language for organization design, parts I and II. *Management Science* 17: 705–31.

Arlacchi, Pino. 1986. *Mafia Business: The Mafia Ethic and the Spirit of Capitalism*. London: Verso.

Bayor, Ronald. 1978. *Neighbors in Conflict*. Baltimore: Johns Hopkins University Press.

Becker, Howard S. 1963. *Outsiders: Studies in the Sociology of Deviance*. New York: Free Press.

Becker, Howard S., B. Geer, E.C. Hughes, and A.L. Strauss. 1961. *Boys in White: Student Culture in a Medical School*. Chicago: University of Chicago Press.

Bell, Daniel. 1963. The myth of the Cosa Nostra. *The New Leader*. (December 23): 12–15.

_____. 1964. *The End of Ideology*. Glencoe, IL: The Free Press.

Bell, Gerald D. 1967. Determinants of pan of control. *American Journal of Sociology* 73: 90–101.

Bequai, August. 1979. *Organized Crime: The Fifth Estate*. Lexington, MA: Heath.

Blau, Peter M. 1956. *Bureaucracy in Modern Society 2d ed*. New York: Random House.

_____. 1964. *Exchange and Power in Social Life*. New York: John Wiley.

Block, Alan A. 1978. History and the study of organized crime. *Urban Life* 6 (January): 455–74.

_____. 1979a. *East Side-West Side: Organizing Crime in New York, 1939–1959.* Swansea, U.K.: Christopher Davis Publishers.

_____. 1979b. The snowman cometh: Coke in progressive New York. *Criminology* 17.

_____. 1986. A modern marriage of convenience: A collaboration between organized crime and U.S. intelligence. In R.J. Kelly (ed.), *Organized Crime: A Global Perspective.* Totowa, NJ: Rowan and Littlefield.

Block, Alan A. and William J. Chambliss. 1981. *Organizing Crime.* New York: Elsevier.

Block, Alan A. and Frank R. Scarpitti. 1985. *Poisoning for Profit: The Mafia and Toxic Waste.* New York: William Morrow.

Blok, Anton. 1971. *The Mafia of a Sicilian Village, 1860–1960.* London: William Clowes and Sons.

Boissevain, Jeremy. 1974. *Friends of Friends: Networks, Manipulators and Coalitions.* Oxford: Basil Blackwell.

Bonnano, Joseph. 1983. *A Man of Honor: The Autobiography of Joseph Bonnano.* New York: Simon and Schuster.

Brecher, Edward M. 1972. *Licit and Illicit Drugs.* Mount Vernon, NY: Consumers Union.

Brodeur, Paul. 1985. Annals of law: The asbestos industry on trial. *New Yorker*, (June 10, June 17, June 24, July 1).

Cady, Steve. 1976. Illegal bets in America exceed legal ones, 3–1, study shows. *New York Times* (June 27): 5, 9.

Campbell, D.T. and J.C. Stanley. 1963. *Experimental and Quasi-Experimental Designs for Research.* Chicago: Rand McNally.

Capeci, Jerry. 1978. Tieri: The most powerful Mafia chieftain. *New York* (August 21): 22–26.

Cartey, Desmond. 1970. How black enterprisers do their thing: An odyssey through ghetto capitalism. In G. Jacobs (ed.), The *Participant Observer: Encounters with Social Reality.* New York: George Braziller.

Chambliss, William J. 1964. A sociological analysis of the law of vagrancy. *Social Problems* 12 (Summer).

_____. 1971. Vice, corruption, bureaucracy and power. *Wisconsin Law Review* 4.

_____. 1976a. Vice, corruption, bureaucracy and power. In W. Chambliss and M. Mankoff *Whose Law? What Order?* New York: John Wiley and Sons.

_____. 1976b. The state, the law, and the definition of behavior as criminal or delinquent. In D. Galser (ed.), *Handbook of Criminology.* Chicago: Rand McNally.

_____. 1978. *On the Take: From Petty Crooks to Presidents.* Bloomington: Indiana University Press.

Chambliss, William J. and Alan Block. 1981. *Organizing Crime.* New York: Elsevier.

Chandler, David L. 1975. *Brothers in Blood: The Rise of the Criminal Brotherhoods.* New York: Dutton.

Clinard, Marshall, and Richard Quinney. 1973. *Criminal Behavior Systems.* New York: Holt, Rinehart and Winston.

Cloward, Richard A. and Lloyd E. Ohlin. 1960. *Delinquency and Opportunity.* New York: Free Press.

Cohen, Albert K. 1965. The sociology of the deviant act: Anomie theory and beyond. *American Sociological Review* 30 (February).

Commission on the Review of the National Police Toward Gambling. 1976. *Gambling in America.* Washington, D.C.: U.S. Government Printing Office.

Conklin, John E. 1973. *The Crime Establishment: Organized Crime and American Society.* Englewood Cliffs, N.J.: Prentice-Hall.

Cook, Fred J. 1973. *Mafia!* Greenwich, CT: Fawcett.

Cook, J. and J. Carmichael. 1980. The invisible enterprise. *Forbes* 126, issues 7–11.

Cooley, Charles H. 1902. *Human Nature and Social Order.* New York: Charles Scribner's Sons.

Cressey, Donald R. 1967a. The functions and structure of criminal syndicates. In *Task Force Report: Organized Crime.* President's Commission on Law Enforcement and the Administration of Justice. Washington, D.C.: U.S. Government Printing Office: 25–60.

———. 1967b. Methodological dilemmas in the study of organized crime as a social problem. *The Annals of the American Academy of Political and Social Science.* 374: 101–112.

———. 1969. *Theft of the Nation: The Structure and Operations of Organized Crime in America.* New York: Harper and Row.

DeFranco, Edward J. 1973. *Anatomy of a Scam: A Case Study of a Planned Bankruptcy by Organized Crime.* Washington, D.C.: U.S. Government Printing Office.

Dean, J. P., R. L. Eichorn, and L. P. Dean. 1967. Observation and interviewing. In J. T. Dolby (ed.), *An Introduction to Social Research.* New York: Appleton-Century-Crofts: 274–304.

Demaris, Ovid. 1981. *The Last Mafioso.* New York: Bantam.

———. 1986. *The Boardwalk Jungle.* New York: Bantam.

Department of Justice, National Institute of Law Enforcement and Criminal Justice. 1977. *The Development of the Law of Gambling: 1776–1976.* Washington, D.C.: U.S. Department of Justice.

Donner, Frank J. 1980. *The Age of Surveillance: Aims and Methods of America's Political Intelligence System.* New York: Alfred A. Knopf.

Dorsett, Lyle. 1968. *The Prendergast Machine.* New York: Oxford University Press.

Durkheim Emile. 1947. *The Division of Labor in Society.* Glencoe, IL: The Free Press.

Eitzen, Stanley, D. 1983. *Social Problems.* Boston: Allyn and Bacon.

Emery, Fred W. and Eric L. Trist. 1965. The causal texture of organizational environment. *Human Relations* 18: 21–31.

Fleishman, Edwin A. and Edwin F. Harris. 1962. Patterns of leadership behavior related to employee grievances and turnover. *Personnel Psychology* 15 (Spring): 43–56.

Form, William H. and Delbert C. Miller. 1960. *Industry, Labor, and Community.* New York: Harper & Brothers.

Fried, Albert. 1980. *The Rise and Fall of the Jewish Gangster in America.* New York: Holt, Rinehart and Winston.

Fund for the City of New York. 1972. *Legal Gambling in New York: A Discussion of Numbers and Sports Betting.* New York: Fund for the City of New York.

Gage, Nicholas. 1971. *The Mafia is Not an Equal Opportunity Employer.* New York: McGraw-Hill.

———. 1974. Questions are raised on Lucky Luciano book. *New York Times* (December 17): 1, 28.

Galliher, John F. and J. A. Cain. 1974. Citation support for the Mafia myth in criminology textbooks. *The American Sociologist* 9: 68–74.

Gardiner, John A. 1967. Public attitudes toward gambling and corruption. *Annals of the American Academy of Political and Social Science* 374.

———. 1970. *The Politics of Corruption: Organized Crime in an American City.* New York: Russell Sage Foundation.

Gardiner, John A. and Theodore R. Lyman. 1978. *Decisions for Sale: Corruption and Reform in Land-Use and Building Regulations.* New York: Praeger.

Geis, Gilbert. 1972. *Not the Law's Business? An Examination of Homosexuality, Abortion, Prostitution, Narcotics and Gambling in the United States.* Rockville, MD: National Institute of Mental Health, Center for Studies of Crime and Delinquency.

Geis, Gilbert and Robert F. Meier. 1977. *White Collar Crime: Offenses in Business, Politics and the Professions.* New York: The Free Press.

Gibb, Cecil A. 1968. Leadership. In G. Lindzey and E. Aronson (eds.), *Handbook of Social Psychology.* 2d ed. vol. IV. Reading, MA: Addison-Wesley: 205–82.

Glazer, B. G. 1965. The constant comparative method of quantitative analysis. *Social Problems* 12: 436–445.

Gold, R. L. 1958. Roles in sociological field observations. Social Forces 36: 217–223.

Gosch, Martin and Richard Hammer. 1974. *The Last Testament of Lucky Luciano.* New York: Dell.

Gouldner, Alvin W. 1959. Organizational analysis. In Robert K. Merton, Leonard Broom, and Leonard S. Cottrell (eds.), *Sociology Today.* New York: Basic Books: 400–428.

Gusfield, Joseph R. 1963. *Symbolic Crusade: Status Politics and the American Temperance Movement.* Urbana: University of Illinois Press.

Hage, Jerald and Michael Aiken. 1970. *Social Change in Complex Organizations.* New York: Random House.

Hagan, Frank E. 1983. The organized crime continuum: A further specification of a new conceptual model. *Criminal Justice Review* 8: 52–57.

Hall, Edward T. 1972. *The Silent Language.* Greenwich, CT: Fawcett Books.

Haller, Mark H. 1971. Organized crime in urban society: Chicago in the twentieth century. *Journal of Social History* 5.

_____. 1979. Changing structure of American gambling in the twentieth century. *Journal of Social Issues* 3.

_____. 1987. Business partnerships in the coordination of illegal enterprise. Paper presented at the annual meetings of the American Society of Criminology, Montreal (November).

Hammer, Richard. 1975. *Playboy's Illustrated History of Organized Crime.* Chicago: Playboy Press.

Harring, Sidney L. 1977. Class conflict and the suppression of tramps in Buffalo, 1892–1894. *Law and Society Review* 11 (Summer).

_____. 1983. *Policing a Class Society.* New Brunswick: Rutgers University Press.

Hellman, Daryl A. 1980. *The Economics of Crime.* New York: St. Martin's Press.

Hess, Henner. 1973. *Mafia and Mafiosi; The Structure of Power.* Lexington, MA: D.C. Heath.

Hillery, George A., Jr. 1955. Definitions of community: Areas of agreement. *Rural Sociology* XX, 2 (June).

Hills, Stuart. 1971. *Crime, Power and Morality: The Criminal Law Process in the United States.* Scranton, PA: Chandler Publishing.

Hindus, Michael Stephen. 1977. The contours of crime and justice in Massachusetts and South Carolina, 1767–1878. *The American Journal of Legal History* 21 (July).

Hollingshead, August B. 1941. The concept of social control. *American Sociological Review* XXIV, 5 (October).

Homans, George C. 1961. *Social Behavior: Its Elementary Forms.* New York: Harcourt, Brace and World.

Homer, F. 1974. *Guns and Garlic.* West Lafayette: Purdue University Press.

Hunter, Floyd. 1953. *Community Power Structure: A Study of Decision Makers.* Chapel Hill: University of North Carolina Press.

Ianni, Francis A. J. 1972a. *A Family Business: Kinship and Social Control in Organized Crime.* New York: Russell Sage Foundation.

_____. 1972b. *Ethnic Succession in Organized Crime.* Washington, D.C.: U.S. Government Printing Office.

_____. 1974. *Black Mafia: Ethnic Succession in Organized Crime.* New York: Simon and Schuster.

Inciardi, James A., Alan A. Block, and Lyle A. Hallowell. 1977. *Historical Approaches to Crime.* Beverly Hills, CA: Sage.

Janes, R. W. 1969. A note on the phases of the community role of the participant observer. *American Sociological Review* 26: 446–450.

James, Jennifer. 1976. Motivations for entrance in prostitution. In L. Crites (ed.), *The Female Offender.* Lexington, Mass: Lexington Books.

_____. 1977. Prostitutes and prostitution. In Edward Sagarin and Fred Montanino (eds.), *Deviants: Voluntary Actors in a Hostile World.* Morristown, NJ: General Learning Press.

Jenkins, Philip and Gary W. Potter. 1986. Organized crime in London. *Corruption and Reform* 1 (3).

_____. 1987. The politics and mythology of organized crime: A Philadelphia case study. *Journal of Criminal Justice* 15 (4).

_____. 1989. Before the Krays: Organized crime in London 1920–1960. *Criminal Justice History* (January).

Kahler, Kathryn, 1986. The Mob is winning: Organized crime in the United States is richer than ever. *Gannett Westchester Newspapers* (May 25): B1, B6.

Katz, Daniel and Robert L. Kahn. 1978. *The Social Psychology of Organizations* 2d ed. New York: Wiley.

King, Rufus. 1969. *Gambling and Organized Crime*. Washington, D.C.: Public Affairs Press.

Kirk, Stephen, Peter Mancust, Thomas Palmer, and M. E. Malone. 1983. How two FBI agents stalked the top U.S. porn dealers. *Boston Globe* (February 18).

Knapp Commission. 1972. *Report of the Commission to Investigation Alleged Police Corruption*. New York: Braziller.

Kruger, Henrik. 1980. *The Great Heroin Coup: Drugs, Intelligence, and International Fascism*. Nost: South End Press.

Kwitny, Jonathan. 1979. *Vicious Circles: The Mafia in the Marketplace*. New York: W.W. Norton.

Landesco, John. 1968. *Organized Crime in Chicago: Part III of the Illinois Crime Survey, 1929*. Chicago: University of Chicago Press.

Laswell, Harold D. and Jeremiah McKenna. 1971. *The Impact of Organized Crime on an Inner-City Community*. New York: Policy Sciences Center.

Lernoux, Penny. 1984. *In Banks We Trust*. Garden City, NY: Anchor/Doubleday.

Levine, J. P., M. C. Musheno, and D. J. Palumbo. 1986. *Criminal Justice in America: Law in Action*. New York: John Wiley & Sons.

Light, Ivan. 1977. Numbers gambling among blacks: A financial institution. *American Sociological Review* 42 (December).

Linder, Lee. 1987. Scarfo charged with 2nd murder. *Associate Press* (April 11).

Luksetich, William A. and Michael D. White. 1982. *Crime and Public Policy: An Economic Approach*. Boston: Little, Brown.

Lynd, Robert S. and Helen Merrell Lynd. 1929. *Middletown: A Study in Contemporary American Culture*. New York: Harcourt, Brace.

Maas, Peter. 1968. *The Valachi Papers*. New York: G.P. Putnam's Sons.

Maitland, L. 1983. President's anti-drug task forces are falling behind. *New York Times* (March 11): A1.

Mann, Floyd C. 1965. Toward an understanding of the leadership role in formal organization. In F.C. Mann, and D.C. Miller (eds.), *Leadership and Productivity*. San Francisco: Chandler: 68–103.

Mansfield, Roger. 1973. Bureaucracy and centralization: an examination of organizational structure. *Administrative Science Quarterly* 18: 477–88.

Martin, W. A. 1981. Toward specifying a spectrum-based theory of enterprise. *Criminal Justice Review* 6: 54–57.

Mastrofski, Stephen and Gary W. Potter. 1986. Evaluating law enforcement efforts to control organized crime: The Pennsylvania Crime Commission as a case study. *Policy Studies Review* 6, 1.

McCaghy, Charles H. and Stephen A. Cernkovich. 1987. *Crime in American Society*. New York: Macmillan.

McCall, G. J. 1969. Data quality control in participant observation. In G. J. McCall and J. L. Simmons (eds.), *Issues in Participant Observation: A Text and Reader*. London: Addison-Wesley.

McFadden, Robert D. 1987. The Mafia of the 1980s: Divided and under siege. *New York Times* (March 11): A1.

Mead, George H. 1937. *Mind, Self, and Society*. Chicago: University of Chicago Press.

Merton, Robert. 1938. Social structure and anomie. *American Sociological Review* 3.

———. 1967. *On Theoretical Sociology*. New York: The Free Press.

Messick, Hank. 1967. *Silent Syndicate*. New York: Free Press.

———. 1973. *Lansky*. New York: Berkeley Publishing Company.

Mieczkowski, Thomas. 1986. Geeking up and throwing down: Heroin street life in Detroit. *Criminology* 24 (Nov.): 645–66.

Miller, James G. 1960. Information input, overload, and psychopathology. *American Journal of Psychiatry* 116: 695–704.

Miller, Judith Droitcour and Ira H. Cisin. 1983. *Highlights From the National Survey on Drug Abuse: 1982*. Rockville, MD: National Institute on Drug Abuse.

Miller, Walter B. 1958. Lower class culture as a generating milieu of gang delinquency. *Journal of Social Issues* 14.

Mills, James. 1986. *The Underground Empire*. New York: Doubleday.

Moldea, James. 1986. *Dark Victory: Ronald Reagan, MCA, and the Mob*. New York: Viking.

Moore, Mark H. 1986. Organized crime as a business enterprise. Paper presented at the American Society of Criminology Meetings.

Moore, W. H. 1974. *Kefauver and the Politics of Crime*. Columbus: University of Missouri Press.

Morris, Norval and Gordon Hawkins. 1970. *The Honest Politician's Guide to Crime Control*. Chicago: University of Chicago Press.

Musto, David F. 1973. *The American Disease: Origins of Narcotics Control*. New Haven: Yale University Press.

National Advisory Committee on Criminal Justice Standards and Goals. 1976. *Report of the Task Force on Organized Crime*. Washington, D.C.: U.S. Government Printing Office.

Nelli, Humbert S. 1976. *The Business of Crime*. New York: Oxford University Press.

Nisbet, Robert A. 1953. *The Quest for Community: A Study in the Ethics of Order and Freedom*. New York: Oxford University Press.

Organized Crime Digest. 1985. (November).

_____. 1986a. (May).

_____. 1986b. (August).

_____. 1987a. (March 25).

_____. 1987b. (December 23).

Pace, Denny F. and Jimmie C. Styles. 1975. *Organized Crime: Concepts and Control.* Englewood Cliffs, NJ: Prentice-Hall.

Parsons, Talcott. 1960. *Structure and Process in Modern Societies.* New York: Free Press.

Paul, B. 1957. Interview techniques and field relationships. In A.L. Kroeber et. al. (eds.) *Anthropology Today.* Chicago: University of Chicago Press.

Pearce, Frank. 1976. *Crimes of the Powerful.* London: Pluto Press.

Pennsylvania Crime Commission. 1970. *Report on Organized Crime.* St. David's, PA: Commonwealth of Pennsylvania.

_____. 1974. *Corruption in the Philadelphia Police Department.* St. David's, PA: Commonwealth of Pennsylvania.

_____. 1980. *A Decade of Organized Crime.* St. David's, PA: Commonwealth of Pennsylvania.

_____. 1981. *Annual Report.* Harrisburg, PA: Commonwealth of Pennsylvania.

_____. 1981. *Health Care Fraud: A Rising Threat.* St. David's PA: Commonwealth of Pennsylvania.

_____. 1982. *Annual Report.* Harrisburg, PA: Commonwealth of Pennsylvania.

_____. 1983. *Annual Report.* Harrisburg, PA: Commonwealth of Pennsylvania.

_____. 1984. *Annual Report.* Harrisburg, PA: Commonwealth of Pennsylvania.

_____. 1985. *Report.* Conshohocken, PA: Commonwealth of Pennsylvania.

_____. 1986. *Report.* Conshohocken, PA: Commonwealth of Pennsylvania.

_____. 1987. *Annual Report.* Harrisburg, PA: Commonwealth of Pennsylvania.

Perrow, Charles. 1967. A framework of the comparative analysis of organizations. *American Sociological Review* 32: 195–08.

_____. 1972. *Complex Organizations: A Critical Essay.* Glenview, IL: Scott Foresman.

Peters, T. J. and R. H. Wakeman, Jr. 1982. *In Search of Excellence: Lessons from America's Best-Run Companies.* New York: Warner Books.

Peterson, Virgil. 1983. *The Mob: 200 Years of Organized Crime in New York.* Ottawa, Ill.: Green Hill.

Pileggi, Nicholas. 1985. *Wise Guy: Life in a Mafia Family.* New York: Pocket Books.

Plate, T. et. al. 1982. *The Mafia at War.* New York: New York Magazine Press.

Potter, Gary W. 1986. *The Porn Merchants.* Dubuque, IA: Kendall Hunt.

Potter, Gary W. and Philip Jenkins. 1985. *The City and the Syndicate: Organizing Crime in Philadelphia.* Lexington, MA: Ginn Press.

Potter, Gary W. and Philip Jenkins. 1984. *Organized Crime in "Morrisburg": Final Report*. University Park: Institute for the Study of Human Development.

President's Commission on Law Enforcement and the Administration of Justice. 1967. *Task Force Report: Organized Crime.*, Washington, D.C.: U.S. Government Printing Office.

President's Commission on Organized Crime. 1986. *The Impact: Organized Crime Today*. Washington, D.C.: U.S. Government Printing Office.

_____. 1984. *Asian Organized Crime*. Washington, D.C.: U.S. Government Printing Office.

_____. 1985. *Gambling*. Washington, D.C.: U.S. Government Printing Office.

_____. 1983. *Organized Crime Federal Law Enforcement Perspective*. Washington, D.C.: U.S. Government Printing Office.

Pugh, D. S., D. J. Hickson, C. R. Hinings, and C. Turner. 1968. Dimensions of organizational structure. *Administrative Science Quarterly* 13: 65–105.

Quinney, Richard. 1975. *Criminology*. Boston: Little, Brown and Company.

Reimer, Svend and John McNamara. 1957. Contact patterns in the city. *Social Forces* XXXVI, 2 (December).

Reiss, Albert J., Jr. 1957. Functional specialization of cities. In P. Hatt and A. Reiss, Jr. (eds), *Cities and Society: The Revised Reader in Urban Sociology*. Glencoe, IL: The Free Press.

Reuss-Ianni, Elizabeth. 1973. *A Community Self-Study of Organized Crime*. New York: Criminal Justice Coordinating Council.

Reuter, Peter. 1983. *Disorganized Crime: The Economics of the Visible Hand*. Cambridge: The MIT Press.

_____. 1986. Methodological and institutional problems in organized crime research. Paper prepared for the conference on Critical Issues in Organized Crime Control. Washington, D.C.: The Rand Corporation.

Reuter, Peter, Jonathan Rubinstein, and Simon Wynn. 1983. *Racketeering in Legitimate Industries: Two Case Studies, Executive Summary*. Washington, D.C.: U.S. Department of Justice, National Institute of Justice.

Rowan, Roy. 1986. The 50 biggest Mafia bosses. *Fortune* (November 10): 24–38.

Rubinstein, Jonathan, and Peter Reuter. 1977. *Numbers: The Routine Racket*. New York: Policy Sciences Center, Inc.

_____. 1978a. Fact, fancy and organized crime. *The Public Interest*. 53.

_____. 1978b. *Bookmaking in New York*. New York: Policy Sciences Center, Inc.

Salerno, Ralph and John S. Tompkins. 1969. *The Crime Confederation*. Garden City, NY: Doubleday.

Satchell, Michael. 1979. The big business of smut. *Parade* (August 19).

Schatzman, L., and Strauss, A. L. 1973. *Field Research: Strategies for a Natural Sociology*. Englewood Cliffs, NJ: Prentice-Hall.

Schur, Edwin M. 1965. *Crimes Without Victims*. Englewood Cliffs, N.J.: Prentice-Hall.

Schur, Edwin M. and Hugo A. Bedau. 1974. *Victimless Crimes: Two Sides of a Controversy*. Englewood Cliffs, N.J.: Prentice-Hall.

Seeley, John R., R. Alexander Sim, and Elizabeth W. Loosely. 1956. *Crestwood Heights: A Study of the Culture of Suburban Life*. New York: Basic Books.

Shaw, Clifford and Henry D. McKay. 1972. *Juvenile Delinquency and Urban Areas*. Chicago: University of Chicago Press.

Silberman, Charles E. 1978. *Criminal Violence, Criminal Justice*. New York: Random House.

Simon, Carl P. and Anna D. Witte. 1982. *Beating the System: The Underground Economy*. Boston: Auburn House Publishing.

Skolnick, Jerome H. 1978. *House of Cards: Legalization and Control of Casino Gambling*. Boston: Little, Borwn and Co.

Smith, Dwight C., Jr. 1975. *The Mafia Mystique*. New York: Basic Books.

_____. 1976. Mafia: The prototypical alien conspiracy. *The Annals of the American Academy of Political and Social Science* 423 (January): 75–88.

_____. 1978. Organized crime and entrepreneurship. *International Journal of Criminology and Penology* 6.

_____. 1980. Paragons, pariahs, and pirates: A spectrum-based theory of enterprise. *Crime and Delinquency* 26.

Sondern, Frederick. 1959. *Brotherhood of Evil: The Mafia*. New York: Farrar, Straus and Cuday.

Sutherland, Edwin H. 1973. *Edwin H. Sutherland: On Analyzing Crime*. Karl Schuessler, ed. Chicago: University of Chicago Press.

Suttles, Gerald D. 1968. *The Social Order of the Slum*. Chicago: University of Chicago Press.

Task Force on Organized Crime. 1967. *Task Force Report: Organized Crime*. Washington, D.C.: U.S. Government Printing Office.

Taylor, Ian, Paul Walton, and Jock Young. 1973. *The New Criminology*. New York: Harper and Row.

Thompson, James D. 1967. *Organizations in Action*. New York: McGraw-Hill.

Tonnies, Ferdinand. 1940. *Fundamental Concepts of Sociology*. New York: American Book.

United States Senate, Special Committee to Investigate Organized Crime in Interstate Commerce. 1951. *Investigation of Organized Crime in Interstate Commerce*. Washington, D.C.: U.S. Government Printing Office. (Kefauver).

United States Senate, Permanent Subcommittee on Investigation. 1964. *Organized Crime and Illicit Traffic in Narcotics*. Washington, D.C.: U.S. Government Printing Office. (McClellan).

Villano, Anthony. 1978. *Brick Agent*. New York: Ballantine.

Vold, George and Thomas J. Bernard. 1986. *Theoretical Criminology*. New York: Oxford University Press.

Walsh, Marilyn E. 1977. *The Fence.* Westport, CT: Greenwood.

Warner, W. Lloyd and J. O. Low. 1947. *The Social System of the Modern Factory: The Strike, A Social Analysis.* New Haven: Yale University Press.

Warren, Roland L. 1973. *The Community in America.* New York: Rand McNally.

Weber, Max. 1968. *Economy and Society.* G. Roth and C. Witich (eds.), New York: Bedminster Press.

Whyte, William Foote. 1961. *Street Corner Society.* Chicago: University of Chicago press.

Wieland, George F. 1969. The determinants of clarity in organization goals. *Human Relations* 22: 161–72.

Wisotsky, Stephen. 1986. *Breaking the Impasse in the War on Drugs.* New York: Greenwood Press.

Wolf, Eric R. 1966. Kinship, friendship and patron-client relations in complex societies. In M. Banton (ed.), *The Social Anthropology of Complex Societies.* London: Tavistock Publications.

Yeager, M. C. 1975. The political economy of illegal drugs. *Contemporary Drug Problems* 4.

Index